CHUANG-TZÜ

A. C. Graham, who was Professor of Classical Chinese at the
School of Oriental and African Studies, London University,
has worked for many years on the thought and the textual
and linguistic problems of Chinese philosophical literature
in general and Chuang-tzŭ in particular.

He is an experienced translator of Chinese poetry (Poems
of the late T'ang, London 1965) and is interested in the
problems of transmitting Chuang-tzŭ's qualities as writer as
well as thinker.

A. C. Graham, who was Professor of Classical Chinese at the School of Oriental and African Studies, London University, has worked for many years on the thought and the textual and linguistic problems of Chinese philosophical literature in general and Chuang-tzǔ in particular.

He is an experienced translator of Chinese poetry (Poems of the late T'ang, London 1965) and is interested in the problems of transmitting Chuang-tzǔ's qualities as writer as well as thinker.

CHUANG-TZŬ
The Inner Chapters

A.C. Graham

A Mandala Book

UNWIN PAPERBACKS
London   Boston   Sydney   New Zealand

First published in Great Britain by George Allen & Unwin in 1981
First published in paperback by Unwin® Paperbacks, an imprint of
Unwin Hyman Limited, in 1986
Re-issued in 1989

Unwin Hyman Limited
15–17 Broadwick Street, London W1V 1FP, UK

Unwin Hyman Inc
8 Winchester Place, Winchester, Massachusetts 01890, USA

Allen & Unwin Australia Pty Ltd
8 Napier Street, North Sydney, NSW 2060, Australia

Allen & Unwin New Zealand Pty Ltd with the Port Nicholson Press
Compusales Building, 75 Ghuznee Street, Wellington, New Zealand

ISBN 0 04 299013 0

British Library Cataloguing in Publication Data

Chuang-tzŭ: the seven Inner Chapters
and other writings: from the book
Chuang-tzŭ.—(Mandala)
1. Philosophy
I. Graham, A. C.   II. Series
181'.11   B126

Printed in Great Britain by Guernsey Press Co. Ltd,
Guernsey, Channel Islands

For Dawn

Contents

Preface

The textual notes to this translation have been published separately as *Chuang-tzŭ: Textual notes to a partial translation*, School of Oriental and African Studies, 1981. My conclusions on the date and composition of the book are presented in '*How much of 'Chuang-tzŭ' did Chuang-tzŭ write?*', in *Studies in Classical Chinese thought*, edited Henry Rosemont Jr and Benjamin I. Schwartz, *Journal of the American Academy of Religion Thematic Issue*, Sept 1979, 47/3, 459–502.

I would like to thank Douglas Hewitt and Henry Rosemont Jr for reading and commenting on the translation of the *Inner chapters* and John Hardy for introducing me to Oscar Wilde's review of Giles' version.

Extracts or earlier drafts from this translation have appeared in *History of Religions* v. 9 and in *Montemora* Nos 1, 3, 4.

Part One

Introduction

1

Chuang-tzŭ and the origins of Taoism

We know very little about the life of Chuang Chou (commonly called Chuang-tzŭ), who wrote the nucleus of what Arthur Waley described as 'one of the most entertaining as well as one of the profoundest books in the world'.[1] The book is the longest of the classics of Taoism, the philosophy which expresses the side of Chinese civilisation which is spontaneous, intuitive, private, unconventional, the rival of Confucianism, which represents the moralistic, the official, the respectable. The *Historical records* of Ssŭ-ma Ch'ien (*c.* 145–*c.* 89 BC), in a brief biographical note, date Chuang-tzŭ in the reigns of King Hui of Liang or Wei (370–319 BC) and King Hsüan of Ch'i (319–301 BC). They say that he came from the district of Meng in the present province of Honan, and held a minor post there in Ch'i-yüan ('Lacquer Garden', perhaps an actual grove of lacquer trees) which he abandoned for private life. For further information we have only the stories in the book which carries his name, a collection of writings of the fourth, third and second centuries BC of which at least the seven *Inner chapters* are generally recognised as his work.

Whether we take the stories about Chuang-tzŭ as history or as legend, they define him very distinctly as an individual. In this he is unique among Taoist heroes, of whom even Lao-tzŭ, the supposed founder of the school, never in anecdote displays any features but those of the Taoist ideal of a sage. Most of the tales about Chuang-tzŭ fall into three types: we find him mocking logic (always in debate with the sophist Hui Shih), or scorning office and wealth, or ecstatically contemplating death as part of the universal process of nature. Only the second of these themes belongs to conventional Taoist story-telling, and even here he strikes a distinctive note, at once humorous and deep. Whatever the historical worth of the stories, in reading the *Inner chapters* one has the impression of meeting the same very unusual man. It is not simply that he is a remarkable thinker and writer; he is someone with an absolutely fearless eye like the William Blake of *The marriage of heaven and hell*, he gives that slightly hair-raising sensation of the man so much himself that, rather than rebelling against conventional modes of thinking, he seems free of them by birthright. In the landscape which he shows us, things somehow do not have the relative importance which we are accustomed to assign to them. It is as though he finds in animals and trees as much significance as in people; within the human sphere, beggars, cripples and freaks are seen quite without pity and with as much interest and respect as princes and sages, and death with the same equanimity as life. This sense of a truly original vision is not diminished by familiarity with other ancient Chinese literature, even that in which his influence is deepest. Though both men were firmly grounded in their own place and time, there was never another Englishman like Blake or another Chinese like Chuang-tzŭ.

The more closely one reads the disconnected stories and fragmentary jottings in the *Inner chapters*, the more aware one becomes of the intricacy of its texture of contrasting yet reconciled strands, irreverent humour and awe at the mystery and holiness of everything, intuitiveness and subtle, elliptical flights of intellect, human warmth and inhuman impersonality, folkiness and sophistication, fantastic unworldly raptures and down-to-earth observation, a vitality at its highest intensity in the rhythms of the language which celebrates death, an effortless mastery of words and a contempt for the inadequacy of words, an invulnerable confidence and a bottomless scepticism. One can read him primarily as a literary artist, as Confucians have done in China. However, one cannot get far in exploring his sensibility as a writer without finding one's bearings in his philosophy.

The great creative period of Chinese philosophy lasted from the time of Confucius (551–479 BC) to the reunification of the empire by the Ch'in dynasty in 221 BC. Political disunity and rapid social and technological change, at a pace never afterwards equalled in Chinese history until the nineteenth century, had undermined the religion, moral code and political institutions of the declining Chou dynasty, and thrown open the question 'What is the Way?' – the way that the empire should be ordered and individuals should conduct their lives. Confucius was a conservative who set out to restore the moral and cultural heritage of the Chou, himself unaware of the originality of his own reinterpretations of the tradition which he was refining and clarifying. Late in the fifth century BC his earliest rival Mo Ti (Mo-tzŭ) was the first to propose new foundations; he laid down the principle of universal love, and submitted traditional rules and institutions to the test of whether in practice they benefit men or harm them, or benefit everyone or some at the expense of the rest. The rivalry between Confucians and Mohists continued until the end of the age of the philosophers. For Chuang-tzŭ, it only confirmed that moralists arguing from different standpoints can never reach agreement, and encouraged him in his uncompromising moral relativism.

In the nearer background of Chuang-tzŭ's thought are philosophers of the fourth century BC, whose writings do not survive. A minor one is Sung Hsing (also called Sung Jung), who in spite of his moralism is respected by Chuang-tzŭ for his thesis that 'To be insulted is not disgraceful', implying that a man's worth has nothing to do with the approval or disapproval of others.[2] More important is the 'Nurture of life' school led by Yang Chu (*c.* 350 BC), whom the moralistic schools condemned as an egoist. In a world in which members of the upper class were expected to pursue a public career, Yang Chu was the first spokesman of those who preferred the tranquillity of private life to the cares and dangers of office. His philosophy, although it contributed to Taoism, had nothing mystical about it. Just as much as the Mohists, the Yangists judged conduct by the test of practical benefit and harm, but drew a different conclusion – that life is more important than the things which sustain it, and that to pursue riches and power may be danger-ous to health and survival. Four chapters of *Chuang-tzŭ*, which we call the 'Yangist miscellany', seem to be late writings of this school, and there is even some evidence, which we shall consider in introducing the stories about Chuang-tzŭ,[3] that at one time he belonged to it himself. Certainly he agreed with Yang Chu in preferring health and peace of mind to worldly success, but he was looking for a philosophy – and this is perhaps the deepest impulse behind his thinking – which instead of imprisoning him in the self and its worries about survival would reconcile him to the mutability of fortune and the certainty of death.

As the rival schools multiplied, debate became progressively more rational, until late in the fourth century BC sophists appeared who studied logical puzzles for their own sake. Chuang-tzŭ was a younger acquaintance, perhaps at some time a disciple, of the greatest of the sophists, Hui Shih. But he turned away from him, towards the cult of intuitiveness and spontaneity in both political and private action which was to become characteristic of Taoism. Unlike the Confucians and the Mohists, the early Taoists did not form an organised school; the name was applied to them retrospectively, and is first attested in the classification of 'Six Schools' by Ssŭ-ma T'an (died 110 BC). As far as our information goes, Chuang-tzŭ himself may have been the very first of them. The great Taoist classic *Lao-tzŭ* is traditionally ascribed to Lao Tan ('Old Tan'), supposed contemporary of Confucius and founder of the school, but is not attested until late in the third century BC, and there is no trace of its influence in the *Inner chapters*. In taking the side of spontan-eity against Hui Shih's logic Chuang-tzŭ helped to tip the scale at that critical moment when the Chinese glimpsed the rationalist path which unknown to them was already being followed by the Greeks, but did not take it.

2
Spontaneity

Although it is not easy to offer a definition of Taoism, thinkers classed as philosophical Taoists do share one basic insight – that, while all other things move spontaneously on the course proper to them, man has stunted and maimed his spontaneous aptitude by the habit of distinguishing alternatives, the right and the wrong, benefit and harm, self and others, and reasoning in order to judge between them. To recover and educate his knack he must learn to reflect his situation with the unclouded clarity of a mirror, and respond to it with the immediacy of an echo to a sound or shadow to a shape. For Chuang-tzǔ the fundamental error is to suppose that life presents us with issues which must be formulated in words so that we can envisage alternatives and find reasons for preferring one to the other. People who really know what they are doing, such as a cook carving an ox, or a carpenter or an angler, do not precede each move by weighing the arguments for different alternatives. They spread attention over the whole situation, let its focus roam freely, forget themselves in their total absorption in the object, and then the trained hand reacts spontaneously with a confidence and precision impossible to anyone who is applying rules and thinking out moves. 'When I chisel a wheel,' says the carpenter to Duke Huan,[4] 'if the stroke is too slow it slides and does not grip, if too fast it jams and catches in the wood. Not too slow, not too fast; I feel it in the hand and respond from the heart, the tongue cannot put it into words, there is a knack in it somewhere which I cannot convey to my son and which my son cannot learn from me.'

In another tale[5] a swimmer is asked how he stays afloat in a whirlpool, and answers: 'I enter with the inflow and emerge with the outflow. I follow the Way of the water and do not impose my selfishness on it . . . That it is so without me knowing why it is so is destiny.' Such stories about special knacks were popular in the school of Chuang-tzǔ; only one of them, the tale of Cook Ting carving the ox,[6] belongs to the *Inner chapters* which can be confidently ascribed to Chuang-tzǔ himself, but as concrete illustrations of the Taoist approach they are as instructive to the modern reader as they evidently were to ancient apprentices of the school.

In responding immediately and with unsullied clarity of vision one hits in any particular situation on that single course which fits no rules but is the inevitable one (Chuang-tzǔ is fond of the term 'inevitable',[7] which he uses rather as when we speak of the inevitability of an artist's casually drawn line). This course, which meanders, shifting direction with varying conditions like water finding its own channel, is the *Tao*, the 'Way', from which Taoism takes its name; it is what patterns the seeming disorder of change and multiplicity, and all things unerringly follow where it tends except that inveterate analyser and wordmonger man, who misses it by sticking rigidly to the verbally formulated codes which other philosophical schools present as the 'Way of the sage' or 'Way of the former kings'. The spontaneous aptitude is the *te*, the 'Power', the inherent capacity of a thing to perform its specific functions successfully. (As an English equivalent of *te* many translators prefer 'virtue', to be understood however as in 'The virtue of cyanide is to poison' rather than as in 'Virtue is its own reward'). Like the Way, it belongs to man no more or less than to other things; we read in one *Chuang-tzǔ* story that the training of a fighting cock ends when its *te* is complete.[8] In ancient Chinese thinking, which has no dichotomy of mind and body, the 'Power' even in man includes not only the full potentialities of the sage but such physical powers as eyesight and hearing, and Chuang-tzǔ sees it as a difficulty requiring explanation that perfection of Power does not ensure that the body will grow up strong and beautiful.[9] The concepts of *Tao* and *te* make a pair, as in the alternative title of *Lao-tzǔ*, the *Tao te ching*, 'Classic of the Way and of Power'.[10]

How am I to train the Power in me so that I am prompted to act without the aid of reasons, ends, moral and prudential principles? By cultivating the spontaneous energies, which Chuang-tzǔ conceives in terms of the physiological ideas current in his time. He assumes that the organ of thought is not the brain but the heart, and also that everything in motion in the universe is activated by *ch'i*, 'breath, energy', conceived as a fluid which in its purest state is the breath which vitalises us. Inside the body the *ch'i* alternates between phases of activity, as the 'Yang', and of passivity, as the 'Yin', as in breathing out and in. He shares such assumptions of Chinese medicine as that birth and growth are Yang and ageing is Yin, that illness is an imbalance of the two, and that changes of mood from exhilaration to depression are the Yang energies climaxing and reverting to the Yin phase.[11] In the main tradition of Chinese cosmology (already represented in the *Outer chapters* of *Chuang-tzǔ*) all energies not only in the body but throughout the cosmos are classed as Yin or Yang, accounting for the alternations of dark and light and of all other opposites. Chuang-tzǔ himself, however, seems to follow an older scheme of 'Six Energies', Yin and Yang, wind and rain, dark and light.[12] Thinking in terms of the traditional physiology, he recommends us to educate the spontaneous energies rather than use the heart to think, name, categorise and conceive ends and principles of action. (But the only specific technique which he mentions, and that only casually, is controlled breathing.)[13] Then we shall respond anew to the totality of every new situation, as the swimmer adapts to the varying pulls and pressures of the whirlpool, aware that it would not help but harm him to pause and ask himself 'How shall I escape?', even entertain the thought about himself 'I want to escape'.

With the abandonment of fixed goals, the dissolution of rigid categories, the focus of attention roams freely over the endlessly changing panorama, and responses spring directly from the energies inside us. For Chuang-tzŭ this is an immense liberation, a launching out of the confines of self into a realm without limits. A word which regularly quickens the rhythm of his writing is *yu*, 'roam, travel', used rather like the 'trip' of psychedelic slang in the 1960s. In his first chapter, 'Going rambling without a destination', he begins by imagining the flight of a giant bird and asking how the air can carry its weight, and proceeds to the flight, which does not depend even on the air, of the sage who 'rides a true course between heaven and earth, with the changes of the Six Energies as his chariot, to travel into the infinite'.[14] But he is not thinking only of ecstatic experience; even a diplomat on a difficult mission is advised to consider only the objective conditions and 'let the heart roam with other things as its chariot, and trust yourself to the inevitable in order to nurture the centre of you'.[15]

3

Rejection of logic

Like all great anti-rationalists, Chuang-tzǔ has his reasons for not listening to reason. He develops them in the pieces assembled in 'The sorting which evens things out', a scattered series of notes which conveys more than anything else in ancient Chinese the sensation of a man thinking aloud. We see from this chapter that Chuang-tzǔ learned more than one might have expected from his rationalist mentor Hui Shih. The philosophy of Hui Shih is known primarily by a sequence of ten theses, unfortunately without their explanations, reported in the last chapter of *Chuang-tzǔ*, 'Below in the empire'.[16] Most of them seem to be paradoxes designed to prove that one cannot make spatial and temporal divisions without contradiction ('The South has no limit yet does have a limit', 'The sun at noon is simultaneously declining, simultaneously with being alive a thing dies'). The last of the theses is different in nature: 'Let your love spread to all the myriad things, heaven and earth are one unit.' This suggests that the point of the whole series is to show that since division leads to self-contradiction everything is one, other persons are the same as oneself, and therefore to be loved equally; it supports the principle of universal love preached by the Mohists. But it is clear that if he is taking this position Hui Shih has come dangerously close to discrediting his own tool, analytic reason. He wishes to discredit only spatial and temporal divisions, but it will take only one more step to observe that all reasoning depends on making distinctions, and to reach the conclusion that we should abandon reason for the immediate experience of an undifferentiated world, transforming 'All are one' from a moral into a mystical affirmation. It is in 'The sorting that evens things out' that Chuang-tzǔ takes this step.

The themes which other schools describe the sophists as exploring are the 'dimensionless' and the 'limitless' (paradoxes of space and time), the 'same' and the 'different' (paradoxes arising from the relativity of similarity and difference), and the 'hard' and the 'white' (paradoxes resulting from treating the mutually pervasive as distinct, for example the hardness and whiteness of a stone). Chuang-tzǔ himself on occasion touches on the first two themes, but uses 'hard and white' only as a contemptuous metonym for chop logic.[17]

Unfortunately we have no writings of Hui Shih and only two genuine essays of the other major sophist Kung-sun Lung, the *White horse* and *Meanings and things*. But we can learn a great deal about current methods of argumentation, and its technical terminology, from the later Mohist manual of disputation, the *Canons*.[18] This document, which contains direct answers to some of Chuang-tzŭ's criticisms of disputation,[19] dates from about 300 BC or a little later. Its theory of naming (the only one in ancient China, as far as our information goes) is strictly nominalistic; a common name such as 'horse' is given to a particular object and extended to all similar to it. When we ask what an object is, we are asking what name fits it. 'Disputation'[20] is the arguing out of alternatives, one right and one wrong, such as 'Is it an ox or not?'; questions in which both alternatives may be right or wrong ('Is it an ox or a horse?', 'Is it a whelp or a dog'?) are excluded from disputation. One party affirms and the other denies that the name fits, by expressions most conveniently translated by 'That's it' and 'That's not'.[21] Apart from 'deeming'[22] the object to be *it*, a horse for example, one may deem something to be 'so'[23] of it (that it is white, that one rides it). By disputation one proves that a claim is or is not 'allowable',[24] ultimately by appealing to the definitions of names. (The *Canons* start by defining no less than seventy-five logical, ethical and geometrical terms and analysing the ambiguities of twelve more.) Among the logical terms of the *Canons* one which is especially prominent in *Chuang-tzŭ* is *yin*, 'go by' (take as a criterion);[25] thus to judge whether a man fits the description 'black man' you have to decide which part of his body to 'go by' (his eyes? his skin?). It may be noticed that the basically demonstrative words 'it' and 'so' (the latter equivalent to 'like it', 'as it') attract attention, as such English words as 'true' and 'valid' do not, to the question whether users of a name are in fact picking out the same thing as *it*.

It is not clear from the scanty documents at what date Chinese thinkers came to appreciate that names have only a conventional relation to objects. Chuang-tzŭ is the earliest whom we know to have made the point explicitly; and throughout 'The sorting which evens things out' one feels the exhilarating shock of the discovery when it was still new, the apparent overthrow of all received ideas when it is first seen that in principle anything might be called anything. What is 'it' for me and what is 'other' than it depend on my choice of standpoint, and when I say 'That's it' I am merely announcing that the thing in question is the thing to which I have chosen to give the name. There is no need of sophistry to prove Kung-sun Lung's theses 'A white horse is not a horse' and 'The meaning is not the meaning'; I merely have to name something else 'horse' and the objects commonly given the name will not be horses.[26]

As far as horses are concerned, no doubt we can easily adapt to other usages by taking into account what speakers 'go by' in applying the name. But with moral terms more serious consequences arise. For example the basic ethical term for all schools was *yi*, translatable as 'duty'. For Confucians it is the conduct traditionally prescribed for the various social relations, for example between father and son or ruler and subject; but the Mohists, who criticised accepted morality on utilitarian grounds, formulated in the *Canons* the new definition 'To be "dutiful" is to be beneficial'.[27] Moralists however cannot afford simply to agree to differ over the definition of the word, and be forced to admit that there is nothing to choose between the Confucian standpoint from which the three-year period of mourning for parents is *it* and the Mohist standpoint from which it is not. Each school thinks it knows what does actually constitute duty, and engages in disputation to justify itself. Chuang-tzŭ calls this the ' "That's it" which deems',[28] which judges that something actually is what we call it (in contrast with the ' "That's it" which goes by circumstance',[29] which is relative to a criterion), and denies that any reasoning can support it. The result of disputation is simply that those with the same starting-point agree and those without differ.

Chuang-tzŭ derides all claims that reason can give us certainty. The only assurances we can have or should want is that of organic process and unanalysed knacks and skills, of whatever we confidently do without knowing how we do it. We have to 'know how to know by depending on that which the wits do not know', otherwise we are projected into 'the ultimate uncertainty'.[30] His objections to analytic thinking are thrown out casually, as insights formulated without being developed, but they are impressively wide in range. In looking for reasons one is caught in an infinite regress, testing by tests which in the end are themselves untested.[31] To call in allies can give only a false confidence, since they agree with us only because they have made the same initial choice of standpoint. If someone shares my standpoint against yours, how can he help me to refute you? Even if he argues from a standpoint shared by both of us, what help is that against others who do not share it?[32] If we could find something to start from on which everyone in the world agreed I still would not *know* it (it would merely be that everyone happens to call the same thing by the same name); I cannot even know what it is I do not know – like Meno in Plato's dialogue *Meno*, Chuang-tzŭ thinks that a contradiction – and I am still contradicting myself if I try to find a rock bottom of scepticism in 'I know that no thing knows anything'.[33] Moreover, there is no guarantee that something I happen to feel sure of is more likely to be true than something I doubt; 'if you use the undoubted to unravel the doubted and transfer it to the undoubted, this is to give an undeserved importance to the undoubted'.[34] Even the greatest thinkers frequently change their minds; how do I know there is anything I now believe which I shall not reject in the future?[35] Chuang-tzŭ is also sceptical about the organ with which we think, which, it may be worth repeating, is not the brain but the heart. Why do we continue to trust its thoughts even in old age when it has decayed with the rest of the body? In any case all men have hearts, and if each of them, wise or foolish, takes his own as the final authority, how can they agree? [36] Does the heart reign over the body at all? Isn't it rather that the body is a system within which the organs take turns as ruler and subject? The body does indeed have a 'genuine ruler' which articulates its members, but that is the Way itself, the mysterious order which runs through all things, which we follow spontaneously as soon as we cease to use the heart to analyse alternatives. [37]

Chuang-tzŭ also shares that common and elusive feeling that the whole is greater than the sum of its parts, that analysis always leaves something out, that neither side of a dichotomy is wholly true. He more than once tries to pin it down in intricate, elliptical arguments which direct attention to the moment of transformation from X into Y. According to one of Hui Shih's theses, at the moment of birth or death a thing is both alive and dead; [38] even the later Mohists, who had no taste for sophisms, seem to have taken the position that at the moment when it begins and ends an ox is both ox and non-ox [39]. Does it not follow then that every statement at the moment when it becomes allowable is also unallowable? [40] Moreover, what of the moment when the totality of existing things began? Disputation assumes that if you add non-oxen to oxen nothing is left out. But you leave out what preceded the moment when there began to be oxen and non-oxen; and if you try to include it you are caught up in the contradiction of both crediting it with and denying it existence. [41]

Does Chuang-tzŭ's rejection of disputation amount to a total dismissal of reason? In the first place, spontaneous behaviour as he conceives it is not 'thoughtless' in the sense of 'heedless', on the contrary it follows close attention to the situation. Nor is it implied that every relevant facet is perceived immediately in a moment of insight; when for example Cook Ting carving an ox arrives at an especially intricate knot of bone and sinew he pauses, concentrates until everything is clear to him, then slices through with a single deft stroke. Although Chuang-tzŭ rejects *pien*, 'disputation', the posing and arguing out of alternatives, he always speaks favourably of *lun*, 'sorting, grading', thought and discourse which orders things in their proper relations. In common usage this word tended to imply grading in terms of relative value, but Chuang-tzŭ's kind of *lun* is, to quote the title attached to his second chapter, the 'sorting which evens things out'. [42] It would cover all common-sense thinking about objective facts in order to arrive at a coherent picture of the conditions before responding. It seems that Chuang-tzŭ does not forbid me to think about my situation. What he does forbid is thinking about what I or others ought to do about it, instead of simply answering with the spontaneous act or spontaneous approval or disapproval. The sage, we are told, 'sorts' everything within the cosmos but does not 'assess' it, he 'assesses' the actions of the great men of history but does not engage in disputation about them; and as for what is outside the cosmos – that remainder left over from the total of oxen and non-oxen – he 'locates' it but does not sort it. [43]

How does Chuang-tzǔ reconcile in practice the rejection of all prudential and moral rules with the need to live in a highly regulated society? The sage as he conceives him is both selfless and amoral, and refuses to distinguish and judge between either benefit and harm or right and wrong. However, the carpenter or angler is at his most dexterous in spontaneous rather than deliberated moves, and similarly it is the act without either selfish or altruistic premeditation which he believes to be both in one's own best interests ('You can protect your body, keep life whole, nurture your parents, last out your years') [44] and in the best interests of all ('The benefits of his bounty extend to a myriad ages, but he is not deemed to love mankind' [45]). As for social conventions, Chuang-tzǔ is alert to the dangers of colliding with them, but sees them as deserving only an outward conformity. But in 'Worldly business among men' one notices with some surprise that Chuang-tzǔ does accept two kinds of convention without reserve. [46] One is the service of parents, which is rooted in a love 'which cannot be dispelled from the heart', and is therefore to be accepted as part of our destiny. Here, unlikely as it may seem in the twentieth century, there is a perfect accord between social custom and the informed spontaneous impulse. The other is the service of minister to ruler. The minister has to accept his duties as belonging to the 'inevitable', to the unalterable facts of his situation, and learn to 'roam free inside the cage'. [47] He can try to improve his ruler, but not like a Confucian by prating to him about moral principles; he must identify the growing point of Power in the rule and deftly guide him towards the Way. But even in 'Worldly business among men' Chuang-tzǔ seems to be looking on from outside at unfortunates trapped in office or rash idealists venturing into court in the hope of reforming the ruler. As far as he is concerned, the sensible man stays as far away as he can from official life and its duties.

A point which seems to me of some theoretical interest in moral philosophy [48] is the unfamiliar manner in which Chuang-tzǔ jumps the gap between fact and value. He everywhere assumes that to know how to act I have only to contemplate the objective situation and let myself respond. Is he not overlooking what is nowadays a commonplace, that one can know all the facts about a situation without knowing how to act in it? The fallacy of leaping from 'is' to 'ought' has been recognised ever since Hume. Surely then Chuang-tzǔ is trying to bind us by a concealed imperative which we are at liberty to reject as soon as we uncover it? We might formulate it as: 'Follow the Way, which is the direction in which you tend if you mirror the concrete situation clearly and react to it spontaneously.' But the attempted formulation at once reveals that we are playing into Chuang-tzǔ's hands. There is indeed an implicit imperative behind his talk about the Way, but it is simply 'Mirror the concrete situation clearly before you let yourself respond.' Granted that one cannot infer from 'is' to 'ought', from statements of fact to imperatives, there is no problem about inferring from an imperative of this sort, cognate with 'Face facts' or 'Know thyself', to imperatives to prefer reactions in awareness to reactions in ignorance of the situation as it objectively is. But in that case the imperative which Chuang-tzŭ has covertly introduced is one which it would be madness to reject. One notices too that Chuang-tzŭ does not owe us a demonstration of the value of spontaneity. If he has succeeded in his endeavour to discredit all principles of choice, there will remain only this single implicit imperative, and nothing to apply it to except spontaneous reactions. Part of the interest of Taoism is that it demonstrates the possibility of deriving a whole philosophy of life from a single imperative to deal with things as they objectively are, not as one would like them to be.

Chuang-tzŭ of course is unaware of the problem of 'is' and 'ought'. Nothing could be further from his intentions than to establish rational foundations for an ethical theory; it is simply that in pursuing his sceptical critique he arrives at an unexpectedly firm rock bottom. The nearest he comes to formulating his implicit principle is a dictum right at the end of the *Inner chapters*: 'The utmost man uses the heart like a mirror; he does not escort things as they go or welcome them as they come, he responds but does not store.' [49] The mirror metaphor is developed farthest in the Syncretist essay *Way of Heaven*. [50] 'In the case of the sage's stillness, it is not that he is still because he says "It is good to be still"; there is nothing among the myriad things which is sufficient to disturb his heart, that is why he is still.' He is like quiescent water which 'shows up plainly the beard and eyebrows'; he is 'the mirror of heaven and earth'. We should expect a Westerner who wrote anything like that to draw nihilistic conclusions. But the Syncretist is describing his ideal mode of action; 'in stillness he is moved, and when he moves he succeeds'. Is there still room to object that he assumes the value of success, which presupposes standards for judging that the sage's ends are good? No, the sage's fluid and temporarily emerging goals are the ones to which he spontaneously tends when he mirrors heaven and earth with perfect clarity, and that is sufficient reason for preferring them to any goals to which he might incline in ignorance.

One may add the further point that, in spite of the Taoist refusal to pose alternatives, the imperative 'Mirror clearly' does distinguish a *wrong* kind of spontaneity, the surrender to passions which distort awareness, from the right kind, responsiveness in the impersonal calm when vision is most lucid. This is precisely the point of divergence between Taoism and the superficially similar cult of spontaneity in our own tradition of Romanticism, which values passion by its intensity however much it distorts reality.

4

Heaven and man

Among the basic concepts which Chuang-tzǔ shares with other Chinese thinkers is the pair 'Heaven' and 'man'.[51] In Confucianism Heaven is the supreme power responsible for everything which is independent of man's will, including his destiny and the moral principles by which he should live. (Destiny is the 'decree of Heaven'.) In human affairs it is one's responsibility as a man to act rightly, but whether the result is success or failure, wealth or poverty, long life or early death, is decreed by Heaven and should be accepted with contentment as one's destiny. Early Mohism grounded its morality in the 'will of Heaven', but rejected the notion of destiny, insisting that good and ill fortune are Heaven's rewards and punishments for our actions.

Around 350 BC it began to be noticed that the dichotomy of Heaven and man presents a fundamental difficulty if one recognises that there is such a thing as human nature. Given that it derives from one or the other, man's nature, being independent of his will, must be ordained for him by Heaven. Should it not follow that man obeys Heaven by following his own nature, which seems to conflict with morality? The Yangist school, abhorred by the others as egoists, had as one of its slogans 'Keeping one's nature intact'.[52] This is the start of the first profound metaphysical doubt in Chinese thought, and stimulated the great advances of the late fourth century BC. Among the Confucians, Mencius tried to close the gap between Heaven and man by the doctrine that human nature is morally good. The later Mohist school ceased to appeal to the authority of Heaven and sought new foundations for morality by developing a highly rationalised utilitarian ethic based on the actual desires and aversions of men.[53]

Chuang-tzǔ is, to modify the cliché about Spinoza, a 'Heaven-intoxicated man'. For him, it is not a matter of obeying Heaven; the sage 'constantly goes by the spontaneous and does not add anything to the process of life', he 'lives the life generated by Heaven'.[54] At first sight one might suppose that like the Yangists he wants us to give full scope to the spontaneous inclinations of man's nature. But we noticed in the last section that the implicit imperative of Taoism, 'Mirror clearly', introduces a rift within human spontaneity, rejecting the passions which blur awareness, exalting the impulses which stir in an impersonal calm which mirrors the situation with utmost clarity. The word 'nature'[55] does not appear at all in the *Inner chapters*, although it is common elsewhere in the book. Chuang-tzŭ is interested not in the nature which a man inherits at birth but in the Power which he develops by intensive training. We do not possess from birth that selfless mirror-like objectivity which ensures that every prompting is the 'impulse from Heaven'. To quote a writer in the *Outer chapters* who does speak of nature, 'By the training of the nature we recover the Power'.[56]

When thinking and putting our thoughts into words we are behaving as men; when attending and responding, in ways which we can never fully express in language or justify by reasons, our behaviour belongs with the birth, growth, decay and death of the body among the spontaneous processes generated by Heaven. We are then doing, without knowing how we do it, what Heaven destines for us. Paradoxically, to enact the destined is, since our egoism is always tempting us to think out a better way, 'the most diffi-cult thing of all'.[57] In one dialogue with Hui Shih, Chuang-tzŭ declares that the sage 'has the shape of a man, is without what is essentially man', and explains that 'Judging "That's it" and "That's not" is what I mean by "what is essentially man"'.[58] In another dialogue Yen Hui, disciple of Confucius, discovers that he has never yet been the agent of his own actions, and when he does become the agent, 'there has never yet begun to be a Hui'.[59]

Shall I say then that I act best when as a man I dissolve and allow Heaven to act through me? Here we find a recurrent tension in Chuang-tzŭ's thinking. He does not in practice expect to live in a permanent ecstasy moving like a sleepwalker guided by Heaven; he recognises that one must be sometimes 'of Heaven's party', sometimes 'of man's party', and declares that 'someone in whom neither Heaven nor man is victor over the other, this is what is meant by the True Man'.[60] The clearest formulation of a compromise stands at the head of 'The teacher who is the ultimate ancestor': 'Whoever knows what is Heaven's doing, lives the life generated by Heaven. Whoever knows what is man's doing, uses what his wits know about to nurture what his wits do not know about.'[61] Man does not know how he is born, engenders, dies, or how he acts with spontaneous assurance, which are the workings of Heaven through him; he does know how to nourish the autonomous processes of his body with food and his spontaneous aptitude by training (and by Chuang-tzŭ's own philosophising).

But immediately after this formulation Chuang-tzŭ recognises that he cannot afford a dichotomy of 'Heaven' and 'man'. It is his deepest certainty that all alternatives are false alternatives. He proceeds to ask 'How do I know that the doer I call "Heaven" is not the man? How do I know that the doer I call the "man" is not Heaven?'[62] As usual he throws off his profound ques-tion without developing it, but we may perhaps risk developing it for him. Granted that there are surrenders to spontaneity in which one seems to be driven by forces from beyond, is not the carpenter or swimmer in full command of his unreasoning skill? Whether the agent is Heaven or the man himself seems to be a matter of degree. The same applies to the specifically human activities, analysing alternatives and conforming to rules. Is it not in some sense natural for man to exercise the gift of reason, an ingratitude to Heaven to refuse it? The dichotomy is elsewhere explicitly rejected: 'For the sage there has never begun to be Heaven, never begun to be man.' [63] But it is never quite resolved, and there are some surprising twists in the discussion. One fragment actually declares that Heaven is agent only in the animal and that the perfect man 'hates Heaven'. [64]

That there are people in whom the habits of thinking in alternatives and living by rules are unbreakable is a point fully understood by Chuang-tzŭ. He sees these habits as fetters or mutilations imposed by Heaven. But what is it that Heaven is punishing? It seems that Heaven has a kind of justice different from man's, and requites not what we deliberately do but what we are. 'The maker of things, when he recompenses a man, recompenses not the man but what is from Heaven in the man.' [65] Chuang-tzŭ's exemplar of the noble man crippled by Heaven is none other than Confucius. His attitude to China's greatest teacher is remarkable, and easily misunderstood if one treats the whole book as a unity. The bitter mockery of Confucius in the Yangist chapters 'Robber Chih' and 'The old fisherman', and the elaborate condescension with which Old Tan instructs him in a cycle of stories in the *Outer chapters*, are quite foreign to Chuang-tzŭ, who never allows any of his characters to treat the Master disrespectfully to his face. Among the landmarks in his intellectual scenery Confucius stands as the great moralist, Hui Shih as the great rationalist, and he has respect for both. He sees a funny side to them of course, but Chuang-tzŭ was a man who could joke about death on his own deathbed. [66]

Very curiously, while the Hui Shih of the *Inner chapters* and elsewhere in the book talks like the logician that he is, Confucius is a moralist only in his behaviour; his thoughts are Chuang-tzŭ's own. But he understands them only in the abstract, and calmly accepts that he himself is irrevocably condemned to live by the conventions. As he tells a disciple, he is 'one of those under sentence from Heaven'; [67] and a pupil whose foot has been chopped recognises him as mutilated by Heaven as he himself has been crippled by human justice. [68] A Western reader may well see Confucius as a tragic figure. But the tragic sense assumes that the conflict between fate and human hope cannot be resolved, while a Taoist sees it as a weakness even to wish that the inevitable could be otherwise. Confucius is credited with having the dignity to accept himself as he is. But why Chuang-tzŭ chooses to present Confucius as sympathising in theory with his own philosophy is a puzzling question. It was common enough for thinkers of competing schools to put their own opinions into the mouths of the same legendary ancient sages, but to do this to the fully historical and comparatively recent founder

of a rival school, whose doctrines are publicly known, is quite a different
matter. Nobody else does it, apart from later Taoists writing new stories
about Confucius. Psychological speculation is hardly in order here, but it is
almost as though Confucius were a father-figure whose blessing the rebellious son likes to imagine would have been granted in the end.

Although Chuang-tzŭ shares the general tendency of Confucians and Taoists to think of Heaven as an impersonal power rather than as an emperor
issuing his decrees up in the sky, his attitude has a strong element of
numinous awe, a sense of man's littleness before an incomprehensible power
which he likes to personify as 'the maker of things'.[69] This concept, and the
related metaphor of man as metal moulded by a smith,[70] hardly attracts a
Westerner's attention, since they are familiar in our own Christian background. But there is no Creator in Chinese religion or philosophy (Heaven
continually 'generates' things, after the analogy of a father rather than a
craftsman, he does not create things out of nothing), and Chuang-tzŭ himself
is thinking of his maker as moulding and remoulding in an endless process of
transformation. Later when the 'maker of things' appears in Chinese literature it is as a poetic conceit borrowed from *Chuang-tzŭ*, and inside the book it
belongs exclusively to Chuang-tzŭ himself. He also uses the word *Ti*,[71] here
translated 'God', a supreme ruler who belongs to the culture of the older
Shang dynasty rather than to the Chou, which replaced him by Heaven. It is
clear that Chuang-tzŭ does not in any simple sense believe in a personal God,
but he does think of Heaven and the Way as transcending the distinction
between personal and impersonal (which would be as unreal to him as other
dichotomies), and of awe as though for a person as an appropriate attitude to
the inscrutable forces wiser than ourselves, throughout the cosmos and in
the depths of our own hearts, which he calls 'daemonic'.[72] One of his names
for the highest kind of man is the 'daemonic man', and he thinks of man as
lifted above himself by infusion of the daemonic from outside when the heart
is cleared of all accretions of past knowledge.[73]

Quite apart from the Taoist rejection of all dichotomies, within Chinese
cosmology the distinction between personal and impersonal is not absolute
but relative. A Western grappling with the concept of Heaven is likely to
presuppose that it is either a person living up in the sky or an impersonal and
physical Nature named by metaphor after the sky. But the Heaven which
ordains everything beyond the scope of man's powers is simply the sky itself.
We have already noticed the concept of *ch'i*, 'energy',[74] which has the place
which 'matter' holds in our own cosmology, and is at the root of some of the
profoundest differences of viewpoint between the ancient Chinese and ourselves. The universe is not constituted from inert matter, it is a pool of energetic fluid, the *ch'i*, out of which through their endless cycles things
condense and into which they dissolve. At its purest, most transparent and
active, it is the breath of the living man and the vitalising 'quintessence'[75]
which in physiological terms is his semen. Within the cosmos as a whole it of

course ascends as the air we breathe, while the more massive and inert *ch'i* settles down below as the earth (as in man it coheres as the body). Within this cosmology the universe will be activated by the insubstantial free-moving air of Heaven, and the extent to which any thinker chooses to personify it will depend on how far he pushes the analogy between the cosmos and man.

The experience of achieving without knowing how, living from moment to moment without knowing why, trusting to Heaven and to one's daemon, is crucial to the Taoist attitude. It is a surrender to the incomprehensible which could easily lead to the conviction of possessing magical powers. Chuang-tzŭ refers more than once to walking through fire and water or riding the wind.[76] How literally does he wish us to take him? The references are general, in contexts where we can easily take them as metaphorical. It is remarkable that throughout the thirty-three chapters of *Chuang-tzŭ* we never find a story of an admired figure exercising or pursuing unusual powers, with the exception perhaps of Lieh-tzŭ, in whom it is derided as a weakness.[77] The tale of Cook Ting's prowess with the chopper exhibits the workings of the daemonic as vividly as any miracle-story, of which there is not a single example in all the narrative variety of *Chuang-tzŭ*.

5

The unifying vision

As long as he is thinking as a man, the sage differentiates self from other and thing from thing; but in surrendering to Heaven he treats everything as one. Since all language differentiates, distinguishing by names the things of which one says 'That's it' or 'That's not', the sage, like the carpenter talking to Duke Huan, cannot find words for the totality which he experiences. Might he perhaps at least say 'Everything is one', as Hui Shih did in the last of his paradoxes? Chuang-tzŭ considers this possibility in 'The sorting which evens things out',[78] but rejects it on the grounds that in adding to what is one the proposition that it is one we arrive at two (a point similar to Plato's about the One and its name in *Sophist* 244D). In practice he speaks only of the sage treating things as one, never of things truly being one.[79] Even without the logical point it is plain from the concrete examples in the knack stories that 'Everything is one' would be an inadequate formula. Granted that the carpenter does not pose alternatives, he is making finer discriminations than he can define in language, which is what Chuang-tzŭ means when he says that 'the greatest discrimination is unspoken';[80] the oneness of the wood he chisels and his hand and his eye is more like the 'Unity within variety' of Western aesthetics.

To think in terms of 'Unity within variety' helps to resolve the apparent contradiction that the process by which the sage ceases to differentiate is conceived not as a blending with things but as a detachment from them. Ordinary people become entangled in circumstance, sink under the burden of their possessions, but the sage, to quote a slogan of the *Outer chapters*,[81] 'treats things as things but is not turned into a thing by things'. He withdraws inwards towards a viewpoint from which even his own body is perceived as external. One adept is described as externalising first the world, then the things which support life, finally life itself.[82] Others are said to 'treat their own flesh-and-bone as external to them', to 'travel on the inside of the flesh-and-bone'.[83] Not that the withdrawal is an exploration of inward experience, for Chuang-tzŭ's attitude to the world is uncompromisingly extroverted. The sage as he steps back into himself is still looking outwards; he 'uses the eye to look at the eye', he 'has ears and eyes as images he perceives', he takes his stand at the 'ultimate eye'.[84]

Here it would be a mistake to impose a mind/body dichotomy and conceive the sage as withdrawing to a realm of pure spirit from which he looks out on matter. In detaching himself from the many he is returning to the 'root' or 'trunk' or 'seed' from which they grow, into the 'ancestor' from which they descend, the 'gate' out of which they emerge, the 'axis' round which they revolve. It is at the common point from which all start that they are found to merge together and with oneself in a single whole (just as different branches turn out when traced back to be one and the same tree, not that Chuang-tzŭ develops his 'root' metaphor in this direction). There is a notable difference between the conceptualisations of this underlying ground in Chinese and in Western thought. The goal which Western philosophy has pursued has been the reality beyond appearances, on the assumption (until doubts arose as to the possibility of inferring from 'is' to 'ought') that once we know the truth about the cosmos we shall know how to live in it. The mystical tradition in the West therefore identifies the ground of things as pure Being or ultimate Reality, the vision of which is also a personal salvation. But the goal of Chinese philosophy is the Way by which to live and die, achievement of which may or may not incidentally involve exposure of illusion in our everyday vision of the world in which we act. For Taoism what matters is that the man who withdraws to the 'gate' (to pick the most relevant of the metaphors) has a clear course ahead of him, and all his actions become 'Doing Nothing',[85] spontaneous motion which is plumb with the Way. He also becomes capable of lucidly mirroring heaven and earth, but if that is an illumination of reality it is of the reality of the concrete.

We cannot name the undifferentiated, since names all serve to distinguish, and even to call it 'Way' reduces it to the path which it reveals to us. However, since that path is what one seeks in it, the 'Way' is the most apposite makeshift term for it. According to the *Outer chapters*, the term 'Way' is 'borrowed in order to walk it'.[86] *Lao-tzŭ* sometimes calls it the 'nameless', and also says 'I do not know its name, I style it the "Way"'.[87] As for Being and Reality, the existential verbs in Classical Chinese are *yu*, 'there is', and *wu*, 'there is not', nominalisable as 'what there is/something' and 'what there is not/nothing'; the words used for pronouncing something real or illusory are *shih*, 'solid/full', and *hsü*, 'tenuous/empty'. Only differentiated things may be called 'something' or 'solid'; as for the Way, it may be loosely described as 'nothing' or 'tenuous', but in the last resort it transcends these with all other dichotomies, since the whole out of which things have not yet divided will be both 'without anything' and 'without nothing'.[88] In so far as we can co-ordinate the Chinese concepts with our own, it seems that the physical world has *more* being and reality than the Way. However it is only by grasping the Way that we mirror the physical world clearly, and our illusory picture of a multiple world is compared with a dream from which the sage awakens.[89] The famous story of Chuang-tzŭ's dream of being a butterfly[90] seems, however, to make a different point, that the distinction between waking and dreaming is another false dichotomy. If I distinguish them, how can I tell whether I am now dreaming or awake?

6

Death and mutilation

Chuang-tzŭ writes sometimes of the withdrawal from the many into the one as a detachment from the entire world of change and multiplicity, one's own body included, into a solitude beyond the reach of life and death; at others he sees it rather as a bursting out of the limits of the single body, to be born and die with every new generation. It would be pointless to ask which is his true position, since in trying to put it into words he is caught up in another dichotomy which he can transcend only by moving freely between the alternatives. The liberation from selfhood is seen above all as a triumph over death. His position is not that personal consciousness will survive death, but rather than in grasping the Way one's viewpoint shifts from 'I shall no longer exist' to something like 'In losing selfhood I shall remain what at bottom I always was, identical with everything conscious or unconscious in the universe'. In the exaltation with which Chuang-tzŭ confronts death he seems to foresee the end of his individuality as an event which is both an obliteration and an opening out of consciousness. To come to feel that extinction of self does not matter since at bottom I am everything and have neither beginning nor end is (together with acceptance of annihilation and faith in individual survival) one of the three classic solutions of the problem of death; no thinker in Chinese literature, nor for all I know in the literature of the world, has experienced it as deeply and expressed it as eloquently as Chuang-tzŭ.

Nothing in Chuang-tzŭ's unusual sensibility is more striking than the ecstatic, rhapsodic tone in which he writes of death. This does not reflect a disgust with life; like most Chinese thinkers he is neither an optimist nor a pessimist, and thinks of joy and sorrow as alternating and inseparable like day and night or birth and death. Nor is it a matter of treating death as a beautiful abstraction. In 'The teacher who is the ultimate ancestor' we read of a dying man dragging himself to a well to look at his disfigured body and wonder what it will turn into, of a sage who lolls carelessly against the doorpost talking to his dying friend after shooing away his weeping family, of others who appal a disciple of Confucius by playing the zither and doing odd jobs by the corpse. In the stories about Chuang-tzŭ later in the book he goes to sleep pillowed on a skull, is found thumping a pot (the most vulgar kind of music-making) on the death of his wife, and on his deathbed laughs at his disciples for preferring to have him decently buried and eaten by the worms rather than left in the open to be eaten by the birds. This physical confrontation with death, and mockery of the rites of mourning, for Chinese the most sacred of all, is characteristic of the *Inner chapters* and of stories about Chuang-tzŭ himself, but is very rare elsewhere in Taoist literature, even in the rest of *Chuang-tzŭ*. It is quite without the morbidity of the stress on corruption in the late Medieval art of Europe, which reminds us of the horrors of our mortality for the good of our souls. It seems rather that for Chuang-tzŭ the ultimate test is to be able to look directly at the facts of one's own physical decomposition *without* horror, to accept one's dissolution as part of the universal process of transformation. 'The test that one holds fast to the Beginning is the fact that one is not afraid.' [91]

Unlike death, suffering does not much preoccupy Chuang-tzŭ. The disaster which he ranks as second only to death is deformity or mutilation of the body (not its pain, surprising as this may seem to us moderns, persuaded by the medical progress of the last century or so to think of pain as exceptional and avoidable). The ancient Chinese imputed not only a practical but a moral value to wholeness of body; for a Confucian, it was a duty when he died to return his body to his ancestors intact as when he received it from them. The school of Yang Chu, to which Chuang-tzŭ may once have belonged, laid down the principle that one should not sacrifice any part of the body, even a hair, for any external benefit, even the throne of the empire. How to reconcile oneself to disaster to the body is therefore a crux for Chuang-tzŭ. The *Inner chapters* show a remarkable interest, not shared by later Taoists even in *Chuang-tzŭ* itself, in cripples, freaks, mutilated criminals, who are able to accept and remain inwardly unaltered by their condition. The criminal with a chopped foot carries about with him the visible proof of his crime and betrayal of his ancestors. For conventional opinion, he is of all men farthest from the Way. On the contrary, says Chuang-tzŭ, if he can accept the catastrophe as his destiny, care nothing for the demeaning judgement of others, remain inwardly unbound by the rules while recognising that it will be safer to conform to them in future, he is nearer to the Way than Confucius was. To quote the title of the chapter in which these stories are collected, he possesses the 'Signs of fullness of Power'.

7
Language

The denial that the Way is communicable in words is a familiar paradox of Taoism. *Lao-tzŭ* begins with the line 'The Way that can be told is not the constant Way', which has always tempted humorists Chinese or Western to ask why the author went on to write the book.[92] The irony is especially acute in the case of Chuang-tzŭ, a master of rhapsodic prose, sophisticated argument, aphorism, anecdote, and gnomic verse, who professes a boundless scepticism as to the possibility of ever saying anything.

On closer inspection the joke loses most of its point. Taoists are trying to communicate a knack, an aptitude, a way of living, and when the carpenter tells Duke Huan that he cannot put into words how much pressure to exert in chiselling wood we both understand and agree. With philosophers who profess to know unformulable truths, an ineffable reality, no doubt we have the right to become impatient, but Taoists, as we have noticed already,[93] do not think in terms of discovering Truth or Reality. They merely have the good sense to remind us of the limitations of the language which they use to guide us towards that altered perspective on the world and that knack of living. To point the direction they use stories, verses, aphorisms, any verbal means which come to hand. Far from having no need for words they require all available resources of literary art, which is why all the classics of philosophical Taoism (*Lao-tzŭ*, *Chuang-tzŭ*, *Lieh-tzŭ*) have won important places in the literary history of China.

A classification of three modes of language is developed in a 'Mixed chapters' episode closely related to 'The sorting which evens things out', and in the account of Chuang-tzŭ in the historical chapter 'Below in the empire' his own writing is said to exhibit all of them.[94] The three terms belong to a special vocabulary developed by Chuang-tzŭ in criticising disputation, did not outlast him, and were soon misunderstood. But their meaning can be clarified in the light of the relativism of 'The sorting which evens things out', according to which the sage moves freely between temporary 'lodging-places' instead of being trapped in a permanent standpoint.

(1) 'Saying from a lodging-place' appears to be persuasion by *argumentum*

ad hominem, the only kind of victory in debate which could have any point
for Chuang-tzŭ. You temporarily 'lodge' at the other man's standpoint,
because the meanings he gives to words are for him the only meanings, and
he will not debate on any other basis.

(2) 'Weighted saying' is 'what is said on one's own authority', backed by
depth of experience, not merely the respect given to age. The aphorism
would be the most concentrated example.

(3) 'Spillover saying' is traditionally and plausibly supposed to be named
after a kind of vessel which tips over when filled to the brim and then rights
itself. This is discussed at greater length than the other two taken together.
We are told that it is for daily use, says most when it says least and least when
it says most, that it shifts freely from one standpoint to another, and that we
cannot prolong discourse or live out our lives without it. Presumably this is
the ordinary language in which meanings fluctuate but right themselves in
the spontaneous flow of discourse, providing that the speaker has the knack
of using words, can 'smooth it out on the whetstone of Heaven'.

Chuang-tzŭ's regular mode is the language which spontaneously rights
itself like the spilling vessel; he uses words not like a philosopher but like a
poet, sensitive to their richness, exploiting their ambiguities, letting conflicting meanings explode against each other in apparent contradiction. Thus
Chuang-tzŭ and his school delight in using 'know' in different senses in a
single sentence. When, for example, we are advised to 'know by depending
on what the wits do not know',[95] we can see that knowing *how*, which is
good, is being contrasted with knowing *that*, which is bad. But Taoists do
not analyse such meanings, unlike the later Mohists, who in their *Canons*
distinguish four kinds of knowing: knowing names, objects, how to relate
them and how to act.[96]

The crucial point for Chuang-tzŭ is that words have no fixed meanings
except in the artificial conditions of intellectual debate, in which one may as
well accept the opponent's definitions, since they are no more or less arbitrary than any others. 'Saying is not blowing breath, saying says something;
the only trouble is that what it says is never fixed. Do we really say something? Or have we never said anything? If you think it different from the
twitter of fledgelings, is there proof of the distinction? Or isn't there any
proof?'[97] Yet words do order themselves in speech, not according to any
rules of disputation, but by that unanalysable knack which he discerns at the
bottom of all successful behaviour, and which is the sign that Heaven is
working through us. The meanings of discourse spontaneously right themselves as long as we 'smooth it out on the whetstone of Heaven'; even the
competing voices of philosophers are the 'pipes of Heaven', which blows
through them as the wind blows different noises from hollows of different
shapes.[98]

8

The book Chuang-tzŭ *and the problem of translation*

Chuang-tzŭ illustrates to perfection the kind of battering which a text may suffer between being written in one language and being transferred to another at the other end of the world some two thousand years later. In the first place ancient Chinese thinkers did not write books, they jotted down sayings, verses, stories, thoughts and by the third century BC composed essays, on bamboo strips which were tied together in sheets and rolled up in scrolls. A chapter of *Chuang-tzŭ* would have originated as an item or collection of items making up a single scroll. Collections of scrolls ascribed on good or bad authority to one author or school grew up gradually and did not assume a standard form until Liu Hsiang (77−6 BC) edited them for the Imperial library of the Han dynasty. From his reports on the books, some of which survive, we learn that each copy available to him would have a different number of scrolls, and his method was to collate them and cut out duplicates. We do not have his report on *Chuang-tzŭ*, but according to the bibliographical chapter of the *Han history* the Imperial library copy had 52 chapters. Our present *Chuang-tzŭ* is an abridgement in 33 chapters by Kuo Hsiang (died AD 312), who may be suspected of having tacked the more interesting parts of discarded chapters on to the ones which he retained. The book as we have it from him is divided into three parts.

1 INNER CHAPTERS (chapters 1−7)

Each consists of discontinuous episodes grouped round a common theme which is summed up in a three-word chapter title. This series is homogeneous in thought and style and generally recognised as substantially the work of Chuang-tzŭ himself.

(2) OUTER CHAPTERS (chapters 8−22)

None can be plausibly ascribed to Chuang-tzŭ. These have two-word titles which are mere labels, taken from words in the first sentence. They comprise:

(a) Four complete essays (chapters 8−10 and the first part of chapter 11) by an author idiosyncratic in thought and style whom we call the 'Primitivist' and date about 205 BC.

(b) Three chapters related by their titles, 'Heaven and earth', 'Way of Heaven' and 'Circuits of Heaven' (chapters 12−14), each starting with an exposition of ideas which we class as 'Syncretist' and believe to be those of the editors of the book, probably in the second century BC. But from the Primitivist chapter 11 as far as chapter 14 only the introductory passages are homogeneous; each chapter has been filled out with all kinds of miscellaneous material. Thus the last item of chapter 11 is Syncretist, of chapter 12 Primitivist.

(c) Two complete essays (chapters 15 and 16), the first Syncretist, the next unrelated to anything elsewhere in the book.

(d) Six chapters (chapters 17−22) in which the editor seems to be trying to group materials of multiple authorship around the same themes as in the *Inner chapters*. For this, as for much else in the book, we have no better label than 'School of Chuang-tzŭ'.

(3) MIXED CHAPTERS (chapters 23−33)

Like the *Outer chapters* these have two-word titles which (except in chapters 28−31) are taken from the opening sentence. They are:

(a) Five 'ragbag' chapters (chapters 23−27), quite heterogeneous, much so badly fragmented as to suggest that they have been assembled from broken or misplaced strips in other scrolls. Some of this material looks like Chuang-tzŭ's own writing, and bits of it can be fitted with varying degrees of plausibility into mutilated parts of the *Inner chapters*.

(b) The block we call the 'Yangist miscellany' (chapters 28−31), distinguished by chapter titles summing up their content. Su Shih (AD 1036−1101) already saw that they are not the work of Chuang-tzŭ, and a modern scholar, Kuan Feng, has pointed out that they are not even Taoist, and that most (in my own opinion, all) come from another school, that of Yang Chu. They probably date from a little before and after 200 BC.

(c) The collection ends with another ragbag chapter (chapter 32) and another Syncretist essay (chapter 33) with a title related to those of chapters 12−14, 'Below in the empire' (*T'ien-hsia*, literally 'Below Heaven'). The titles are from the opening sentences as in chapters 8−27. Why have these been separated off and put at the end of the book? Probably because chapter

32 ends with a story about the death of Chuang-tzǔ, while chapter 33 is a general description and evaluation of the pre-Han philosophers down to Chuang-tzǔ, suitable as a conclusion to the book.

The themes of Chuang-tzǔ's own *Inner chapters* are summed up in their titles:

Chapter 1, 'Going rambling without a destination' – the joy of soaring above the realm of conventional judgements and practical concerns;

Chapter 2, 'The sorting which evens things out' – criticism of analytic thinking in terms of right and wrong alternatives;

Chapter 3, 'What matters in the nurture of life' – the knack of living spontaneously;

Chapter 4, 'Worldly business among men' – living in the world without compromising with it;

Chapter 5, 'The signs of fullness of Power' – evaluating the Power in a man without regard for conventional opinion;

Chapter 6, 'The teacher who is the ultimate ancestor' – reconciliation with the loss of individual identity in death;

Chapter 7, 'Responding to emperors and kings' – the government of the empire.

In the Chinese text these are the only chapters which have titles of not two but three words, resembling those of the Confucian apocrypha (*wei-shu*) of the Former Han dynasty (from 206 BC to AD 24). The terms 'even things out', the 'ultimate ancestor' and 'emperors and kings' do not occur in the *Inner chapters* themselves, only in the latest, the Syncretist stratum of the book. Probably Chuang-tzǔ left behind only disjointed pieces, mixed up perhaps with his disciples' records of his oral teaching, and it was a Syncretist editor of the second century BC who devised the headings, grouped the relics under them, and relegated the unusable bits to the *Mixed chapters*. In the last of the *Inner chapters*, centred on a theme in which Chuang-tzǔ was hardly interested, the government of the empire, one has an especially strong impression, not of an author approaching his topic from different directions, but of an editor going to great pains to find even remotely relevant passages.[99]

We can at least say that we have the Chinese text of *Chuang-tzǔ* very much as it was about AD 300, when it was already becoming difficult to understand. Kuo Hsiang, who at that time prepared the abridgement of the text which survives, also wrote the first commentary extant in full. This and other annotations and commentaries written between the third and seventh centuries AD provide explanations of varying plausibility for the many words which had already become obsolete, together with philosophical comments inevitably tinged with the neo-Taoism or Buddhism of their own times. Studied in Chinese with these traditional aids, the book has been something of a lucky dip, in which magnificent episodes mingle with obscure or unintelligible fragments for which the commentators have nothing to offer us but guesses. Further progress requires the full apparatus of modern scholarship, which Chinese, Japanese and Western specialists have only recently begun to deploy, to distinguish the different strata in the writing, restore the corrupt or dislocated text, add to the deplorably little yet known about the grammar of the classical language, make sense of the philosophical terminology. We need also to relate the book to the other philosophical literature of the age. For example, to understand Chuang-tzŭ's criticisms of disputation we have to explore the only surviving manual of disputation, the Mohist *Canons*, which textually is in even worse shape than *Chuang-tzŭ* itself. There are similar difficulties of course with all those ancient writers, Western and Eastern, who miraculously remain living voices although their words survive only in mutilated texts in imperfectly understood languages, like the statues in museums which are still living presences in spite of their broken noses and stumps of arms. However, sinology in the West has a much shorter and sparser tradition than Greek or Hebrew studies, and it will be a long time before we can share the confidence of translators of Homer or Genesis that the preliminary problems, if not solved, have at least been explored up to the limits of present knowledge.

How should we set about turning this extraordinary hotchpotch into English? There are several complete versions, three of them by the best translators of Classical Chinese of their respective generations, James Legge, H. A. Giles and Burton Watson.[100] Giles's version, first published in 1889, has a place on the margins of literary history, as a minor influence on English and American writers from Oscar Wilde to Henry Miller.[101] Watson's, which appeared in 1968, is admirable for his consistent treatment of the main philosophical terms as well as for his deftness in picking the apt and vivid word. All have the limitation that for the most part they follow the traditional commentators without coming to grips with the outstanding textual, linguistic and philosophical problems. This conservatism has not prevented them from doing justice to some of Chuang-tzŭ's best passages, but all three come to grief on a single basic error of policy. They treat *Chuang-tzŭ* as though it were what is nowadays understood by a 'book', and present it as written in prose and divided into chapters composed of paragraphs; and they assume that, however disjointed, mutilated, even frankly unintelligible the original may be, however much its parts may differ in date, in thought and style, it is their duty to trudge forward from sentence to sentence, disguising the breaks, blurring the differences, assimilating the verse to the prose, in order to sustain the illusion of a smooth flow. The trouble with this approach is not simply that it forces the translator to break down now and then and write nonsense, but that it throws him into a defensive stance which corrupts his whole style. He finds himself slipping against his will into a bland evasive English which does not commit him as to

whether any one sentence follows on to the last – an English which no
serious, let alone great artist could ever write. Any literary skill he may
possess will become positively dangerous, enabling him to weave sense and
nonsense into a seamless robe. A quite eerie effect is that the smoother the
English the more Chuang-tzŭ will assume the persona of someone who could
have written that English – intermittently lively, more often verbiage,
expressing even at its most coherent incompatible opinions from 200 years
of Chinese intellectual history. It is in the *best* translations that Chuang-tzŭ
suffers a strange mutation into a whimsical, garrulous old wiseacre to whose
ramblings you listen with half an ear in the confidence that every now and
then he will startle you awake with a vivid phrase, a striking aphorism or a
marvellous story. But this image of the great Taoist, at once affectionate and
profoundly insulting, has no relation to Chuang-tzŭ or any other writer in
the book, no relation to anything except the situation of a translator cracking
under the multiple strains of his craft.

The problem is how to break out of the crippling convention of complete,
sentence-by-sentence prose translation. Arthur Waley, the greatest of translators from Chinese, and the only one who always knew what he was doing,
was a lover of Chuang-tzŭ who had the good sense to offer only carefully
selected extracts embedded in exposition, in his *Three ways of thought in
ancient China*. If we are to risk something more ambitious, it is our duty to
remember that the ideal of integral translation is in this case meaningless,
and that the danger is that the more of the book we think we are translating
the less of it will be conveyed.

In the present venture I start from the following decisions:

(1) It is pointless to offer integral translations except of homogeneous
blocks in the corpus, such as the *Inner chapters* and the Primitivist and
Yangist sequences; but these must be presented complete. So must the other
chapters which are single essays (chapters 15, 16 and 33), and any episode
extracted from chapters which are miscellanea; everything translated must
have its entire identifiable context.

(2) The reader must be informed of what is specific to the thought of
Chuang-tzŭ, the Primitivist, the Yangists, and the Syncretists, so that he can
distinguish them and find his way around them.

(3) Only the chapters which are true essays (such as the Primitivist's)
should be treated as consecutive paragraphed prose. The *Inner chapters* are
collections of isolated episodes probably grouped together by a later editor,
and including, for example, sequences of rhymed quatrains, stories in which
speakers may burst into song, didactic verses with scattered prose comments,
strings of aphorisms, provisional formulations of ideas followed by criticisms,
propositions which Chuang-tzŭ (or a disciple perhaps) proceeds to annotate
phrase by phrase. Each requires a corresponding form in English, with a
typographic layout suited to its structure.

(4) Prose must be translated as prose and verse as verse. It may seem

surprising that all the translators except Waley neglect this surely self-evident principle. However, in a Chinese text verse is not distinguished from prose by its layout on the page, and the formal differences between them are a matter of degree and are obscured by, for example, difficulties in identifying rhymes in the ancient pronunciation. Might it not after all be sufficient to render rhymed passages as poetic prose? In the not infrequent cases of sentences of uneven length which are rhymed but by every other criterion are prose, this defence is quite reasonable. But we also have verse interludes in the four-word measures of the old *Book of songs*, which interrupt the linear development of the thought to allow interactions between parallel members of a couplet or between corresponding lines in successive quatrains. Unless spaced out line by line these will appear as soggy patches in the prose where Chuang-tzŭ seems to have forgotten what he is talking about. Rhyme as such is not the essential test, for the same applies to strings of parallelised aphorisms which differ from didactic verses only in being unrhymed.

(5) The order of the episodes in the *Inner chapters* and the other homogeneous blocks can for the most part be left as it is. But it is not sacred, since there is no reason to suppose that Chuang-tzŭ ever did put his jottings in a definitive order. The occasional passages which break recognisable continuities may be moved to more suitable contexts. We may also use *Mixed chapter* fragments which seem on internal grounds to be Chuang-tzŭ's to fill gaps in the *Inner chapters*. All such transpositions will be identified.[102]

(6) With the mass of varied materials in the *Outer* and *Mixed chapters* which in the present state of scholarship can only be classed as 'School of Chuang-tzŭ', the most convenient policy is to select and group by topic. Every episode chosen must be presented complete, as must such cycles as the tales about Chuang-tzŭ and about the meetings of Confucius and Old Tan. Otherwise, I recognise no duty to supply even easily translatable episodes which do not seem to me to add to the philosophical or literary value of the book. In theory it would be possible to reproduce and regroup all the items, concluding with a collection of scraps decorated with scholarly question marks and rows of dots; but to go on adding to the translated passages brings diminishing returns. A reader curious to know what I have left out (which amounts to a fifth of the book, and since tastes differ may well include some people's favourite passages) will probably also want to check my rearrangements, and will be better served by the existing versions than by an expanded translation on the present lines.

(7) The ideal version would, like the original, have items which are delightful and illuminating at first reading, and others which are elliptical, difficult, enigmatic, to be skipped or to be wrestled with in the light of introduction and notes. But it would never amble between sense and nonsense in that inconsequential meander to a faultering rhythm which should always be taken as a warning that the translator is losing his grip, yet is so easily

mistaken for the mysterious workings of the Oriental mind. Not that I am confident of having attained that ideal myself, for some of the worst problems are raised by the *Inner chapters*, which I am committed to translate entire. I offer in advance my apologies to the ghost of Chuang-tzŭ.

There remains one obstinate problem for which only compromise solutions are possible. How is one to do equal justice to Chuang-tzŭ as a philosopher and as a poet? Most versions show a bias towards one side or the other. A primarily literary translator (such as Giles or Watson) will probably have some liking for the Taoist view of life but also a Taoist distaste for the analysis of concepts, without which he cannot select and manipulate his English equivalents effectively. More intellectual translators (such as Legge, or the great historian of Chinese philosophy Fung Yu-lan, who published a version of the *Inner chapters*) are inclined to neglect the literary aspect as though it were mere decoration of the ideas. But a Taoist is a thinker who despises *thoughts*, yet values, and finds the imagery and rhythm to convey, any spontaneously emerging process of thinking which he senses is orienting him in the direction of the Way. My own private final test of whether translation is really working is whether it catches any of the extraordinary rhythmic energy of Chuang-tzŭ's writing, not merely for the lift of the heart which it gives but because to lose it falsifies the pace and shifts and stresses of his thinking.

In the Chinese original the thinker and the poet are one. But in the effort to make him speak our language we are constantly faced with a choice between the ugly expression and the inexact. If we are to come to grips with the key terms of Taoist vocabulary we need regular equivalents, which will often sound awkward, and will assume their full meaning only after being experienced repeatedly in context. In 'The sorting which evens things out' one may translate, as in non-philosophical contexts, *shih pi* by 'this' and 'that', *shih fei* by 'right' and 'wrong', and the English will flow very smoothly (that precious sparing of the nerves from the shock of jarring words for which translators are tempted to sacrifice every other value); but the argument, which turns on the single word *shih*, will drop out of sight. Having vowed not to give the impression that Chuang-tzŭ writes mellifluous nonsense, I render *shih pi* by 'it' and 'other' and *shih fei* by 'That's it' and 'That's not'. These expressions are not easy to manipulate, especially since Chuang-tzŭ appears to make a distinction, crucial throughout the chapter, between two kinds of *shih* – *yin shih* ('going by circumstance and *shih*-ing') and *wei shih* ('deeming and *shih*-ing'). These I am reduced to rendering 'the "That's it" which goes by circumstance' and 'the "That's it" which deems'. Here the coherence of the conceptual structure has to be respected at any cost. But the cost is considerable, for Chuang-tzŭ is writing as a poet just as much here as anywhere else. The translator of a complex text is a juggler with a dozen balls to keep in simultaneous flight, and some of them are always bouncing on the floor.

NOTES TO PART ONE

1 Arthur Waley, *Three ways of thought in ancient China* (London, 1939), p. 163.

2 cf. p. 44 below.

3 cf. p. 117 below.

4 cf. p. 140 below.

5 cf. p. 136 below.

6 cf. p. 63f below.

7 *Pu te yi*.

8 cf. p. 135f below.

9 cf. pp. 79-81 below. When Confucius flatters Robber Chih he professes to see in his strong and handsome body the supreme proof of the Power in him (p. 236 below).

10 There is an unfortunate slip in the phrasing of the title of Arthur Waley's translation of this text (*The Way and its Power*, London, 1934) which has misled some readers into supposing that the Power belongs to the Way; it belongs to the sage and to the fighting cock.

11 cf. pp. 50, 67, 70, 71, 88 below.

12 cf. p. 44 below.

13 cf. pp. 48, 84, 97 below.

14 cf. p. 44 below.

15 cf. p. 71 below.

16 cf. pp. 283-5 below.

17 We in fact translate the phrase as 'chop logic' on pp. 55, 82 below.

18 Translated in A. C. Graham, *Later Mohist logic, ethics and science* Hong Kong and London 1978.

19 *Canons* B. 35, 48, 68, 71, 72, 79, 82 (ut sup. n. 18).

20 *Pien*, literally 'distinguishing' (between right and wrong alternatives). The term we translate by 'sophist' is *pien-che* 'distinguisher'.

21 The demonstrative pronoun *shih*, 'this' (the aforementioned/the one in question), used verbally ('is-this') and the negative copula *fei*, 'is-not'. In ordinary contexts they can be translated quite conveniently as 'right' and 'wrong'; for the considerations which force us to use the unwieldy 'That's it' and 'That's not', cf. p. 33 above.

22 *Wei*.

23 *Jan*.

24 *K'o*.

25 Ut sup. n. 18, pp. 214-16 and *passim*.

26 cf. p. 53 below.

27 *Canons* A 8.

28 *Wei shih*, 'deem and judge to be *shih*'.

29 *Yin shih*, 'go by and judge to be *shih*'.

30 cf. p. 102 below.

31 cf. p. 63 below.

32 cf. p. 60 below.

33 cf. p. 58 below.

34 cf. p. 63 below.

35 cf. p. 102 below.

36 cf. p. 50f below.

37 cf. p. 51 below.

38 cf. p. 283 below.

39 Ut sup. n. 18, pp. 299, 341.

40 cf. p. 52 below.

41 cf. p. 55 below.

42 cf. p. 48 below.

43 cf. p. 57 below.

44 cf. p. 62 below.

45 cf. p. 91 below.

46 cf. p. 70 below.

47 cf. p. 69 below.

48 I have developed this argument in '*Taoist spontaneity and the dichotomy of "is" and "ought"*', in *Experimental essays on Chuang-tzŭ*, edited Victor H. Mair, forthcoming University Press of Hawaii.

49 cf. p. 98 below.

50 cf. p. 259 below.

51 *T'ien*, 'Heaven, sky' and *jen*, 'man'.

52 cf. p. 221 below.

53 Ut sup. n. 18, pp. 44-52.

54 cf. pp. 82, 84 below.

55 *Hsing*.

56 cf. p. 156 below.

57 cf. p. 71 below.

58 cf. p. 82 below.

59 cf. p. 68f below.

60 cf. p. 85 below.

61 cf. p. 84 below.

62 cf. p. 84 below.

63 cf. p. 111 below.

64 cf. p. 100 below.

65 cf. p. 108 below.

66 cf. p. 125 below.

67 cf. p. 90 below.

68 cf. p. 79 below.

69 cf. pp. 88f, 91, 95, 108 below.

70 cf. p. 88f below.

71 cf. pp. 65, 86 below.

72 *Shen*, primarily verbal, '(be) daemonic': nominalised, 'the daemonic, daemon'. Rudolph Otto in *The idea of the Holy* (translated by John W. Harvey, Oxford, 1925) coined the word 'numinous' to identify a power and intelligence higher than and alien to man, which refuses quite to fit our categories of the rational, the personal and the moral, and can enter into man and raise him above himself. In modern vocabulary the moralising and rationalising use of 'God', 'holy', 'sacred', 'glory' has eroded the sense of it, and it is trivialised in the 'uncanny', 'eerie' and 'haunted' of ghost stories. 'Numinous' is hardly usable in literary translation, being a coined word without resonance, but Otto himself calls attention to Goethe's use of 'daemonic' in such passages as the following: 'The Daemonic is that which cannot be accounted for by understanding or reason ... In Poetry there is from first to last something daemonic, and especially in its unconscious appeal, for which all intellect and reason is insufficient, and which therefore has an efficacy beyond all concepts.'' ... And in general it is manifested throughout nature, visible and invisible, in the most diverse ways. Many creatures in the animal kingdom are of a wholly daemonic kind ...'. 'This daemonic character appears in its most *dreadful* form when it stands out dominatingly in some *man*. Such are not always the most remarkable men ... But an incredible force goes forth from them, and they exercise an incredible power over all creatures, nay, perhaps even over the elements' (quoted Otto, op. cit. 155–7). 'Daemonic' seems to me to be the modern word closest to *shen*, but I use it with the warning that its restless, anguished quality is foreign to the Chinese word, not to mention the malign associations which it tends to collect by confusion with 'demoniac'.

73 cf. pp. 69, 105 below.

74 cf. p. 7 above.

75 *Ching*.

76 cf. pp. 44, 46, 58, 84 below.

77 cf. p. 44 below.

78 cf. p. 56 below.

79 cf. pp. 46, 53, 77 below. In one 'School of Chuang-tzŭ' episode the Yellow Emperor does say that 'the myriad things are one', but then confesses that by expounding the Way in words he has displayed his own ignorance of it (p. 160 below).

80 cf. p. 57 below.

81 There is evidence that at some stage the slogan also appeared in the *Inner chapters* (p. 184 below).

82 cf. p. 87 below.

83 cf. pp. 78, 89 below.

84 cf. pp. 62, 77, 85 below.

85 *Wu wei*, 'Doing Nothing' (a paradoxical expression which some translators soften by such equivalents as 'Non-action'), is a basic concept in *Lao-tzŭ* but less prominent throughout most of *Chuang-tzŭ*. *Wu wei* is refraining from trying to force spontaneous trends by deliberate action. It implies letting most things alone – the ruler leaving government to his ministers and intervening only at the strategic points where the minimum effort will achieve the maximum result, or the hermit withdrawing into private life. It also implies that when one does move, it is not 'doing' (as the execution of a reasoned project with a fixed end), but tending towards fluid goals in response to changing circumstances, as spontaneously as the unwilled processes of heaven and earth.

86 cf. p. 153 below.

87 Lao Tzu: *Tao te ching*, translated D. C. Lau (Penguin Classics, 1963), ch. 1, 32, 37, 41; and 25.

88 cf. p. 157 below.

89 cf. p. 91 below.

90 cf. p. 61 below.

91 cf. p. 77 below.

92 cf. *The philosophers*, a satirical verse by Po Chü-yi (AD 722–846) translated by Arthur Waley, *Chinese poems* (London, 1946), 173.

93 cf. p. 21 above.

94 cf. p. 283 below.

95 cf. p. 102 below.

96   *Canons* A 80.
97   cf. p. 52 below.
98   cf. p. 48f below.
99   cf. p. 94 below.
100   Complete English translations are: F. H. Balfour, *The divine classic of Nan-hua* (Shanghai, 1881); H. A. Giles, *Chuang-tzŭ* London, 1926 (1st edition 1889); James Legge, *Texts of Taoism* (*Sacred books of the East* vols. 39, 40) (Oxford, 1891); James R. Ware, *The sayings of Chuang Chou* (New York, 1963); Burton Watson, *Complete works of Chuang Tzu* (New York and London, 1968) (cf. also his selection, *Chuang Tzu: basic writings* (New York, 1964).

The *Inner chapters* have been translated by Fung Yu-lan, *Chuang-tzŭ* (Shanghai, 1933); Gia-fu Feng and Jane English, *Chuang Tseu: Inner chapters* (New York, 1974).

101   There is a strong tinge of Chuang-tzŭ in Wilde's *Soul of man under social-ism*, first published in 1891, and one direct quotation: '...as a wise man once said many centuries before Christ, there is such a thing as leaving mankind alone; there is no such thing as governing mankind'. The reference is to the opening sentence of ch. 11, 'Keep it in place and within bounds (p. 211 below), in Giles's version: 'There has been such a thing as letting mankind alone; there has never been such a thing as governing mankind.' Wilde had reviewed the book enthusiastically in the *Speaker* 8 Feb. 1890, describing it as 'the most caustic criticism of modern life I have met with for some time'. *Musings of a Chinese mystic*, a selection from H. A. Giles's translation by Lionel Giles (*Wisdom of the East series*, London, 1906), is mentioned among 'the books in my life' in Henry Miller's *A devil in paradise*.

102   cf. pp. 36–39 below.

Finding list for the Chinese text

3/10   *Miscellaneous*

189f	18/29−39
190	26/48f
190	23/70−2
191	19/35−8
191f	19/38−46
192f	14/30−44

4   *Essays of the Primitivist*

200−203	8/1−26 + 12/95−102 + 8/26−33
204−206	9
207−210	10/(Delete 8−10, 14, 21f, 26)
211−213	11/1−28 (Delete 28)
214f	14/60 74
216f	12/83−95 + 11/57−61

5   *Yangist miscellany*

224−233	28
234−243	29
244−247	30
248−253	31

6   *Syncretist writings*

259 263	13/1−45
264−267	15
268	11/66−74
269	12/1−6
269f	14/1−5
271f	12/6−12
272	12/12−18
273	13/60−4
274−285	33

Text (Translation)

ch. 1 (pp. 43−7)
ch. 2/1−9 (pp. 48f), 9−90 (pp. 50−60), 90f (p. 60), 91f (p. 60), 92−6 (pp. 60f)
ch. 3/1f (p. 62), 2−19 (pp. 63−5)
ch. 4 (pp. 66−75)
ch. 5/1−31 (pp. 76−9), 31−40 (pp. 79f), 41−7 (p. 80), 47−9 (p. 81), 49−52 (p. 80), 52−60 (p. 82)
ch. 6/1−11 (pp. 84f), 11−14 (pp. 91f), 14−17 (p. 85), 17−19 (p. 79), 19−22 (pp. 85f), 22−4 (p. 90), 24−73 (pp. 86−91), 73−89 (p. 90f), 89−97 (pp. 92f)
ch. 7/1−26 (pp. 94−7), 26f (p. 81), 27−35 (pp. 97f)
ch. 8/1−26 (pp. 200−2), 26−33 (pp. 202f)
ch. 9 (pp. 204−6)
ch. 10, deleting 8−10, 14, 21f, 26 (pp. 207−10)
ch. 11/1−28, deleting 28 (pp. 211−13), 28−44 (pp. 177−9), 57−61 (pp. 216f), 61−3 (p. 185), 63−6 (p. 150), 66−74 (p. 268)

ch. 12/1−6 (p. 269), 6−18 (pp. 271f), 26−33 (pp. 179t), 33−7 (pp. 174t), 37−41
(p. 156), 41−5 (pp. 130f), 52−69 (pp. 186f), 77−83 (p. 174), 83−95 (p. 216),
95−102 (p. 202)

ch. 13/1−45 (pp. 259−263), 45−53 (p. 128), 60−4 (p. 273), 64−74 (pp. 139f)

ch. 14/1−5 (pp. 269f), 13−30 (pp. 164−166), 30−44 (pp. 192f), 44−56 (pp. 129f),
56−60 (pp. 128f), 60−74 (pp. 214f), 74−82 (pp. 133f)

ch. 15 (pp. 264−7)

ch. 16 (pp. 171f)

ch. 17/1−24 (pp. 144f), 24−28 (p. 150), 28−48 (pp. 146−148), 48−53 (p. 149),
65−81 (pp. 154−6), 81−91 (pp. 122f)

ch. 18/15−19 (pp. 123f), 22−9 (pp. 124f), 29−39 (pp. 189f), 40−6 (p. 184)

ch. 19/1−7 (pp. 181f), 7−15 (p. 137), 15−17 (p. 174), 17−21 (p. 138), 22−6
(pp. 136f), 35−46 (pp. 191f), 46−54 (pp. 135f), 54−9 (p. 135), 62−4 (p. 138)

ch. 20/1−9 (p. 121), 9−22 (p. 173), 22−4 (p. 142), 45−50 (p. 120), 50−61
(pp. 167f), 61−8 (p. 118), 68−70 (pp. 141f)

ch. 21/14−24 (pp. 168f), 24−38 (pp. 129f), 38−44 (p. 122), 45−7 (p. 139), 47−57
(pp. 140f)

ch. 22/1−16 (pp. 159f), 16−21 (pp. 148f), 21−8 (pp. 160f), 28−43 (pp. 132f),
43−68 (pp. 161−164), 68−70 (p. 139), 70−6 (p. 164)

ch. 23/42−4 (p. 103), 52−8 (pp. 102f), 58−66 (p. 104), 66f (pp. 81f), 70−2 (p. 190),
72−74 (p. 106)

ch. 24/38−48 (p. 101), 48−51 (p. 124), 61−5 (p. 105), 70−73 (pp. 149f), 88−96
(pp. 109f), 96f (p. 85), 97f (p. 85), 101f (p. 81), 102f (p. 81), 103−5 (p. 63),
105−111 (pp. 62f)

ch. 25/9−15 (p. 141), 15−20 (pp. 110f), 20−33 (pp. 153f), 33−8 (p. 109), 43−50
(p. 188), 51−54 (p. 102), 54−59 (pp. 108f), 59−82 (pp. 151−153).

ch. 26/6−11 (p. 119), 31−33 (p. 100), 48f (p. 190)

ch. 27/1−10 (pp. 106f), 10−14 (p. 102), 16−21 (p. 105)

ch. 28−31 (pp. 224−253)

ch. 32/10f (p. 142), 11−15 (pp. 107f), 22−6 (pp. 119f), 41f (p. 182), 42−6 (p. 120),
46f (pp. 118f), 47−50 (p. 125), 50−2 (p. 63)

ch. 33 (pp. 274−285)

Part Two

The Writings of Chuang-tzŭ

The *Inner chapters* (chapters 1–7) of *Chuang-tzŭ* and passages related to the *Inner chapters*

1

Going rambling without a destination

The pieces which the compilers of *Chuang-tzǔ* assembled in 'Going rambling without a destination' are all on the theme of soaring above the restricted viewpoints of the worldly. Escape the fixed routes to worldly success and fame, defy all reproaches that you are useless, selfish, indifferent to the good of the Empire, and a perspective opens from which all ordinary ambitions are seen as negligible, the journey of life becomes an effortless ramble.

In the North Ocean there is a fish, its name is the K'un; the K'un's girth measures who knows how many thousand miles. It changes into a bird, its name is the P'eng; the P'eng's back measures who knows how many thousand miles. When it puffs out its chest and flies off, its wings are like clouds hanging from the sky. This bird when the seas are heaving has a mind to travel to the South Ocean. (The South Ocean is the Lake of Heaven.) In the words of the *Tall stories*, 'When the P'eng travels to the South Ocean, the wake it thrashes on the water is three thousand miles long, it mounts spiralling on the whirlwind ninety thousand miles high, and is gone six months before it is out of breath.' (The *Tall stories of Ch'i* is a record of marvels.) Is the azure of the sky its true colour? Or is it that the distance into which we are looking is infinite? It never stops flying higher till everything below looks the same as above (heat-hazes, dust-storms, the breath which living things blow at each other).

If a mass of water is not bulky enough it lacks the strength to carry a big boat. When you upset a bowl of water over a dip in the floor, a seed will make a boat for it, but if you put the bowl there it jams, because your boat is too big for such shallow water. If the mass of the wind is not bulky enough it lacks the strength to carry the great wings. So it is only when the bird is ninety thousand miles high, with the wind underneath it, that it rests its weight on the wind; and it must have the blue sky on its back and a clear view ahead before it will set its course for the South.

A cicada and a turtle-dove laughed at it, saying, 'We keep flying till we're

bursting, stop when we get to an elm or sandalwood, and sometimes are
dragged back to the ground before we're there. What's all this about being
ninety thousand miles up when he travels south?'

Someone off to the green of the woods, with enough for three meals will be
home with his belly still full; someone going thirty miles pounds grain for the
days he will be away; someone going three hundred miles lays in grain to last
three months. What do these two creatures know? Little wits cannot keep up
with great, or few years with many. How would we know that this is so? The
mushroom of a morning does not know old and new moon, the cricket does not
know spring and autumn; their time is too short. South of Ch'u there is the tree
Ming-ling, which grows through a spring of five hundred years, declines
through an autumn of five hundred years; in the remotest past there was the
great tree Ch'un, with eight thousand years for its spring and eight thousand
for its autumn; it is only nowadays that P'eng-tsu is uniquely famous for living
long, and is it not sad that common men should think him insurpassable?

(T'ang's questions to Chi were about this. 'In the North where nothing
grows there is a vast sea, which is the Lake of Heaven. There is a fish there,
several thousand miles broad, no one knows how long; its name is the K'un.
There is a bird there, its name is the P'eng, its back is as big as Mount T'ai,
its wings are like clouds hanging from the sky. It mounts the whirlwind in a
ram's horn spiral ninety thousand miles high, and only when it is clear of the
clouds, with the blue sky on its back, does it set its course southward to
journey to the South Ocean. A quail laughed at it, saying ''Where does he
think he's going? I do a hop and a skip and up I go, and before I've gone more
than a few dozen yards come fluttering down among the bushes. That is the
highest one can fly, where does he think he's going?'' ' This was in disputation about the small and the great.)

Those, then, who are clever enough to do well in one office or efficient
enough to protect one district, whose powers suit one prince and are put to
the test in one state, are seeing themselves as the little birds did, and Sung
Jung smiled at them in disdain. Not only that, he refused to be encouraged
though the whole world praised him, or deterred though the whole world
blamed him, he was unwavering about the division between inward and outward, discriminating about the boundary between honour and disgrace – but
then he soared no higher. (He was too concerned about the world to break
clean away.) Or that Lieh-tzŭ now, he journeyed with the winds for his
chariot, a fine sight it must have been, and did not come back for fifteen days.
(Even so, there was something he failed to plant in his own soil.) The former
of them, in the hope of bringing blessings to the world, failed to break clean
away; the latter, even if he did save himself the trouble of going on foot, still
depended on something to carry his weight. As for the man who rides a true
course between heaven and earth, with the changes of the Six Energies for
his chariot, to travel into the infinite, is there anything that he depends on?
As the saying goes,

> The utmost man is selfless,
> The daemonic man takes no credit for his deeds,
> The sage is nameless.

NOTE The passages we have bracketed look like afterthoughts of Chuang-tzŭ or later annotations, and in the Chinese text three of them seem out of place; in the translation they have been pushed forward a little.

Sung Jung is the philosopher Sung Hsing of 'Below in the empire' (pp. 278f below), one of whose doctrines was that 'To be insulted is not disgraceful'. Chuang-tzŭ sees his refusal to feel devalued by other men's judgements as a first step to escape from the world, but regrets that he still thought it his duty to get involved in politics for the good of the empire. Lieh-tzŭ, later ranked among the greatest Taoist sages, is apparently seen by Chuang-tzŭ as a man who missed the final liberation by mistakenly seeking the Way through magic; in the single story about him in the *Inner chapters* (pp. 96–8 below) he is misled by a sorcerer before he attains the true Way. Neither of them quite achieves a selflessness indifferent to winning credit for deeds and having an honoured name.

The 'Six Energies' which activate the cyclic motions of heaven and earth are traditionally enumerated as Yin and Yang, wind and rain, dark and light.

· · ·

Yao resigned the Empire to Hsü Yu, saying

'When the sun or the moon is up, if the torch fires are not put out, aren't we taking too much trouble to light the world? When the timely rains fall, if we go on flooding the channels, aren't we working too hard to water the fields? While you, sir, are in your place the Empire is in order, yet here I still am in the seat of honour. In my own eyes I do not deserve it; let me make you a present of the Empire.'

'If you order things as Emperor, it's that already the Empire is in order; and if I were to see any point in taking your place, would it be for the sake of the name? The name is the guest of the substance. Would it be for the sake of the substance? The tit that nests in the deep forest wants no more than one branch, the mole that drinks in the Yellow River no more than a bellyful. Go back where you belong, my lord, the Empire is no use to me. Even when the chief cook does run a disorderly kitchen, the priest and the medium will not step over the jars and dishes to take his place.'

NOTE In Confucian legend the pre-dynastic emperor Yao is a sage who when his time is over abdicates to the man best fitted to rule in his place, Shun. Yangists and Taoists delighted in imagining a recluse Hsü Yu who disdained the offer of Yao's throne. In this and the next episode Chuang-tzŭ introduces a further refinement: Yao himself understood that the good order of his reign came not from his own policies but from individuals cultivating the Power in them in private, Hsü Yu and the nameless man on Mount Ku-yi. In ancient Chinese thought political order results directly from the mysterious influence of the Power in the ruler, and his political acts are merely its by-products. For a modern reader, this is a strange conceptualisation, but we may express Chuang-tzŭ's insight in more familiar terms – the social fabric coheres or dissolves by the action of influences which have little to do with the deliberate policies of rulers, and which may be emanating from humble, publicly unnoticed individuals.

.   .   .

Chien Wu put a question to Lien Shu,

'I heard Chieh Yü say something, he talked big but there was no sense in it, he left the firm ground and never came back. I was amazed and frightened by his words, which streamed on into the infinite like the Milky Way, wild extravagances, nothing to do with man as he really is.'

'What did he say?'

'In the mountains of far-off Ku-yi there lives a daemonic man, whose skin and flesh are like ice and snow, who is gentle as a virgin. He does not eat the five grains but sucks in the wind and drinks the dew; he rides the vapour of the clouds, yokes flying dragons to his chariot, and roams beyond the four seas. When the daemonic in him concentrates it keeps creatures free from plagues and makes the grain ripen every year.'

'I thought him mad and wouldn't believe him.'

'Yes, the blind can never share in the spectacle of emblems and ornaments, nor the deaf in the music of drums and bells. Is it only in flesh-and-bone that there is blindness and deafness? The wits have them too. When he spoke these words he was like a girl who waits for a suitor to come. This man, this Power that is in him, would merge the myriad things and make them one. The age has an incessant urge towards misrule, who are these people so eager to make the business of the empire theirs? This man no other thing will wound; though the great floods rise to the sky he will not drown, though metal and stone fuse in the great droughts and moors and mountains char he will not burn. From this man's very dust and siftings you could smelt and mould a Yao or Shun. Who are these people so determined to make other things their business?

'A man of Sung who traded in ceremonial caps travelled to the Yüeh tribes, but the men of Yüeh who cut their hair short and tattoo their bodies had no use for them. Yao who reduced the people of the Empire to order, and imposed regular government on all within the seas, went off to see the Four in the mountains of far-off Ku-yi, on the north bank of Fen River, and in a daze forgot his empire there.'

NOTE   Chieh Yü, the madman of Ch'u who mocked Confucius, is Chuang-tzŭ's favourite character in the Confucius story (pp. 74, 95 below). The 'Four' have not been plausibly identified.

.   .   .

Said Hui Shih to Chuang-tzŭ

'The King of Wei gave me the seeds of a great calabash. I planted them,

they grew up, with gourds of five bushels. When you filled them with water
or soup they weren't solid enough to stay upright, if you split them to make
ladles they sagged and spilled over. It's not that they weren't impressively
big, but because they were useless I smashed them to bits.'

'You really are clumsy, sir, in finding uses for something big. There was a
man of Sung who was expert in making a salve to keep hands from chapping.
For generations the clan had been silk-bleachers by trade. A stranger heard
about it, and asked to buy the secret for a hundred pieces of gold. The man
assembled his clan and talked it over. "For generations", he said, "we have
been silk bleaching, for no more than a few pieces. Now in one morning we
can sell the art for a hundred. I propose we give it to him."

'The stranger when he got it recommended it to the King of Wu. There
was trouble with Yüeh, and the King of Wu made him a general. That
winter he fought a battle by water with the men of Yüeh. He utterly defeated
the men of Yüeh, and was enfiefed in a bit of the conquered territory.

'In their ability to keep hands from chapping, there was nothing to choose
between them; if one of them got a fief for it while the other stayed a silk-
bleacher, it's that they put it to different uses. Now if you had five-bushel
calabashes, why didn't it occur to you to make them into those big bottles
swimmers tie to their waists, and go floating away over the Yangtse and the
Lakes? If you worried because they sagged and wouldn't hold anything, isn't
it that you still have a heart where the shoots grow up tangled?'

* * *

Said Hui Shih to Chuang-tzŭ

'I have a great tree, people call it the tree-of-heaven. Its trunk is too
knobbly and bumpy to measure with the inked line, its branches are too curly
and crooked to fit compasses or L-square. Stand it up in the road and a
carpenter wouldn't give it a glance. Now this talk of yours is big but useless,
dismissed by everyone alike.'

'Haven't you ever seen a wild cat or a weasel? It lurks crouching low in
wait for strays, makes a pounce east or west as nimble uphill or down, and
drops plumb into the snare and dies in the net. But the yak now, which is as
big as a cloud hanging from the sky, this by being able to be so big is unable to
catch as much as a mouse. Now if you have a great tree and think it's a pity
it's so useless, why not plant it in the realm of Nothingwhatever, in the wilds
which spread out into nowhere, and go roaming away to do nothing at its
side, ramble around and fall asleep in its shade?

> Spared by the axe
> No thing will harm it.
> If you're no use at all,
> Who'll come to bother you?'.

2

The sorting which evens things out

The last word in the title *Ch'i wu lun* is sometimes understood as 'discourse' ('The discourse on evening things out'), sometimes in its more basic sense of 'sort out (in coherent discourse)'. Comparison with the three-word titles of the other *Inner chapters* favours the latter alternative. *Lun*, 'sorting out', is the one kind of thinking always mentioned with approval in *Chuang-tzŭ*. Outside Taoism it suggests grading in superior and inferior categories, but Chuang-tzŭ detaches it from valuation, turns it into 'the sorting which evens things out'.

The theme of the chapter is the defence of a synthesising vision against Confucians, Mohists and Sophists, who analyse, distinguish alternatives and debate which is right or wrong. It contains the most philosophically acute passages in the *Inner chapters*, obscure, fragmented, but pervaded by the sensation, rare in ancient literatures, of a man jotting the living thought at the moment of its inception. It is a pity that the Syncretist who assembled the chapter seems to have been out of sympathy with these intellectual subtleties designed to discredit the intellect, for he has relegated a number of closely related passages to the *Mixed chapters* (pp. 101–8, 110f below).

Tzŭ-ch'i of Nan-kuo reclined elbow on armrest, looked up at the sky and exhaled, in a trance as though he had lost the counterpart of himself. Yen-ch'eng Tzŭ-yu stood in waiting before him.

'What is this?' he said. 'Can the frame really be made to be like withered wood, the heart like dead ashes? The reclining man here now is not the reclining man of yesterday.'

'You do well to ask that, Tzŭ-yu! This time I had lost my own self, did you know it? You hear the pipes of men, don't you, but not yet the pipes of earth, the pipes of earth but not yet the pipes of Heaven?'

'I venture to ask the secret of it.'

'That hugest of clumps of soil blows out breath, by name the "wind". Better if it were never to start up, for whenever it does ten thousand hollow places burst out howling, and don't tell me you have never heard how the hubbub swells! The recesses in mountain forests, the hollows that pit great trees a hundred spans round, are like nostrils, like mouths, like ears, like sockets, like bowls, like mortars, like pools, like puddles. Hooting, hissing, sniffing, sucking, mumbling, moaning, whistling, wailing, the winds ahead sing out AAAH!, the winds behind answer EEEH!, breezes strike up a tiny chorus, the whirlwind a mighty chorus. When the gale has passed, all the hollows empty, and don't tell me you have never seen how the quivering slows and settles!'

'The pipes of earth, these are the various hollows; the pipes of men, these are rows of tubes. Let me ask about the pipes of Heaven.'

'Who is it that puffs out the myriads which are never the same, who in their self-ending is sealing them up, in their self-choosing is impelling the force into them?

'Heaven turns circles, yes!
Earth sits firm, yes!
Sun and moon vie for a place, yes!
Whose is the bow that shoots them?
Whose is the net that holds them?
Who is it sits with nothing to do and gives them the push that sends them?

'Shall we suppose, yes, that something triggers them off, then seals them away, and they have no choice?
Or suppose, yes, that wheeling in their circuits they cannot stop themselves?
Do the clouds make the rain?
Or the rain the clouds?
Whose bounty bestows them?
Who is it sits with nothing to do as in ecstasy he urges them?

'The winds rise in the north,
Blow west, blow east,
And now again whirl high above.
Who breathes them out, who breathes them in?
Who is it sits with nothing to do and sweeps between and over them?'

NOTE Chuang-tzŭ's parable of the wind compares the conflicting utterances of philosophers to the different notes blown by the same breath in the long and short tubes of the pan-pipes, and the noises made by the wind in hollows of different shapes. It is natural for differently constituted persons to think differently; don't try to decide between their opinions, listen to Heaven who breathes through them.

The trance of Tzŭ-ch'i reappears in a *Mixed chapter* fragment (p. 105 below), where he speaks of a progressive objectivisation of successive selves from which he detaches himself. Here he has finally broken out of the dichotomy, losing both 'the counterpart of himself' and 'his own self'.

'That hugest of clumps of soil', a phrase peculiar to the *Inner chapters* (pp. 86–8 below), seems to conjure up an image of the universe so far in the distance that it is no bigger than a clod you could hold in your hand.

The poem which we identify as the conclusion of the dialogue survives only in one of the *Outer chapters*, the 'Circuits of Heaven' (chapter 14). But the Buddhist *Chih-kuan fu-hsing ch'uan-hung chüeh* (preface dated AD 766) cites it from the *Inner chapters* (*Taishō Tripitaka* No. 1912, p. 440C), from which it would have been excised when *Chuang-tzŭ* was abridged, to avoid duplication. The fit is so neat that it can be located here with some confidence.

•   •   •

'Great wit is effortless,
Petty wit picks holes.
Great speech is flavourless,
Petty speech strings words.

'While it sleeps, the paths of souls cross:
When it wakes, the body opens.
Whatever we sense entangles it:
Each day we use that heart of ours for strife.'

The calm ones, the deep ones, the subtle ones.

'Petty fears intimidate,
The supreme fear calms.
It shoots like the trigger releasing the string on the notch',

referring to its manipulation of 'That's it, that's not'.

It ties us down as though by oath, by treaty',

referring to its commitment to the winning alternative.

'Its decline is like autumn and winter',

speaking of its daily deterioration. As it sinks, that which is the source of its deeds cannot be made to renew them.

'It clogs as though it were being sealed up',

speaking of its drying up in old age. As the heart nears death, nothing can make it revert to the Yang.

Pleasure in things and anger against them, sadness and joy, forethought and regret, change and immobility, idle influences that initiate our gestures – music coming out of emptiness, vapour condensing into mush-rooms – alternate before it day and night and no one knows from what soil they spring. Enough! The source from which it has these morning and evening, is it not that from which it was born?

NOTE   Chuang-tzŭ might be either the author or the annotator of these verses about the heart, the organ of thought. The 'supreme fear' which calms would be the fear of death, reconciliation with which is Chuang-tzǔ's central concern.

• • •

'Without an Other there is no Self, without Self no choosing one thing rather than another.'

This is somewhere near it, but we do not know in whose service they are being employed. It seems that there is something genuinely in command, and that the only trouble is we cannot find a sign of it. That as 'Way' it can be walked is true enough, but we do not see its shape; it has identity but no shape. Of the hundred joints, nine openings, six viscera all present and complete, which should I recognise as more kin to me than another? Are you people pleased with them all? Rather, you have a favourite organ among them. On your assumption, does it have the rest of them as its vassals and concubines? Are its vassals and concubines inadequate to rule each other? Isn't it rather that they take turns as each other's lord and vassals? Or rather than that, they have a genuine lord present in them. If we seek without success to grasp what its identity might be, that never either adds to nor detracts from its genuineness.

NOTE   Chuang-tzǔ starts from a quotation or a provisional formulation of his own. His theme is again the heart, the organ of thought. Should it be allowed to take charge of our lives? Isn't it merely one of many organs each with its own functions within an order which comes from beyond us, from the Way?

• • •

Once we have received the completed body we are aware of it all the time we await extinction. Is it not sad how we and other things go on stroking or jostling each other, in a race ahead like a gallop which nothing can stop? How can we fail to regret that we labour all our lives without seeing success, wear ourselves out with toil in ignorance of where we shall end? What use is it for man to say that he will not die, since when the body dissolves the heart dissolves with it? How can we not call this our supreme regret? Is man's life really as stupid as this? Or is it that I am the only stupid one, and there are others not so stupid? But if you go by the completed heart and take it as your authority, who is without such an authority? Why should it be only the man who knows how things alternate and whose heart approves its own judgements who has such an authority? The fool has one just as he has. For there to be 'That's it, that's not' before they are formed in the heart would be to 'go to Yüeh today and have arrived yesterday'. This would be crediting with existence what has no existence; and if you do that even the daemonic Yü could not understand you, and how can you expect to be understood by me?

NOTE   'I go to Yüeh today but came yesterday' is a paradox of the Sophist Hui Shih (p. 283 below), here mentioned only for its absurdity.

•   •   •

Saying is not blowing breath, saying says something; the only trouble is that what it says is never fixed. Do we really say something? Or have we never said anything? If you think it different from the twitter of fledgelings, is there proof of the distinction? Or isn't there any proof? By what is the Way hidden, that there should be a genuine or a false? By what is saying darkened, that sometimes 'That's it' and sometimes 'That's not'? Wherever we walk how can the Way be absent? Whatever the standpoint how can saying be unallowable? The Way is hidden by formation of the lesser, saying is darkened by its foliage and flowers. And so we have the 'That's it, that's not' of Confucians and Mohists, by which what is *it* for one of them for the other is not, what is *not* for one of them for the other is. If you wish to affirm what they deny and deny what they affirm, the best means is Illumination.

No thing is not 'other', no thing is not 'it'. If you treat yourself too as 'other' they do not appear, if you know of yourself you know of them. Hence it is said:

> '"Other" comes out from "it", "it" likewise goes by "other"',

the opinion that 'it' and 'other' are born simultaneously. However,

> 'Simultaneously with being alive one dies',

and simultaneously with dying one is alive, simultaneously with being allowable something becomes unallowable and simultaneously with being unallowable it becomes allowable. If going by circumstance that's it then going by circumstance that's not, if going by circumstance that's not then going by circumstance that's it. This is why the sage does not take this course, but opens things up to the light of Heaven; his too is a 'That's it' which goes by circumstance.

NOTE   In disputation if an object fits the name 'ox' one affirms with the demonstrative word *shih*, '(That) is it'; if it is something other than an ox one denies with a *fei*, '(That) is not'. Here Chuang-tzŭ tries to discredit disputation by the objection that at any moment of change both alternatives will be admissible. He appeals to a paradox of Hui Shih, 'The sun is simultaneously at noon and declining, a thing is simultaneously alive and dead' (p. 283 below), and generalises to the conclusion that any statement will remain inadmissible at the moment when it has just become admissible. It was also recognised in current disputation (as we find it in the Mohist *Canons*) that one can say both 'Y is long' (in relation to X) and 'Y is short' (in relation to Z), and that even with words such as 'black' and 'white' which are not comparative one has to decide whether to 'go by' (*yin*) the black parts or the white when deeming someone a 'black man'. Chuang-tzǔ sees it as the lesson of disputation that one is entitled to affirm or deny anything of anything. He thinks of Confucians and Mohists who stick rigidly to their affirmations and denials as lighting up little areas of life and leaving the rest in darkness; the Illumination of the sage is a vision which brings everything to light.

• • •

What is It is also Other, what is Other is also It. There they say 'That's it, that's not' from one point of view, here we say 'That's it, that's not' from another point of view. Are there really It and Other? Or really no It and Other? Where neither It nor Other finds its opposite is called the axis of the Way. When once the axis is found at the centre of the circle there is no limit to responding with either, on the one hand no limit to what is *it*, on the other no limit to what is not. Therefore I say: 'The best means is Illumination.' Rather than use the meaning to show that

'The meaning is not the meaning',

use what is *not* the meaning. Rather than use a horse to show that

'A horse is not a horse'

use what is *not* a horse. Heaven and earth are the one meaning, the myriad things are the one horse.

NOTE   There are extant essays by the Sophist Kung-sun Lung arguing that 'A white horse is not a horse' and 'When no thing is not the meaning the meaning is not the meaning'. Chuang-tzǔ thinks he was wasting his time; since all disputation starts from arbitrary acts of naming, he had only to pick something else as the meaning of the word, name something else 'horse', and then for him what the rest of us call a horse would not be a horse.

• • •

Allowable? – allowable. Unallowable? – unallowable. The Way comes about as we walk it; as for a thing, call it something and that's so. Why so? By being so. Why not so? By not being so. It is inherent in a thing that from somewhere that's so of it, from somewhere that's allowable of it; of no thing is it not so, of no thing is it unallowable. Therefore when a 'That's it' which deems picks out a stalk from a pillar, a hag from beautiful Hsi Shih, things however peculiar or incongruous, the Way interchanges them and deems them one. Their dividing is formation, their formation is dissolution; all things whether forming or dissolving in reverting interchange and are deemed to be one. Only the man who sees right through knows how to inter-change and deem them one; the 'That's it' which deems he does not use, but finds for them lodging-places in the usual. The 'usual' is the usable, the 'usable' is the interchangeable, to see as 'interchangeable' is to grasp; and once you grasp them you are almost there. The 'That's it' which goes by circumstance comes to an end; and when it is at an end, that of which you do not know what is so of it you call the 'Way'.

To wear out the daemonic-and-illumined in you deeming them to be one without knowing that they are the same I call 'Three every morning'. What do I mean by 'Three every morning?'. A monkey keeper handing out nuts said, 'Three every morning and four every evening.' The monkeys were all in a rage. 'All right then,' he said, 'four every morning and three every evening.' The monkeys were all delighted. Without anything being missed out either in name or in substance, their pleasure and anger were put to use; his too was the 'That's it' which goes by circumstance. This is why the sage smooths things out with his 'That's it, that's not', and stays at the point of rest on the potter's wheel of Heaven. It is this that is called 'Letting both alternatives proceed'.

NOTE 'The "That's it" which deems' (*wei shih*): in disputation over whether an object fits the name 'ox', the object is 'deemed' (*wei*) an ox by the judgement 'That's it' (*shih*). Chuang-tzŭ allows the flexible ' "That's it" which goes by circumstance' (*yin shih*), but rejects absolutely the rigid ' "That's it" which deems'.

'Letting both alternatives proceed': in disputation a decision to call an object 'X' 'proceeds' (*hsing*) to all objects of the same kind. But for Chuang-tzŭ one never loses the right to shift from one alternative to the other and allow either to 'proceed' from the instance to the kind.

       •   •   •

The men of old, their knowledge had arrived at something: at what had it arrived? There were some who thought there had not yet begun to be things – the utmost, the exhaustive, there is no more to add. The next thought there were things but there had not yet begun to be borders. The next thought there were borders to them but there had not yet begun to be 'That's it, that's not'. The lighting up of 'That's it, that's not' is the reason why the Way is flawed. The reason why the Way is flawed is the reason why love becomes complete. Is anything really complete or flawed? Or is nothing really complete or flawed? To recognise as complete or flawed is to have as model the Chao when they play the zither; to recognise as neither complete nor flawed is to have as model the Chao when they don't play the zither. Chao Wen strumming on the zither, Music-master K'uang propped on his stick, Hui Shih leaning on the sterculia, had the three men's knowledge much farther to go? They were all men in whom it reached a culmination, and therefore was carried on to too late a time. It was only in being preferred by them that what they knew about differed from an Other; because they preferred it they wished to illumine it, but they illumined it without the

Other being illumined, and so the end of it all was the darkness of chop logic: and his own son too ended with only Chao Wen's zither string, and to the end of his life his musicianship was never completed. May men like this be said to be complete? Then so am I. Or may they not be said to be complete? Then neither am I, nor is anything else.

Therefore the glitter of glib implausibilities is despised by the sage. The 'That's it' which deems he does not use, but finds for things lodging-places in the usual. It is this that is meant by 'using Illumination'.

NOTE Systems of knowledge are partial and temporary like styles on the zither, which in forming sacrifice some of the potentialities of music, and by their very excellence make schools fossilise in decline. Take as model Chao Wen *not* playing the zither, not yet committed, with all his potentialities intact.

. . .

'Now suppose that I speak of something, and do not know whether it is of a kind with the "it" in question or not of a kind. If what is of a kind and what is not are deemed of a kind with one another, there is no longer any difference from an "other".'

However, let's try to say it.

There is 'beginning', there is 'not yet having begun having a beginning'.

– There is 'there not yet having begun to be that "not yet having begun having a beginning"'.

There is 'something', there is 'nothing'.

– There is 'not yet having begun being without something'.

– There is 'there not yet having begun to be that "not yet having begun being without something"'.

All of a sudden '*there is* nothing', and we do not yet know of something and nothing really which there is and which there is not. Now for my part I have already referred to something, but do not yet know whether my reference really referred to something or really did not refer to anything.

NOTE In this and the next passage Chuang-tzǔ criticises two supposed examples of describing in words the whole out of which things divide. He thinks that analysis always leaves an overlooked remainder, and that the whole cannot be recovered by putting the parts together again. According to the current logic, an object either is an ox or is not, so that having distinguished the alternatives we ought to be able to recover the totality by adding non-oxen to oxen. Chuang-tzǔ's refutation of this assumption is highly elliptical, and it is possible that he intends his effect of making the mind fly off in a new direction at every re-reading. But in Chinese as in other philosophy a gap in the argument which hinders understanding (as distinct from a flaw in an argument which we do understand) can generally be filled by exploring implicit questions and presuppositions in the background. Here Chuang-tzǔ is picking out points in common between oxen and non-oxen which distinguish them both from a still remaining Other. In the first place both have a beginning, which excludes from them whatever preceded the beginning of things. Can we continue, by negating and adding, to incorporate this remainder into the totality? What preceded things is that in which they 'had not yet begun to have a beginning'. But in saying this retrospectively we speak as though things were somehow present before they began; we are driven to a further negation, 'There had not yet begun to be that "not yet having begun having a beginning"'.

It is also common to oxen and non-oxen that they are 'something', what there is, in contrast with 'nothing', what there is not. As empty space nothingness is a measurable part of the cosmos; but can we not arrive at the totality by adding Nothing to Something? Here Chuang-tzŭ assumes a position far from obvious to a modern reader but implicit throughout early Taoist literature. There can be Nothing only when there is Something, a void only when there are objects with intervals between them, and both divide out from a whole which is neither one nor the other. Each thing has limited properties, is 'without something', but the whole out of which it differentiates is both 'without anything', since things have not yet emerged, and 'without nothing', since everything emerges from it. Then having added Nothing to Something, I have still to add a remainder which 'has not yet begun to be without something'. But again we are speaking retrospectively as though there were already things to be present or absent, and again we have to negate: 'There had not yet begun to be that "not yet having begun to be without something".' Both Chuang-tzŭ's sequences are no doubt intended to lead to an infinite regress.

He concludes with the simpler point that as soon as we introduce Nothing as the remainder we contradict ourselves by saying 'There is' even of what there is not, Nothing.

.   .   .

'Nothing in the world is bigger than the tip of an autumn hair, and Mount T'ai is small; no one lives longer than a doomed child, and P'eng-tsu died young; heaven and earth were born together with me, and the myriad things and I are one.'

Now that we are one, can I still say something? Already having called us one, did I succeed in not saying something? One and the saying makes two, two and one make three. Proceeding from here even an expert calculator cannot get to the end of it, much less a plain man. Therefore if we take the step from nothing to something we arrive at three, and how much worse if we take the step from something to something! Take no step at all, and the 'That's it' which goes by circumstance will come to an end.

NOTE   Hui Shih had said that 'Heaven and earth are one unit' (p. 284 below). At first sight one might expect Chuang-tzŭ to agree with that at least. But to refuse to distinguish alternatives is to refuse to affirm even 'Everything is one' against 'Things are many'. He observes that in saying it the statement itself is additional to the One which it is about, so that already there are two (Plato makes a similar point about the One and its name in *The Sophist*). It may be noticed that Chuang-tzŭ never does say that everything is one (except as one side of a paradox (p. 77)), always speaks subjectively of the sage treating as one.

.   .   .

The sorting which evens things out

The Way has never had borders, saying has never had norm

'That's it' which deems that a boundary is marked. Let me s

about the marking of boundaries. You can locate as there and enclose by

line, sort out and assess, divide up and discriminate between alternatives,

compete over and fight over: these I call our Eight Powers. What is outside

the cosmos the sage locates as there but does not sort out. What is within the

cosmos the sage sorts out but does not assess. The records of the former

kings in the successive reigns in the Annals the sage assesses, but he does not

argue over alternatives.

To 'divide', then, is to leave something undivided: to 'discriminate

between alternatives' is to leave something which is neither alternative.

'What?' you ask. The sage keeps it in his breast, common men argue over

alternatives to show it to each other. Hence I say: "To "discriminate

between alternatives" is to fail to see something'.

. . .

> The greatest Way is not cited as an authority,
> The greatest discrimination is unspoken,
> The greatest goodwill is cruel,
> The greatest honesty does not make itself awkward,
> The greatest courage does not spoil for a fight.
>
> When the Way is lit it does not guide,
> When speech discriminates it fails to get there,
> Goodwill too constant is at someone's expense,
> Honesty too clean is not to be trusted,
> Courage that spoils for a fight is immature.

These five in having their corners rounded off come close to pointing the
direction. Hence to know how to stay within the sphere of our ignorance is to
attain the highest. Who knows an unspoken discrimination, an untold Way?
It is this, if any is able to know it, which is called the Treasury of Heaven.
Pour into it and it does not fill, bale out from it and it is not drained, and you
do not know from what source it comes. It is this that is called our Benetnash
Star.

NOTE 'Benetnash Star': The standard text has the obscure *Pao kuang* ('Shaded
light'(?)), but there is a plausible variant, *Yao-kuang*, 'Benetnash', the star at the far
end of the handle of the Dipper. The Dipper by turning its handle up, down, east and
west, marks the progress of the four seasons (cf. Joseph Needham, *Science and civilization in China*, 3/250). As a metaphor for the prime mover of things Chuang-tzŭ
chooses not the stationary North Star but the circumpolar star which initiates the
cyclic motions.

. . .

Therefore formerly Yao asked Shun

'I wish to smite Tsung, K'uai and Hsü-ao. Why is it that I am not at ease on the south-facing throne?'

'Why be uneasy', said Shun, 'if these three still survive among the weeds? Formerly ten suns rose side by side and the myriad things were all illumined, and how much more by a man in whom the Power is brighter than the sun!'

NOTE This story seems out of place. Perhaps it was intended as an illustration of 'This is why the sage does not take this course but opens things up to the light of Heaven' (p. 52 above).

•   •   •   •

Gaptooth put a question to Wang Ni.

'Would you *know* something of which all things agreed "That's it"?'

'How would I know that?'

'Would you know what you did not know?'

'How would I know that'?

'Then does no thing know anything?'

'How would I know that? However, let me try to say it – "How do I know that what I call knowing is not ignorance? How do I know that what I call ignorance is not knowing?"'

'Moreover, let me try a question on you. When a human sleeps in the damp his waist hurts and he gets stiff in the joints; is that so of the loach? When he sits in a tree he shivers and shakes; is that so of the ape? Which of these three knows the right place to live? Humans eat the flesh of hay-fed and grain-fed beasts, deer eat the grass, centipedes relish snakes, owls and crows crave mice; which of the four has a proper sense of taste? Gibbons are sought by baboons as mates, elaphures like the company of deer, loaches play with fish. Mao-ch'iang and Lady Li were beautiful in the eyes of men; but when the fish saw them they plunged deep, when the birds saw them they flew high, when the deer saw them they broke into a run. Which of these four knows what is truly beautiful in the world? In my judgement the principles of Goodwill and Duty, the paths of "That's it, that's not", are inextricably confused; how could I know how to discriminate between them?'

'If you do not know benefit from harm, would you deny that the utmost man knows benefit from harm?'

'The utmost man is daemonic. When the wide woodlands blaze they cannot sear him, when the Yellow River and the Han freeze they cannot chill him, when swift thunderbolts smash the mountains and whirlwinds shake the seas they cannot startle him. A man like that yokes the clouds to his chariot, rides the sun and moon and roams beyond the four seas; death and life alter nothing in himself, still less the principles of benefit and harm!'

NOTE In the opening exchange Gaptooth is pressing for an admission that there must be something which is knowable: (1) Would you know something which everyone agrees on? Wang Ni denies it, perhaps because there could be no independent viewpoint from which to judge a universally shared opinion. (2) Then at least one knows what one does not know. But that is a contradiction, or so Chuang-tzŭ thinks (like Meno in Plato's dialogue); the Mohist *Canon* B 48 discusses this problem, and points out that one can know something by name without knowing what objects fit the name. (3) Then one knows that no one knows anything – another contradiction.

.   .   .

Ch'ü-ch'üeh-tzŭ asked Ch'ang-wu-tzŭ

'I heard this from the Master: "The sage does not work for any goal, does not lean towards benefit or shun harm, does not delight in seeking, does not fix a route by a Way, in saying nothing says something and in saying something says nothing, and roams beyond the dust and grime." The Master thought of the saying as a flight of fancy, but to me it seemed the walking of the most esoteric Way. How does it seem to you?'

'This is a saying which would have puzzled the Yellow Emperor, and what would old Confucius know about it? Moreover you for your part are counting your winnings much too soon; at the sight of the egg you expect the cock-crow, at the sight of the bow you expect a roasted owl. Suppose I put it to you in abandoned words, and you listen with the same abandon:

> "Go side by side with the sun and moon,
> Do the rounds of Space and Time.
> Act out their neat conjunctions,
> Stay aloof from their convulsions.
> Dependents each on each, let us honour one another.
> Common people fuss and fret,
> The sage is a dullard and a sluggard.
> Be aligned along a myriad years, in oneness,
>   wholeness, simplicity.
> All the myriad things are as they are,
> And as what they are make up totality."

How do I know that to take pleasure in life is not a delusion? How do I know that we who hate death are not exiles since childhood who have forgotten the way home? Lady Li was the daughter of a frontier guard at Ai. When the kingdom of Chin first took her the tears stained her dress; only when she came to the palace and shared the King's square couch and ate the flesh of hay-fed and grain-fed beasts did she begin to regret her tears. How do I know that the dead do not regret that ever they had an urge to life? Who banquets in a dream at dawn wails and weeps, who wails and weeps in a dream at dawn goes out to hunt. While we dream we do not know that we are dreaming, and in the middle of a dream interpret a dream within it; not until we wake do we know that we were dreaming. Only at the ultimate awakening shall we know that this is the ultimate dream. Yet fools think they are awake, so confident that they know what they are, princes, herdsmen, incorrigible! You and Confucius are both dreams, and I who call you a dream am also a dream. This saying of his, the name for it is 'a flight into the extraordinary'; if it happens once in ten thousand ages that a great sage knows its explanation it will have happened as though between morning and evening.'

·   ·   ·

You and I having been made to argue over alternatives, if it is you not I that wins, is it really you who are on to it, I who am not? If it is I not you that wins, is it really I who am on to it, you who are not? Is one of us on to it and the other of us not? Or are both of us on to it and both of us not? If you and I are unable to know where we stand, others will surely be in the dark because of us. Whom shall I call in to decide it? If I get someone of your party to decide it, being already of your party how can he decide it? If I get someone of my party to decide it, being already of my party how can he decide it? If I get someone of a party different from either of us to decide it, being already of a party different from either of us how can he decide it? If I get someone of the same party as both of us to decide it, being already of the same party as both of us how can he decide it? Consequently you and I and he are all unable to know where we stand, and shall we find someone else to depend on?

It makes no difference whether the voices in their transformations have each other to depend on or not. Smooth them out on the whetstone of Heaven, use them to go by and let the stream find its own channels; this is the way to live out your years. Forget the years, forget duty, be shaken into motion by the limitless, and so find things their lodging-places in the limitless.

What is meant by 'Smooth them out on the whetstone of Heaven'? Treat as 'it' even what is not, treat as 'so' even what is not. If the 'it' is really it, there is no longer a difference for disputation from what is not it; if the 'so' is really so, there is no longer a difference for disputation from what is not so.

NOTE   Since anything may at one time or another be picked out as 'it', if it were really the name of something (in Western grammatical terms, if it were not a pronoun but a noun) it would be the name of everything. Chuang-tzŭ likes the thought that instead of selecting and approving something as 'it' one may use the word to embrace and approve everything, to say 'Yes!' to the universe; we find him doing so in p. 102 below.

·   ·   ·

The penumbra asked the shadow:
    'Just then you were walking, now you stop; just then you were sitting,

now you stand. Why don't you make up your mind to do one thing or the other?'

'Is it that there is something on which I depend to be so? And does what I depend on too depend on something else to be so? Would it be that I depend on snake's scales, cicada's wings? How would I recognise why it is so, how would I recognise why it is not so?

. . .

Last night Chuang Chou dreamed he was a butterfly, spirits soaring he was a butterfly (is it that in showing what he was he suited his own fancy?), and did not know about Chou. When all of a sudden he awoke, he was Chou with all his wits about him. He does not know whether he is Chou who dreams he is a butterfly or a butterfly who dreams he is Chou. Between Chou and the butterfly there was necessarily a dividing; just this is what is meant by the transformations of things.

NOTE 'Showing what he was' seems to connect with the earlier reference to 'showing' that a horse is not a horse (p. 53 above). If so, the point is that the Taoist does not permanently deem himself a man or a butterfly but moves spontaneously from fitting one name to fitting another. cf. 'At one moment he deemed himself the logician's "horse", at another his "ox"' (p. 94 below).

3

What matters in the nurture of life

The theme of this chapter is the recovery of the spontaneity of vital process when we abandon analytic knowledge and trust to the daemonic insight and aptitude which enters us from beyond, from Heaven. The chapter is short and scrappy, surely because of textual mutilation; it is unlikely that the compilers were short of material on so basic a theme. The opening section is badly damaged, but three more fragments of it can be identified by affinities of theme and phrasing; they are tacked on at the very ends of two of the ragbag chapters, chapters 24 and 32. We have used them to restore an introductory essay, not necessarily complete.

My life flows between confines, but knowledge has no confines. If we use the confined to follow after the unconfined, there is danger that the flow will cease; and when it ceases, to exercise knowledge is purest danger.

> Doer of good, stay clear of reputation.
> Doer of ill, stay clear of punishment.
> Trace the vein which is central and make it your standard.
> You can protect the body,
>   keep life whole,
>   nurture your parents,
>   last out your years.

Hence, as the ground which the foot treads is small, and yet, small as it is, it depends on the untrodden ground to have scope to range, so the knowledge a man needs is little, yet little as it is he depends on what he does not know to know what is meant by 'Heaven'. If you know the ultimate One, the ultimate Yin, the ultimate eye, the ultimate adjuster, the ultimate in scope, the ultimately truthful, the ultimately fixed, you have attained the utmost. The ultimate One makes things interchangeable, the ultimate Yin unravels them, the ultimate eye looks out at them, the ultimate adjuster sets a route by them, the ultimate in scope identifies with them, the ultimately truthful verifies them, the ultimately fixed supports them.

If to embrace them all we have Heaven and to stay on course have its light, if in obscurity we have the axis on which things turn, and to start from have that which is other than ourselves, then our unravelling will resemble failing to unravel, our knowing will resemble ignorance. The questions which we put to that which we know only by being ignorant cannot have confines yet cannot be without confines. If when we wrench everything apart there are objects, each in its own position past or present, and we cannot afford to leave any of them out of account, then can it be denied that there is a grand total of all? Why not after all put your questions to *it* ?

Why be bothered by doubts? If you use the undoubted to unravel the doubted and transfer it to the undoubted, this is to have too much respect for the undoubted. Use the unlevel to level and your levelling will not level, use the untested to test and your testing will not test. The sight of the eye is only something which it employs, it is the daemonic in us which tests. It is no new thing that the sight of the eye does not prevail over the daemonic; and is it not sad that fools should depend on what they see and confine themselves to what is of man, so that their achievements are external?

Therefore the capacity of the eye to see presents dangers, the capacity of the ear to hear presents dangers, the capacity of the heart for perilous ambitions presents dangers. All ability in what concerns the organs presents dangers. When the dangers become actual it is too late to mend, as misfortune grows complications multiply, recovery depends on effective action, success depends on prolonged effort; and is it not sad that men should think of the organs as their greatest treasures? Therefore that there is no end to ruined states and massacred peoples is because we do not know how to put our questions to *it*.

NOTE 'The ultimate Yin': Instead of exerting his energies in the active or Yang phase to unravel a problem, the sage lets them withdraw in the passive or Yin phase to an absolute stillness in which he sees problems unravel of themselves. The 'axis': The still point at the centre of us from which we can watch the cycles of events as though from the motionless centre of a rotating wheel (cf. p. 53).

. . .

Cook Ting was carving an ox for Lord Wen-hui. As his hand slapped, shoulder lunged, foot stamped, knee crooked, with a hiss! with a thud! the brandished blade as it sliced never missed the rhythm, now in time with the Mulberry Forest dance, now with an orchestra playing the Ching-shou.

'Oh, excellent!' said Lord Wen-hui. 'That skill should attain such heights!'

'What your servant cares about is the Way, I have left skill behind me. When I first began to carve oxen, I saw nothing but oxen wherever I looked. Three years more and I never saw an ox as a whole. Nowadays, I am in touch through the daemonic in me, and do not look with the eye. With the senses I know where to stop, the daemonic I desire to run its course. I rely on Heaven's structuring, cleave along the main seams, let myself be guided by the main cavities, go by what is inherently so. A ligament or tendon I never touch, not to mention solid bone. A good cook changes his chopper once a year, because he hacks. A common cook changes it once a month, because he smashes. Now I have had this chopper for nineteen years, and have taken apart several thousand oxen, but the edge is as though it were fresh from the grindstone. At that joint there is an interval, and the chopper's edge has no thickness; if you insert what has no thickness where there is an interval, then, what more could you ask, of course there is ample room to move the edge about. That's why after nineteen years the edge of my chopper is as though it were fresh from the grindstone.

'However, whenever I come to something intricate, I see where it will be hard to handle and cautiously prepare myself, my gaze settles on it, action slows down for it, you scarcely see the flick of the chopper – and at one stroke the tangle has been unravelled, as a clod crumbles to the ground. I stand chopper in hand, look proudly round at everyone, dawdle to enjoy the triumph until I'm quite satisfied, then clean the chopper and put it away.'

'Excellent!' said Lord Wen-hui. 'Listening to the words of Cook Ting, I have learned from them how to nurture life.'

. . .

When Kung-wen Hsüan saw the Commander of the Right, he said in astonishment

'What man is this? Why is he so singular? Is it from Heaven or from man?'

'It is from Heaven, not from man. When Heaven engenders something it causes it to be unique; the guise which is from man assimilates us to each other. By this I know it is from Heaven, not from man.'

NOTE   The commentators suppose Kung-wen Hsüan to be singular in the number of his feet, having a chopped foot like the men condemned for crimes in *The signs of fullness of Power*. But the story makes more sense if he is singular in appearance or character, a freak or eccentric.

. . .

The pheasant of the woodlands walks ten paces for one peck, a hundred paces for one drink, but has no urge to be looked after in a cage. One's daemon does not find it good even to be a king.

NOTE   This looks like a misplaced fragment. It would be appropriate to a story about some hermit refusing a throne, like Hsü Yu in 'Going rambling without a destination' (p. 45 above).

. . .

When Old Tan died Ch'in Yi went in to mourn him, wailed three times and came out.

'Were you not the Master's friend?' said a disciple.

'I was.'

'Then is it decent to mourn him like this?'

'It is. I used to think of him as the man, but now he is not. Just now as I came in to mourn him, there were old people bewailing him as they would wail for their sons, young people bewailing him as they would wail for their mothers. As to how he made them gather here – there were surely some who were saying what they had no urge to say, wailing when they had no urge to wail. This is to hide from Heaven and turn away from what we truly are, and forget the gift that we received; of old it was called ''the punishment for hiding from Heaven''. In coming when he did, the Master was on time; in departing when he did, the Master was on course. Be content with the time and settled on the course, and sadness and joy cannot find a way in. Of old this was called ''God's loosing of the bonds''.

'If the meaning is confined to what is deemed the ''firewood'', as the fire passes on from one piece to the next we do not know it is the ''cinders''.'

NOTE If Old Tan had been the great teacher he seemed, his disciples would have learned to take his death with equanimity instead of making all this fuss. The final sentence is obscure. I take it to be using the terminology of disputation. We divide up the changing totality, use names such as 'living' and 'firewood' to detach the partial and temporary, and then suppose that death and burning bring them to an end, forgetting that they are the same thing as what in the next phase in the endless process of transformation will be named 'dead' and 'cinders'.

4

Worldly business among men

This chapter has two sets of episodes. The first considers the devious and intractable problems of the Taoist in office: to what extent can he live the enlightened life and hope to bring his ruler nearer to the Way? The second proclaims the advantages of being useless, unemployable, so that the government leaves you alone.

1 FIRST SERIES

Yen Hui called on Confucius and asked leave to travel.

'Where are you off to?'

'I am going to Wey.'

'What will you do there?'

'I hear that the lord of Wey is young in years and wilful in deeds. He is careless of the cost to his state and blind to his own faults; he is so careless of the cost in men's lives that the dead fill the state to its borders as though it had been ravaged with fire and slaughter. No, the people have nowhere to turn. I have heard you say, sir: ''Never mind the well ruled states, go to the misruled states; at a doctor's gate it is mostly the sick that call.'' I wish to think out what to do in the light of what you taught me, in the hope that the state may be restored to health.'

'Hmm. I am afraid that you are simply going to your execution. One doesn't want the Way to turn into a lot of odds and ends. If it does it becomes multiple, when it's multiple it gets you muddled, when you're muddled you worry, and once you worry there's no hope for you. The utmost man of old established in other people only what he had first established in himself. Until it is firmly established in yourself, what time have you to spare for the doings of tyrants?

'Besides, do you after all understand that the thing by which the Power in us is dissipated is the very thing by which knowledge is brought forth? The

Power is dissipated by making a name, knowledge comes forth from competition. To ''make a name'' is to clash with others, ''knowledge'' is a tool in competition. Both of them are sinister tools, of no use in perfecting conduct.

'Then again, to be ample in Power and solid in sincerity but lack insight into others' temperaments, not enter into competition for reputation but lack insight into others' hearts, yet insist in the presence of the tyrant on preaching about Goodwill and Duty and the lines laid down for us, this amounts to taking advantage of someone's ugliness to make yourself look handsome. The name for it is ''making a pest of oneself''. Make a pest of oneself, and others will certainly make pests of themselves in return. I rather fancy that someone is going to be a pest to you.

'Another thing: if you do think he favours clever people and dislikes fools, will it do you any good to try to be especially clever? Better not get into an argument. A king or duke is sure to pit his wits against one's own with the whole weight of his authority behind him.

> Your eye he'll dazzle,
> Your look he'll cow,
> Your mouth he'll manage,
> Your gesture he'll shape,
> Your heart he'll form.

You will find yourself using fire to quell fire, water to quell water, the name for it is 'going from bad to worse'. Being submissive at the start that is how you will always be. I am afraid that he will lose faith in your fulsome words, and so you'll be sure to die at the tyrant's hands.

'One more point. Formerly Kuan Lung-feng was executed by Chieh and Prince Pi-kan by Chow. Both were men meticulous in their personal conduct who as ministers offended emperors by sympathising with their subjects. Consequently their lords found their meticulousness a reason to get rid of them. These were men who desired a good name. And formerly Yao attacked Tsung, Chih and Hsü-ao, Yü attacked Yu-hu, the countries were reduced to empty wastes and hungry ghosts, the rulers were executed. There was no end to their calls to arms, no respite in their aspiration to great deeds. All these men were seekers of the name or the deed, and don't tell me you haven't heard of them! A good name, a great deed, tempt even the sage, and do you think you're any better?

'However, I am sure you have something in mind. Let me hear about it.'

'Would it do', said Hui, 'to be punctilious and impartial, diligent and single-minded?'

'O no, that's no good at all! To sustain the Yang at its height without reverting to the Yin puts one under great stress, the tension shows in one's face. It is something which ordinary people prefer not to defy, so they suppress what the other man is stirring up in them in order to calm their own hearts. Even what are named "powers which progress from day to day" will not grow to the full in him, let alone the supreme Power! He will stay obstinately as he is and refuse to reform, outwardly agreeing with you but inwardly insensible, and what's the good of that?'

'In that case, said Hui, 'inwardly I shall be straight but outwardly I shall bend, I shall mature my own judgement yet conform to my betters. In being "inwardly straight", I shall be of Heaven's party. One who is of Heaven's party knows that in the eyes of Heaven he is just as much a son as the Son of Heaven is, and is he the only one who, when speaking on his own account, has an urge which carries him away and other people applaud, or which carries him away and other people disapprove? Such a one is excused by others as childlike. It is this that I mean by "being of Heaven's party".

'In "outwardly bending" I shall be of man's party. Lifting up the tablet in his hands and kneeling and bowing from the waist are the etiquette of a minister; everyone else does it, why should I presume to be an exception? If you do what others do, the others for their part will find no fault in you. It is this that I mean by "being of man's party".

'In "maturing my own judgement yet conforming to my betters" I shall be of the party of the men of old. The words, although in substance instructions or criticisms, belong to the men of old, I can't be held responsible for them. Such a person can be as straight as he likes without getting into trouble. It is this that I mean by "being of the party of the men of old". How will that do?'

'Oh no, that's no good at all! Too much organising. If you stick to the forms and don't get too familiar, even if you're stupid you will escape blame. But that's all that can be said for it. How would you succeed in making a new man of him? It's still taking the heart as one's authority.'

'I have nothing more to propose', said Hui. 'I venture to ask the secret of it.'

'Fast, and I will tell you,' said Confucius. 'Doing something thought out in the heart, isn't that too easy? Whoever does things too easily is unfit for the lucid light of Heaven.'

'I am of a poor family, I have not drunk wine or eaten a seasoned dish for months. Would that count as fasting?'

'That kind of fasting one does before a sacrifice, it is not the fasting of the heart.'

'I venture to inquire about the fasting of the heart.'

'Unify your attention. Rather than listen with the ear, listen with the heart. Rather than listen with the heart, listen with the energies. Listening stops at the ear, the heart at what tallies with the thought. As for 'energy', it is the tenuous which waits to be roused by other things. Only the Way accumulates the tenuous. The attenuating is the fasting of the heart.'

'When Hui has never yet succeeded in being the agent, a deed derives from Hui. When he does succeed in being its agent, there has never begun to be a Hui. – Would that be what you call attenuating?'

'Perfect! I shall tell you. You are capable of entering and roaming free inside his cage, but do not be excited that you are making a name for yourself. When the words penetrate, sing your native note; when they fail to penetrate, desist. When there are no doors for you, no outlets, and treating all abodes as one you find your lodgings in whichever is the inevitable, you will be nearly there.

'To leave off making footprints is easy, never to walk on the ground is hard. What has man for agent is easily falsified, what has Heaven for agent is hard to falsify. You have heard of using wings to fly. You have not yet heard of flying by being wingless; you have heard of using the wits to know, you have not yet heard of using ignorance to know.

> 'Look up to the easer of our toils.
> In the empty room the brightness grows.
> The blessed, the auspicious, stills the stilled.
> The about to be does not stay still.

This I call "going at a gallop while you sit". If the channels inward through eyes and ears are cleared, and you expel knowledge from the heart, the ghostly and daemonic will come to dwell in you, not to mention all that is human! This is to transform with the myriad things, here Shun and Yü found the knot where all threads join, here Fu-hsi and Chi Ch'ü finished their journey, not to speak of lesser men!'

NOTE For Yen Hui (the favourite disciple of Confucius) to go to the King full of good intentions and well thought out plans will do harm in stead of good. He must first train the motions in himself which can spontaneously move another in the direction of the Way. He must trust to the *ch'i* (translated 'energies'), the breath and other energising fluids which alternate between activity as the Yang and passivity as the Yin (as in breathing out and in), training them with the meditative technique including controlled breathing which is mentioned elsewhere (pp. 48, 84, 97). When the purified fluid has become perfectly tenuous the heart will be emptied of conceptual knowledge, the channels of the senses will be cleared, and he will simply perceive and respond. Then the self dissolves, energies strange to him and higher than his own (the 'daemonic') enter from outside, the agent of his actions is no longer the man but Heaven working through him, yet paradoxically (and it is in hitting on this paradox that Hui convinces Confucius that he understands) in discovering a deeper self he becomes for the first time truly the agent. He no longer has deliberate goals, the 'about to be' at the centre of him belongs to the transforming processes of heaven and earth. Then he will have the instinct for when to speak and when to be silent, and will say the right thing as naturally as a bird sings.
  'To leave off making footprints': it is easy to withdraw from the world as a hermit, hard to remain above the world while living in it.

•   •   •

Tzŭ-kao the Duke of She, about to go on a mission to Ch'i, consulted Confucius.

'The mission on which His Majesty has sent me is most weighty; and the way Ch'i treats emissaries, you know, is to be most respectful but put things off indefinitely. It is no use forcing the pace even with a commoner, not to speak of the lord of a state! I am very uneasy about it. You once said to me: "There are few enterprises, great or small, in which we are not under pressure to push for success. If the enterprise fails, we are sure to suffer the penalties of the Way of Man, and if it succeeds we are sure to suffer the maladies of the Yin and Yang. To escape ill consequences whether he succeeds or not – only the Man of Power is capable of that." I am one who sticks to a diet of plain and simple foods, no one at my kitchen stove ever grumbles about the heat, but now I get orders in the morning and by evening am drinking iced water; surely I must be getting a fever? Before I even have access to the facts of the case I am already suffering those "maladies of the Yin and Yang"; and if the enterprise fails I shall surely suffer your "penalties of the Way of Man" as well. This is getting the worst of it both ways. I am inadequate to bear my responsibilities as a minister, and only hope you have some advice to give me.'

'In the world there are two supreme commandments,' said Confucius. 'One of them is destiny, the other duty. A child's love of his parents is destined: it cannot be dispelled from the heart. A minister's service to his lord is duty; wherever he may go his lord is his lord. The commandments from which there is no escape between heaven and earth, these are what I call the supreme ones. This is why in the service of parents there is no higher degree of filial conduct than to live contentedly wherever they may dwell, in the service of a lord no fuller measure of loyalty than to perform his tasks contentedly whatever they may be, and in the service of one's own heart no higher degree of Power than, without joy and sorrow ever alternating before it, to know that these things could not be otherwise, and be content with them as our destiny. It is inherent in serving either as a son or as a minister that there is something which is inevitable. If you act on the facts of the situation, forgetful of your own person, how can it ever occur to you that it would please you more to save your life than to die? Go, sir, it is well that you should.

'Allow me to repeat to you some things I have heard. Whenever we are dealing with neighbours we have to rub along with each other on a basis of trust; but with people more distant we have to show our good faith in words, and the words must have some messenger. To pass on the words of parties both of whom are pleased or both of whom are angry with each other is the most difficult thing in the world. In the one case there are sure to be a lot of exaggerated compliments, in the other a lot of exaggerated abuse. Every sort of exaggeration is irresponsible, and if language is irresponsible trust in it fails, and the consequence of that is that the messenger is a doomed man. Therefore the book of rules says: "If you report the straightforward facts and omit the exaggerated language, you will be safe enough."'

'Another point: competitors in a game of skill begin in a bright Yang mood, but it is apt to end up by darkening to Yin; when they have gone too far they play more and more unfair tricks. Drinkers at a formal banquet are mannerly at first, but generally end up too boisterous; when they have gone too far the fun gets more and more reckless. This happens in all sorts of affairs. What begins as courtly is liable to end up vulgar; things which at the start were simple enough sooner or later are sure to get out of hand. Words are wind and waves, deeds fulfil or discredit them. It is easy for wind and waves to make a stir, and as easy for fulfilment or discrediting to endanger. Therefore the anger which is aroused has no other source than the cunning in wording and bias in phrasing.

'When an animal faces death it does not choose its cry, the viciousness is in its very breath, and then it generates the blood lust in hunter and hunted alike. If you go too far in trying to force a conclusion, the other is sure to respond with poor judgement, and he will not even know what is happening to him. If he does not even know what is happening to him, who can guess where it will end? Therefore the book of rules says: ''Do not deviate from the orders, do not push for success. To exceed due measure is to go beyond your commission.'' To deviate from the orders and push for success will endanger the enterprise. A fine success takes time, an ugly outcome is irreparable; can you afford not to be careful?

'Besides, to let the heart roam with other things as its chariot, and by trusting to the inevitable nurture the centre of you, is the farthest one can go. Why should there be anything you have initiated in the reply you bring back? The important thing is to fulfil what is ordained for you; and that is the most difficult thing of all.'

NOTE It is remarkable to find Chuang-tzŭ talking like a moralist about the 'duty' to serve the ruler, especially since elsewhere he always uses the word unfavourably (cf. p. 60 above, 'Forget the years, forget duty'). However, this is the single episode in which an inquirer is under specific orders from his ruler. Chuang-tzŭ does not question the institutions of family and state, although he does not talk about them much. You do in the last resort acknowledge a duty to the state in which you live, and if by choice or necessity you come to be in office you accept its rules as belonging to the 'inevitable'. However narrow the limits, as long as you preserve the responsiveness of your energies you can still, like Hui in the last episode, 'roam free inside the cage'.
'What is ordained for you': the king's decree and/or what Heaven destines for you. Paradoxically, it is supremely difficult to act out your destiny, to surrender to the impulse from Heaven instead of thinking in terms of self-interest and morality (described as 'too easy' on p. 68 above).

·   ·   ·

When Yen Ho was appointed tutor of the heir apparent of Duke Ling of Wey, he inquired of Ch'ü Po-yü
'Let us imagine the case of a man with a Power in him which Heaven has made murderous. If I behave recklessly in his company it will endanger our

country; if I behave decently in his company it will endanger my life. He has just enough wit to know that a man has erred, but not to know why he erred. How would I deal with someone like that?'

'A good question indeed! Be alert, on guard! Get your own person rightly adjusted! In your demeanour what matters is to get close, in your heart what matters is to be at peace. However, there are difficulties on both points. In getting close you don't want to be drawn in, and you don't want the peace in your heart to escape outside. If by your demeanour getting too close you are drawn in, it will be downfall, ruin, collapse, trampling. If the peace in your heart escapes outside, it will become repute, fame, a disaster, a curse.

'When he wants to play the child, join him in playing the child. When he wants to jump the fences, join him in jumping the fences. When he wants to burst the shores, join him in bursting the shores. Fathom him right through, and be drawn into the unblemished in him.

'Don't you know about the praying mantis? It will wave its arms furiously and stand bang in the middle of a rut, it doesn't know that the weight of the wheel is too much for its strength. This is because the stuff it's made of is too noble. Be alert, on guard! If you confront him with something accumulating in you which takes pride in your own nobility, you won't last long. And don't you know what a keeper of tigers does? He daren't give them a live animal because they will get into a rage killing it, or a whole animal either, because they will get into a rage tearing it apart. He keeps track of the times when they will be hungry or full, and has the secret of their angry hearts. Tigers are a different breed from men, but when they fawn on the man who feeds them it is because he goes along with their dispositions; and so if they get murderous it is because he thwarts their dispositions.

'The man who loves his horse will pamper it with a basket for its dung and a clam shell for its piss. But if a fly or mosquito should happen to hover near, and he slaps it unexpectedly, the horse will burst its bit and smash his head and kick in his chest. There was nothing wrong with the intention but the love did damage. You can't be too careful.'

2 SECOND SERIES

When Carpenter Shih was travelling to Ch'i he came to a village at a bend in the road, and saw the chestnut-leaved-oak by the altar of the god of the soil. It was broad enough to give shade to several thousand oxen and measured by the tape a hundred spans round; it was so high that it overlooked the hills and the lowest branches were seventy feet up; boughs from which you might make a boat could be counted by the dozen. The crowd gazing at it was like the throng in a market, but Carpenter Shih did not give it a glance; he walked straight on without a pause.

When his apprentice had had his fill of gazing at it he ran to catch up with Carpenter Shih.

'Since I took up the axe to serve you, sir, I have never seen such noble timber. Why is it that you didn't deign to look at it, didn't even pause as you walked?'

'Enough, don't mention it again. That's good-for-nothing wood. Make a boat from it and it will sink, make a coffin and it will rot at once, make a bowl and it will break at once, make a gate or door and it will ooze sap, make a pillar and it will be worm-holed. This wood is wretched timber, useless for anything; that's why it's been able to grow so old.'

When Carpenter Shih came home, the sacred oak appeared in a dream and said to him

'With what do you propose to compare me? Would it be with the fine-grained woods? As for the sort that bear fruits or berries, the cherry-apple, pear, orange, pumelo, when the fruit ripens they are stripped, and in being stripped they are disgracefully abused, their branches broken, their twigs snapped off. These are trees which by their own abilities make life miserable for themselves; and so they die in mid-path without lasting out the years assigned to them by Heaven, trees which have let themselves be made victims of worldly vulgarity. Such are the consequences with all things. I would add that this quest of mine to become of no possible use to anyone has been going on for a long time: only now, on the verge of death, have I achieved it, and to me it is supremely useful. Supposing that I had been useful too, would I have had the opportunity to grow so big?

'Besides, you and I are both things, what nonsense! that one of us should think it is the other which is the thing: and the good-for-nothing man who is soon to die, what does he know of the good-for-nothing tree?'

When Carpenter Shih woke up he told his dream.

'If it prefers to be useless', said the apprentice, 'why is it serving as the sacred tree?'

'Hush! Don't say it. It's simply using that as a pretext, thinks of itself as pestered by people who don't appreciate it. Aren't the ones which don't become sacred trees in some danger of being clipped? Besides, what that tree is protecting has nothing to do with the vulgar, and if we praise it for doing a duty won't we be missing the point?

· · ·

When Tzŭ-ch'i of Nan-po was rambling on the Hill of Shang, he saw a great tree which stood out from the rest. You could tether a thousand teams of horses to it, and they would all find shelter in its shade.

'What tree is this?' said Tzŭ-ch'i. 'The timber must be quite out of the ordinary, I should think.'

But when he looked up at the slimmer branches, they were too crooked to make beams and rafters. When he looked down at the trunk, the grain was too twisted and loose to make coffins. If you licked a leaf it stung the mouth and left a sore, if you took a sniff it made you delirious for a full three days.

'This indeed is wretched timber,' said Tzŭ-ch'i, 'which is why it has grown to be so big. Aha! That's why the most daemonic of men are made of such poor stuff!'

* * *

There is a place in Sung, Ching-shih, where catalpas, cypresses and mulberries thrive. But a tree an arm-length or two round will be chopped down by someone who wants a post to tether his monkey, a tree of three or four spans by someone seeking a ridge-pole for an imposing roof, a tree of seven or eight spans by the family of a noble or rich merchant looking for a sideplank for his coffin. So they do not last out the years Heaven assigned them, but die in mid-journey under the axe. That is the trouble with being stuff which is good for something. Similarly in the sacrifice to the god of the river it is forbidden to cast into the waters an ox with a white forehead, a pig with a turned-up snout or a man with piles. These are all known to be exempt by shamans and priests, being things they deem bearers of ill-luck. They are the very things which the daemonic man will deem supremely lucky.

* * *

Cripple Shu – his chin is buried down in his navel, his shoulders are higher than his crown, the knobbly bone at the base of his neck points at the sky, the five pipes to the spine are right up on top, his two thighbones make another pair of ribs. By plying the needle and doing laundry he makes enough to feed himself, and when he rattles the sticks telling fortunes for a handful of grain he is making enough to feed ten. If the authorities are press-ganging soldiers the cripple strolls in the middle of them flipping back his sleeves; if they are conscripting work parties he is excused as a chronic invalid: if they are doling out grain to the sick he gets three measures, and ten bundles of firewood besides. Even someone crippled in body manages to support himself and last out the years assigned him by Heaven. If you make a cripple of the Power in you, you can do better still!

* * *

When Confucius travelled to Ch'u, Chieh Yü the madman of Ch'u wandered at his gate crying

'Phoenix! Phoenix!
What's to be done about Power's decline?

Of the age to come we can't be sure,
To the age gone by there's no road back.

When the Empire has the Way
The sage succeeds in it.
When the Empire lacks the Way
The sage survives in it.
In this time of ours, enough
If he dodges execution in it.

Good luck is lighter than a feather,
None knows how to bear its weight.
Mishap is heavier than the earth,
None knows how to get out of the way.

Enough, enough!
Of using Power to reign over men.
Beware, beware!
Of marking ground and bustling us inside.

Thistle, thistle,
Don't wound me as I walk.
My walk goes backward and goes crooked,
Don't wound my feet.

The trees in the mountains plunder themselves,
The grease in the flame sizzles itself.
Cinnamon has a taste,
    So they hack it down.
Lacquer has a use,
        So they strip it off.

All men know the uses of the useful, but no one knows the uses of the useless.'

NOTE   cf. *Analects of Confucius*, chapter 18: 'Chieh Yü the madman of Ch'u sang as he passed Confucius

"Phoenix! Phoenix!
What's to be done about Power's decline?
The past is not worth reproach,
The future we can still pursue.
Enough, enough!
These days to take office is perilous."

Confucius got down from his carriage and tried to talk with him, but the man hurried off to avoid him, and he did not get the opportunity.'
   This ballad ironically welcomes Confucius, preaching ideal government in a decadent age, as the phoenix which comes as an auspicious omen when there is a sage on the throne. Chuang-tzŭ has written a version of his own (it must be his, for the unqualified praise of uselessness is a theme which, even in *Chuang-tzŭ*, is peculiar to his own writings (cf. pp. 47, 100 below). The use of Chieh Yü as a spokesman of Taoism is also confined to him (cf. pp. 46, 95).

5

The signs of fullness of Power

The test that a man lives by the Power in himself, and is wholly independent of everything outside him, is his indifference to the great irreparable disasters, death and bodily deformity, an indifference which makes others too ignore even such an obtrusive sign of mutilation and social condemnation as a foot chopped off for a crime. The theme of death belongs to *The teacher who is the ultimate ancestor*; stories about mutilated criminals, freaks and cripples are collected in this chapter. They are characteristic of Chuang-tzŭ's own writing, almost disappearing from the book after the end of the *Inner chapters*.

There was a man with a chopped foot in Lu, Wang T'ai, who had as many disciples in his retinue as Confucius himself. Ch'ang Chi asked Confucius

'Wang T'ai had his foot chopped off, but the disciples in his train divide Lu down the middle with yours. When he stands up he doesn't teach, when he sits down he doesn't talk things over, yet they go to him empty and come away full. Is there indeed a wordless teaching, or a heart which is whole though the body is deformed? What man is this?'

'The Master is a sage,' said Confucius. 'I should already have gone to him myself if I hadn't been putting it off. And if *I* would want him as teacher, is it surprising that lesser men do? Never mind our country Lu, I'll pull in the whole world to come with me to follow him.'

'If in spite of his chopped foot he is greater than you, sir, he must indeed be quite out of the ordinary. Is there something special about the use to which such a man puts the heart?'

'Death and life are mighty indeed, but he refuses to alter with them; though heaven were to collapse and earth subside he would not be lost with them. He is aware of the Flawless and is not displaced with other things; he does his own naming of the transformations of things and holds fast to their Ancestor.'

'What do you mean?'

'If you look at them from the viewpoint of their differences, from liver to gall is as far as from Ch'u to Yüeh; if you look at them from the viewpoint of their sameness, the myriad things are all one. Such a man cannot even tell apart the functions of eyes and ears, and lets the heart go roaming in the peace which is from the Power. As for other things, he looks into that in which they are one, and does not see what each of them has lost; he regards losing his own foot as he would shaking off mud.'

'His concern is for himself, he uses his wits to discover his own heart, his heart to discover the unchanging heart beyond it. Why should others congregate around him?'

'None of us finds his mirror in flowing water, we find it in still water. Only the still can still whatever is stilled. Among all that owe their destiny to the earth, only the pine and cypress are due on course; winter and summer they are the same green. Among all that owe their destiny to Heaven, only Yao and Shun are due on course; they stand at the head of the myriad things. One blessed with the ability to set life due on course does it for every living thing.

'The test that one holds fast to the Beginning is the fact of not being afraid. A single brave knight will boldly enter a battle of great armies; if this can be done even by a man capable of exerting himself out of ambition to make a name, how much more by one who makes heaven and earth his palace and the myriad things his storehouse, his trunk and limbs a place where he lodges and his eyes and ears images which he perceives, who treats as one all that wit knows and has a heart which never dies! He will pick his own day to rise out of the world. As for other men, it is for them to follow in his train; why should he want to make others his business?'

•   •   •

Shen-t'u Chia, a man with a chopped foot, was fellow student under Po-hun Nobody with Tzǔ-ch'an the Prime Minister of Cheng.

'If I make the first move to leave, you stay,' said Tzǔ-ch'an. 'If you make the first move to leave, I stay.'

Next day he found himself sitting with him again for the same lesson on the same mat.

'If I leave you stay, if you leave I stay. I shall now leave. Would it bother you too much to stay? Or would you rather not? And if you do not make way when you see the Prime Minister, are you putting yourself on a level with the Prime Minister?'

'So there's really the Prime Minister, you say, here among our Master's pupils? That's the one who being you is pleased it's you who's Prime Minister and turns his back on everyone else. I have heard it said: ''If your mirror is bright the dust will not settle, if the dust settles it's that your mirror isn't bright. Keep company long enough with a man of worth and there will be no crime in you.'' The teacher you now acknowledge as the greatest is our Master, yet you can still talk to me like this. Don't you think that's a crime?'

'After *that* happened to you, you would still argue with Yao which of you is the better man. If you reckon it all up, isn't there even enough Power in you to take an honest look at yourself?'

'There are many of us who would freely tell you about their crimes, thinking that they did not deserve to suffer; there are a few of us who would refuse to tell you about their crimes, thinking that they did not deserve to be spared; but as for recognising the inescapable and being content with it as destined, only the man who does have Power in him is capable of that. To stray within the range of archer Yi's bow and not be hit is destiny. Plenty of people who have whole feet laugh at me because I haven't; I get into a furious temper, but if I go to the Master's place the mood has passed before I come home. I do not know whether it is the Master cleansing me by his goodness or my own self-awakening. I have been going around with the Master for nineteen years now, and was never aware that I'm a man with a chopped foot. You and I are roaming now on the inside of the flesh-and-bone, yet you haul me out to take a look from the outside of the flesh-and-bone. Don't you think that's a crime?'

Tzǔ-ch'an, taken aback, corrected his expression and bearing. 'You don't have to say any more,' he said.

NOTE 'If your mirror is bright': If the disciple's mind, unclouded by egoism, lucidly reflects the master's teaching, he will be faultless.

•   •   •

There was a man with a chopped foot in Lu, Shu-shan Choptoes, who came walking on his heels to see Confucius.

'You were careless,' said Confucius. 'After getting into such trouble before, what is the point of coming to me now?'

'I simply did not have the sense to care, and took my own safety for granted, that is how I lost my foot. Coming to you now, what gave the foot its worth still survives in me, which is why I am concerned to keep it intact. There is nothing which heaven refuses to cover over or earth to support; I thought of you, sir, as my heaven and earth, how could I have known that you would turn out like this?'

'That was rude of me, why don't you come in, sir? Allow me to instruct you in what I have heard.'

When Choptoes left, Confucius said

'My disciples, be diligent! That Choptoes was condemned to have his foot chopped off, but he is still concerned to study in order to make amends for his former wicked conduct, and how much more the man in whom Power remains whole!'

Choptoes told Old Tan

'As an aspirant to be the utmost man, Confucius has some way to go, wouldn't you say? Why did he bother to keep coming to learn from you? He still has an urge to have his name bandied about as someone unique and extraordinary. Doesn't he know that the utmost man would think of it as fettering and handcuffing himself?'

'Why not just get him to recognise death and life as a single strand,' said Old Tan, 'and the allowable and the unallowable as strung on a single thread? Surely it's possible to shake off his fetters and handcuffs?'

'When Heaven does the punishing, how can they be shaken off?'

(He thought of the mutilation as a bodily feature, of the rites as his supports, of knowing what to do as a matter of timeliness, of Power as the capacity to stay on course.

'He thought of the mutilation as a bodily feature': he took the truncation for granted.

'Of the rites as his supports': as the means to conduct himself among the worldly.

'Of knowing what to do as a matter of timeliness': of doing whatever is inevitable in the circumstances.

'Of Power as the capacity to stay on course' means that he went to old Confucius with people who had their feet, and that the others genuinely regarded him as heedful in his conduct.)

NOTE   The bracketed passage is some ancient exposition of the story which in the Chinese text has become stranded in the middle of chapter 6, where it is unintelligible.
Choptoes is learning the accepted code of manners as a practical convenience, without any inner allegiance. The real cripple is Confucius himself, who cannot live without the code to support him. Not that it is his fault; he was born a defective man, mutilated and imprisoned by Heaven, as he admits in a later episode (p. 90 below).

．　．　．

Duke Ai of Lu put a question to Confucius.

'In Wey there was a hideous man called Uglyface T'o. Young men who lived with him were so fascinated that they couldn't leave, the girls who when they saw him begged their parents "I would rather be his concubine than anyone else's wife" could be counted in dozens. No one ever heard him say anything new, all he ever did was chime in with others. Without the throne of a lord of men from which to save a man from death, or mounting revenues with which to make waning bellies wax, and on top of that ugly enough to give the whole world a fright, chiming in without saying anything new, in knowledge content to stay within the bounds of the ordinary, none the less wild creatures would couple where he stood. This was obviously a man with something different about him. I summoned him to court to observe him, and he really was ugly enough to frighten the whole world. He stayed with me, and before it was time to start counting in months I was getting interested in the sort of man he was; before a year was up he had all my faith. The state lacked a chief minister, I put him in charge. He accepted only after a hesitation, in an apathetic voice as though he were declining. Embarrassing for me! But in the end I did get the state into his hands. Not long afterwards he left me and went away. I was as moved as if I had been bereaved, as if there were no one left with whom to share the joy of this state. What man was this?'

'To tell a story about myself,' said Confucius, 'I was once sent on a mission to Ch'u, and happened to see some little pigs sucking at their dead mother. Not long after, in the batting of an eye-lid they all abandoned her and ran. It was just that they did not see themselves in her, did not recognise their own kind in her. What they loved in their mother was not her shape, but what made her shape move. Men who die in battle require no coffin plumes at their burial, a man with chopped feet will not grudge you the loan of his shoes; neither possesses what made them matter.

'Cripple Lipless with the crooked legs advised Duke Ling of Wey; the Duke was so pleased with him that when he looked at normal men their legs were too lanky. Pitcherneck with the big goitre advised Duke Huan of Ch'i; the Duke was so pleased with him that when he looked at normal men their necks were too scrawny. To the extent then that Power stands out, we lose sight of the bodily shape. When men do not lose sight of what is out of sight but do lose sight of what is in plain sight, we may speak of "the oversight which is seeing things as they are".

'When a girl becomes a concubine of the Son of Heaven, they will not clip her nails or pierce her ears; a man with a new bride stays away from court and cannot be sent on any more missions. If we have such regard even for the whole in body, how much more for the man who keeps the Power in him whole! Now Uglyface T'o is trusted before he says a word, is accepted as an intimate without any deed to his credit, makes someone hand over his state and fear only that he will not accept it; he is evidently one in whom the stuff is whole but the Power has failed to shape the body.'

'What do you mean by his stuff being whole?'

'Death and life, survival and ruin, success and failure, poverty and riches, competence and incompetence, slander and praise, hunger and thirst, these are the mutations of affairs, the course of destiny. They alternate before us day and night, and knowledge cannot measure back to where they began. Consequently there is no point in letting them disturb one's peace, they are not to be admitted into the Magic Storehouse. To maintain our store in peace and joy, and let none of it be lost through the senses though the channels to them are cleared, to ensure that day and night there are no fissures and it makes a springtime it shares with everything, this is to be a man who at every encounter generates the season in his own heart. This is what I mean by his stuff being whole.'

'What do you mean by the Power failing to shape the body?'

'Being level is the culmination of water coming to rest. That the water-level can serve as standard is because it is protected from within and undisturbed from outside. As the saying goes, ''The wind passing over the river takes some of it away, the sun passing over the river takes some of it away; but even if wind and sun were both to abide with the river, the river would suppose that they had never begun to infringe on it, for it is something which issues forth from springs of its own. The filling of a contour by whirling water, still water, flowing water, water bubbling up, water dripping down, water gushing from the side, water dammed and diverted, stagnant water, water with several sources, makes the same deep pool. Hence the water abiding with the earth fills its contours, the shadow abiding with the shape fills its contours, any thing abiding with another thing fills its contours. The Power is the wholly at peace with itself on the course which is in accord. That the Power fails to shape the body is because other things are unable to keep their distance from it.'

On another day Duke Ai told Min-tzŭ:

'Not so long ago I thought I had nothing to learn about lording it over the empire from the south-facing throne, controlling the people from the centre and worrying how to keep them alive. Now that I have heard the words of the utmost man, I am afraid that I lack the substance of it, and that by neglecting the care of my own person I shall ruin the state. I and Confucius are not lord and vassal, he is simply a friend who has put me in his debt.'

NOTE   The end of the story of Uglyface and the start of the next episode show signs of textual dislocation, with gaps fillable from the 'Ragbag chapters', chapters 23 and 24, as well as with a fragment which has strayed into the story of Lieh-tzŭ and the shaman in chapter 7; the present translation is based on a radical reconstruction.

For ancient Chinese thought, which does not make a distinction in kind between the mental and the physical, it is the Power, the capacity to respond without reflection according to the Way, which enables the body to grow into its proper shape. (cf. p. 236 below, where Confucius hypocritically pretends to regard Robber Chih's strong and handsome figure as the supreme manifestation of the Power in him, and p. 78 above, where he assumes that mutilation impairs Power, mistakenly excluding Choptoes from those 'in whom Power remains whole'.) How then can Power be at its height in cripples and freaks? In according with the Way, the sage is sensitive to and adapts to all pressures from outside. The Power in shaping the body is like the water which, irrespective of its source, has a shape imposed on it by the topography of the place. It seems indeed that it is we ourselves, we ordinary folk, who by crowding round T'o from the day of his birth because the charm of pure spontaneity so attracts us, have forced his superbly sensitive and malleable organism into a shape we judge to be ugly.

·   ·   ·

If you step on someone's foot in the market you make a formal apology for your carelessness; an elder brother says he hopes it didn't hurt; father and mother are too close kin to say anything at all. Hence it is said:

> In utmost courtesy there is something not done as man.
> Utmost duty isn't towards another.
> Utmost knowledge doesn't plan,
> Utmost goodwill is kin to no one,
> Utmost honesty doesn't bother about money.

Hence, wherever the sage roams, for him knowledge is a curse, commitment is a glue, putting others in his debt is trafficking, getting credit for his deeds is peddling. Since the sage does not plan, what use has he for knowledge? Since he does not chop in pieces, what use has he for glue? Since he loses nothing, what use has he for repayments? Since he does not treat things as commodities, what use has he for peddling? For these four things, he buys at the market of Heaven. To "buy at the market of Heaven" is to be fed by Heaven. Having received his food from Heaven, what use has he for man? He has the shape of a man, is without what is essentially man. He has the shape of a man, and therefore congregates with men; he is without what is essentially man, and therefore "That's it, that's not" are not found in his person. Indiscernibly small, that which attaches him to man! Unutterably vast, the Heaven within him which he perfects in solitude!'

Said Hui Shih to Chuang-tzŭ

'Can a man really be without the essentials of man?'

'He can.'

'If a man is without the essentials of man, how can we call him a man?'

'The Way gives him the guise, Heaven gives him the shape, how can we refuse to call him a man?'

'But since we do call him a man, how can he be without the essentials of man?'

'Judging "That's it, that's not" is what I mean by "the essentials of man". What I mean by being without the essentials is that the man does not inwardly wound his person by likes and dislikes, that he constantly goes by the spontaneous and does not add anything to the process of life.'

'If he does not add anything to the process of life, how can there be any such thing as his person?'

'The Way gives us the guise, Heaven gives us the shape: do not inwardly wound yourself by likes and dislikes. But now you

> Go on pushing your daemon outside,
> Wearing your quintessence away.
> You loll on a treetrunk and mumble,
> Drop off to sleep held up by withered sterculia.
> It was Heaven that chose you a shape,
> But you sing chop logic as your native note.'

NOTE 'Withered sterculia': Hui Shih is mentioned elsewhere (p. 54 above) as leaning on wood of the *wu-t'ung* tree (*sterculia platanifolia*), presumably a desk or armrest made of it. One may guess that this is a concrete memory of the exhausted sophist drooping over desiccated wood which for Chuang-tzŭ sums up his impression of the unnatural and sterile effort of purely analytic thinking.

6

The teacher who is the ultimate ancestor

The Taoist does not take the heart, the organ of thought, as his teacher or authority (cf. pp. 51, 68 above); the only instructor he recognises is the ultimate Ancestor who generates all things, whose guidance is discovered in reverting to pure spontaneity. Its profoundest lesson is reconciliation with death, by a surrender without protest to the process of living and dying as mere episodes in the endless transformations of heaven and earth.

'To know what is Heaven's doing and what is man's is the utmost in knowledge. Whoever knows what Heaven does lives the life generated by Heaven. Whoever knows what man does uses what his wits know about to nurture what they do not know about. To last out the years assigned you by Heaven and not be cut off in mid-course, this is perfection of knowledge.'

However, there's a difficulty. Knowing depends on something with which it has to be plumb; the trouble is that what it depends on is never fixed. How do I know that the doer I call 'Heaven' is not the man? How do I know that the doer I call the 'man' is not Heaven? Besides, there can be true knowledge only when there is a true man. What do we mean by the 'True Man'? The True Men of old did not mind belonging to the few, did not grow up with more cock than hen in them, did not plan out their actions. Such men as that did not regret it when they missed the mark, were not complacent when they hit plumb on. Such men as that climbed heights without trembling, entered water without a wetting, entered fire without burning. Such is the knowledge which is able to rise out of the world on the course of the Way. The True Men of old slept without dreaming and woke without cares, found one food as sweet as another, and breathed from their deepest depths. (The breathing of the True Man is from down in his heels, the breathing of plain men is from their throats; as for the cowed, the submissive, they talk in gulps as though retching. Wherever desires and cravings are deep, the impulse which is from Heaven is shallow.)

The True Men of old did not know how to be pleased that they were alive, did not know how to hate death, were neither glad to come forth nor reluctant to go in; they were content to leave as briskly as they came. They did not forget the source where they began, did not seek out the destination where they would end. They were pleased with the gift that they received, but forgot it as they gave it back. It is this that is called 'not allowing the thinking of the heart to damage the Way, not using what is of man to do the work of Heaven'. Such a one we call the True Man. Such men as that had unremembering hearts, calm faces, clear brows. They were cool like autumn, warm like spring; they were pleased or angry evenly through the four seasons, did what fitted in with other things, and no one knew their high point. The True Man of Old –

> His figure looms but suffers no landslides:
> He seems to lack but takes no gifts.
> Assured! his stability, but not rigid:
> Pervasive! his tenuous influence, but it is not on display.
> Lighthearted! Seems to be doing as he pleases:
> Under compulsion! Inevitable that he does it.
> Impetuously! asserts a manner of his own:
> Cautiously! holds in the Power which is his own.
> So tolerant! in his seeming worldliness:
> So arrogant! in his refusal to be ruled.
> Canny! Seems he likes to keep his mouth shut:
> Scatterbrained! Forgets every word that he says.

The True Men of old used what is Heaven's to await what comes, did not let man intrude on Heaven. The True Men of old used the eye to look at the eye, the ear to look at the ear, the heart to recover the heart. Such men as that when they were level were true to the carpenter's line, when they were altering stayed on course. Hence they were one with what they liked and one with what they disliked, one when they were one and one when they were not one. When one they were of Heaven's party, when not one they were of man's party. Someone in whom neither Heaven nor man is victor over the other, this is what is meant by the True Man.

NOTE   At the end of chapter 5, Chuang-tzǔ took the side of Heaven against man; here he tries to resolve the dichotomy. As in several examples in chapter 2, he starts from a preliminary formulation, either his own or quoted from some unknown source, and then raises a doubt. The formulation takes the dichotomy for granted, and lays it down that the purpose of man's thought and action is to nourish the spontaneous process which is from Heaven, as in the support of the body, which is engendered by Heaven to last to a ripe old age provided that the man looks after it properly. But can one make an ultimate distinction between the spontaneous motion and the deliberate action? The reformulation at the end attacks the dichotomy with the paradox that the sage remains fundamentally one with things whether he is being united with them by Heaven or is dividing himself off as a thinking man.

. . .

Death and life are destined; that they have the constancy of morning and evening is of Heaven. Everything in which man cannot intervene belongs to the identities of things. Those have Heaven only as their father, yet still for our part we love them, and how much more that which is exalted above them! A man thinks of his lord merely as better than himself, yet still for his part will die for him, and how much more for the truest of lords!

That hugest of clumps of soil loads me with a body, has me toiling through a life, eases me with old age, rests me with death; therefore that I find it good to live is the very reason why I find it good to die. We store our boat in the ravine, our fishnet in the marsh, and say it's safe there; but at midnight someone stronger carries it away on his back, and the dull ones do not know it. The smaller stored in the bigger has its proper place, but still has room to escape; as for the whole world stored within the world, with nowhere else to escape, that is the ultimate identity of an unchanging thing. To have happened only on man's shape is enough to please us; if a shape such as man's through ten thousand transformations never gets nearer to a limit, can the joys we shall have of it ever be counted? Therefore the sage will roam where things cannot escape him and all are present. That he finds it good to die young and good to grow old, good to begin and good to end, is enough for men to take him as their model; and how much more that to which the myriad things are tied, on which we depend to be transformed just once!

. . .

As for the Way, it is something with identity, something to trust in, but does nothing, has no shape. It can be handed down but not taken as one's own, can be grasped but not seen. Itself the trunk, itself the root, since before there was a heaven and an earth inherently from of old it is what it was. It hallows ghosts and hallows God, engenders heaven, engenders earth; it is farther than the utmost pole but is not reckoned high, it is under the six-way-oriented but is not reckoned deep, it was born before heaven and earth but is not reckoned long-lasting, it is elder to the most ancient but is not reckoned old. Hsi-wei found it, and with it dangled heaven and earth in his hand; Fu-hsi found it, and with it ventured into the Mother of all breath. The Dipper which guides the stars found it, and through all the ages points unerringly; the sun and moon found it, and through all the ages never rest. K'an-p'i found it and ventured into Mount K'un-lun, P'ing-yi found it and swam the great river, Chien Wu found it and settled on Mount T'ai, the Yellow Emperor found it and rose up in the cloudy sky, Chuan Hsü found it and settled in the Black Palace. Yü Ch'iang who found it stands in the farthest North, the Western Queen Mother who found it sits in Shao-kuang; none knows their beginning, none knows their end. P'eng-tsu found it, who lived right back in the time of Shun, right down to the Five Tyrants. Fu Yüeh found it, and used it to minister to Wu Ting, ere long possessor of the Empire; he rides the East Corner and straddles Sagittarius and Scorpio, a neighbour to all the constellated stars.

. . .

Tzŭ-k'uei of Nan-po asked the woman Chü
  'You are old in years, how is it that you look as fresh as a child?'
  'I have heard the Way.'
  'Can the Way be learned?'
  ''Mercy me, it can't be done, you're not the man for it! That Pu-liang Yi had the stuff of a sage but not the Way of a sage, I have the Way of a sage but not the stuff of a sage. I wanted to teach it to him; could it be that he would really become a sage? In any case it's not so hard to tell the Way of a sage to someone with the stuff of a sage. I wouldn't leave him alone until I'd told him: three days in a row and he was able to put the world outside him. When he had got the world outside him I still wouldn't leave him alone, and by the seventh day he was able to put the things we live on outside him. When he got the things we live on outside him, again I wouldn't leave him alone, and by the ninth day he was able to put life itself outside him. Once he had got life itself outside him, he could break through to the daylight, and then he could see the Unique, and then he could be without past and present, and then he could enter into the undying, unliving. That which kills off the living does not die, that which gives birth to the living has never been born. As for the sort of thing it is, it is there to escort whatever departs, is here to welcome whatever comes, it ruins everything and brings everything about. Its name is ''At home where it intrudes''. What is ''at home where it intrudes'' is that which comes about only where it intrudes into the place of something else.'
  'Where did you of all people come to hear of that?'
  'I heard it from Inkstain's son, who heard it from Bookworm's grandson, who heard it from Wide-eye, who heard it from Eavesdrop, who heard it from Gossip, who heard it from Singsong, who heard it from Obscurity, who heard it from Mystery, who heard it from what might have been Beginning.'

. . .

Four men, Masters Ssŭ, Yü, Li, and Lai, were talking together.
  'Which of us is able to think of nothingness as the head, of life as the spine, of death as the rump? Which of us knows that the living and the dead, the surviving and the lost, are all one body? He shall be my friend.'

The four men looked at each other and smiled, and none was reluctant in his heart. So they all became friends.

Soon Master Yü fell ill, and Master Ssŭ went to inquire.

'Wonderful! how the maker of things is turning me into this crumpled thing. He hunches me and stick out my back, the five pipes to the spine run up above my head, my chin hides down in my navel, my shoulders are higher than my crown, the knobbly bone in my neck points up at the sky. The energies of Yin and Yang are all awry.'

His heart was at ease and he had nothing to do. He tottered out to look at his reflection in the well.

'Ugh! The maker of things still goes on turning me into this crumpled thing.'

'Do you hate it?'

'No, why should I hate it? Little by little he'll borrow my left arm to transform it into a cock, and it will be why I am listening to a cock-crow at dawn. Little by little he'll borrow my right arm to transform it into a crossbow, and it will be why I am waiting for a roasted owl for my dinner. Little by little he'll borrow and transform my buttocks into wheels, my daemon into a horse, and they'll be there for me to ride, I'll never have to harness a team again! Besides, to get life is to be on time and to lose it is to be on course; be content with the time and settled on the course, and sadness and joy cannot find a way in. This is what of old was called ''being loosed from the bonds''; and whoever cannot loose himself other things bind still tighter. And it is no new thing after all that creatures do not prevail against Heaven. What would be the point in hating it?'

Soon Master Lai fell ill, and lay panting on the verge of death. His wife and children stood in a circle bewailing him. Master Li went to ask after him.

'Shoo! Out of the way!' he said. 'Don't startle him while he transforms.'

He lolled against Lai's door and talked with him.

'Wonderful, the process which fashions and transforms us! What is it going to turn you into, in what direction will it use you to go? Will it make you into a rat's liver? Or a fly's leg?'

'A child that has father and mother, go east, west, north, south, has only their commands to obey; and for man the Yin and Yang are more than father and mother. Something other than me approaches, I die; and if I were to refuse to listen it would be defiance on my part, how can I blame him? That hugest of clumps of soil loaded me with a body, had me toiling through a life, eased me with old age, rests me with death; therefore that I found it good to live is the very reason why I find it good to die. If today a master swordsmith were smelting metal, and the metal should jump up and say ''I insist on being made into an Excalibur'', the swordsmith would surely think it metal with a curse on it. If now having once happened on the shape of a man, I were to say ''I'll be a man, nothing but a man'', he that fashions and transforms us would surely think me a baleful sort of man. Now if once and for all I think of heaven and earth as a vast foundry, and the fashioner and transformer as the master smith, wherever I am going why should I object? I'll fall into a sound sleep and wake up fresh.'

·   ·   ·

The three men, Master Sang-hu, Meng Tzŭ-fan and Master Ch'in-chang, were talking together.

'Which of us can be *with* where there is no being with, be *for* where there is no being for? Which of us are able to climb the sky and roam the mists and go whirling into the infinite, living forgetful of each other for ever and ever?'

The three men looked at each other and smiled, and none was reluctant in his heart. So they became friends.

After they had been living quietly for a while Master Sang-hu died. Before he was buried, Confucius heard about it and sent Tzŭ-kung to assist at the funeral. One of the men was plaiting frames for silkworms, the other strumming a zither, and they sang in unison

> 'Hey-ho, Sang-hu!
> Hey-ho, Sang-hu!
> You've gone back to being what one truly is,
> But we go on being human, O!'

Tzŭ-kung hurried forward and asked

'May I inquire whether it is in accordance with the rites to sing with the corpse right there at your feet?'

The two men exchanged glances and smiled.

'What does he know about the meaning of the rites?'

Tzŭ-kung returned and told Confucius

'What men are these? The decencies of conduct are nothing to them, they treat the very bones of their bodies as outside them. They sing with the corpse right there at their feet, and not a change in the look on their faces. I have no words to name them. What men are these?'

'They are the sort that roams beyond the guidelines,' said Confucius. 'I am the sort that roams within the guidelines. Beyond and within have nothing in common, and to send you to mourn was stupid on my part. They are at the stage of being fellow men with the maker of things, and go roaming in the single breath that breathes through heaven and earth. They think of life as an obstinate wart or a dangling wen, of death as bursting the boil or letting the pus. How should such men as that know death from life, before from after? They borrow right-of-way through the things which are different but put up for the night in that body which is the same. Self-forgetful right down to the liver and the gall, leaving behind their own ears and eyes, they turn start and end back to front, and know no beginning-point or standard.

Heedlessly they go roving beyond the dust and grime, go rambling through the lore in which there's nothing to *do*. How could they be finicky about the rites of common custom, on watch for the inquisitive eyes and ears of the vulgar?'

'In that case, sir, why depend on guidelines yourself?'

'I am one of those condemned by the sentence of Heaven. However, let us see what we can do together.'

'I venture to ask the secret of it.'

'As fish go on setting directions for each other in the water, men go on setting directions for each other in the Way. For the fish which set directions for each other in the water, you dig a pool and their nurture is provided for. For us who set directions for each other in the Way, if we cease to be busy life fixes its own course. When the spring dries up and the fish are stranded together on land, they spit moisture at each other and soak each other in the foam, but they would be better off forgetting each other in the Yangtse or the Lakes. Rather than praise sage Yao and condemn tyrant Chieh, we should be better off if we could forget them both and let their Ways enter the transformations. As the saying goes, ''Fish forget all about each other in the Yangtse and the Lakes, men forget all about each other in the lore of the Way''.'

'Let me ask about extraordinary men.'

'Extraordinary men are extraordinary in the eyes of men but ordinary in the eyes of Heaven. As the saying goes, ''Heaven's knave is man's gentleman, man's gentleman is Heaven's knave''.'

•   •   •

Yen Hui put a question to Confucius.

'Meng-sun Ts'ai wailed when his mother died but did not shed a tear, in his inward heart he did not suffer, conducting the funeral he did not grieve. In spite of these three failings, he is renowned as the best of mourners throughout the state of Lu. Are there really people who win a name for it without possessing the substance? I am utterly amazed at it.'

'That Meng-sun has the whole secret, he has taken the step beyond knowledge. If you merely simplify it you don't succeed, finishing with it altogether does simplify something. Meng-sun does not know what he depended on to be born, does not know what he will depend on to die, does not know how to be nearer to the time before or the time after. If in transforming he has become one thing instead of another, is it required that what he does not know terminated in being transformed? Besides, at the stage of being transformed how would he know about the untransformed? At the stage of being untransformed, how would he know about the transformed? Is it just that you and I are the ones who have not yet begun to wake from our dream?

'Moreover he has convulsions of the body without damage to the heart, has abodes for no longer than a morning but no true death. It's just that

Meng-sun has come awake. When another man wails he wails too; it is simply that, all the way up from that which they depend on to be-about-to-be, he is with him in recognising him as ''I''. How would I know what it is I call recognising as ''I''?

'You dream that you are a bird and fly away in the sky, dream that you are a fish and plunge into the deep. There's no telling whether the man who speaks now is the waker or the dreamer. Rather than go towards what suits you, laugh: rather than acknowledge it with your laughter, shove it from you. Shove it from you and leave the transformations behind; then you will enter the oneness of the featureless sky.'

· · ·

Yi-erh-tzŭ visited Hsü Yu.

'What riches did you get from Yao?' said Hsü Yu.

'Yao told me: ''Be sure to devote yourself to Goodwill and Duty and say plainly 'That's it, that's not'.'' '

'Then what do you think you're doing here? When that Yao has already branded your hide with Goodwill and Duty, and snipped off your nose with his ''That's it, that's not'', how are you going to roam that free and easy take-any-turn-you-please path?'

'At any rate I should like to roam by its hedges.'

'No. Blind pupils can never share in the sight of beautiful eyebrows and face, nor pupilless eyes in the spectacle of green and yellow vestments.'

'Wu-chuang losing his beauty, Chü-liang his strength, the Yellow Emperor his wisdom, were all simply in the course of being smelted and hammered. How do we know that the maker of things will not make my brand fade and my snipped nose grow, so that finding myself whole again I can be your disciple?'

'Hmm, we can't be sure. Let me put it for you in a few words. My Teacher, O my Teacher! He chops fine the myriad things but it is not cruelty, his bounty extends to a myriad ages but it is not goodwill, he is elder to the most ancient but it is not growing old, he overhangs heaven and bears up earth and cuts up and sculpts all shapes but it is not skill –

'It is over *this* that you have to roam.'

(Therefore when the sage goes to war, though he ruins states he does not lose men's hearts; the benefits of his bounty extend to a myriad ages, but he is not deemed to love mankind. Hence to delight in being expert in things is not sagehood, to be more kin to some than to others is not goodwill, to pry into what is Heaven's is not cleverness. If your benefits and harms do not interchange you are not a gentleman, if in pursuit of a name you lose your own self you are not a knight, if by forgetting what you are you fail to be genuine you are not a master of men. As for such as Hu Pu-hsieh, Wu

Kuang, Po Yi, Shu Ch'i, Chi-tzŭ, Hsü Yü, Chi T'o, Shen-t'u Ti, they were men who served what served others, were suited by what suited others, not by what suited themselves.)

NOTE The rhapsodic address to the Way as 'My Teacher' must have especially appealed to the Syncretist editor, for it has inspired the chapter title 'Teacher who is the ultimate ancestor', and is quoted as Chuang-tzŭ's in a Syncretist essay (p. 260 below). The bracketed passage, which we shift here from earlier in the chapter, seems to be a comment on or development of it, whether by Chuang-tzŭ or by another hand. The list of names at the end is of men who pointlessly sacrificed themselves on trifling points of honour; the 'Yangist Miscellany', which also finds them obnoxious, tells several of their stories (pp. 231–3, 238 below).

· · ·

'I make progress,' said Yen Hui.
'Where?' said Confucius.
'I have forgotten about rites and music.'
'Satisfactory. But you still have far to go.'
Another day he saw Confucius again.
'I make progress.'
'Where?'
'I have forgotten about Goodwill and Duty.'
'Satisfactory. But you still have far to go.'
Another day he saw Confucius again.
'I make progress.'
'Where?'
'I just sit and forget.'
Confucius was taken aback.
'What do you mean, just sit and forget?'
'I let organs and members drop away, dismiss eyesight and hearing, part from the body and expel knowledge, and go along with the universal thoroughfare. This is what I mean by "just sit and forget".'
'If you go along with it, you have no preferences; if you let yourself transform, you have no norms. Has it really turned out that you are the better of us? Oblige me by accepting me as your disciple.'

· · ·

Master Yü was friendly with Master Sang, and it had been raining incessantly for ten days. 'I am afraid Sang will be in trouble,' said Yü, and wrapping up some rice took it him for his dinner. When he reached Sang's gate there was a sound as much like wailing as singing, to the strumming of a zither
'Was it father? – Was it mother? – Heaven? – Man?'

There was something in it of a voice too frail to hold out and in a hurry to finish the verse.

Entering, Master Yü asked

'The verse you were singing, what did you mean by it?'

'I was imagining who it might be that brought me so low, and can't find an answer. How could my father and mother have wanted me to be poor? Heaven is impartial to everything it covers, earth to everything it carries; why would heaven and earth discriminate to make me poor? I can't find out who it is that did it. That nonetheless I have sunk so low – shall we say it's destiny?'

7

Responding to the Emperors and Kings

This last of the *Inner chapters* collects Chuang-tzǔ's few observations on ideal king-ship. For the Syncretist editor this would be the greatest of themes, but it is plain that to find anything remotely relevant in Chuang-tzǔ's literary remains he had to scrape the bottom of the barrel. The first item is the conclusion of a dialogue already used in chapter 2 (p. 58 above); he must have chopped it off and added the introduction which resumes the previous exchanges ('Gaptooth asked questions of Wang Ni, four times asked and four times he did not know').

The editor found only four items directly concerned with kingship, which we distinguish as the 'First series'. The 'Second series' illustrates aspects of sagehood which he perhaps thought especially relevant to government. Thus his reason for including the penultimate episode (p. 98 below) might be that it introduces the metaphor of the sage's heart as a mirror, important in the Syncretist theory of kingship (p. 259 below).

1 FIRST SERIES

Gaptooth asked questions of Wang Ni, four times asked and four times he did not know. So Gaptooth hopped about in great delight, and went on a journey to tell Master Reedcoat.

'Didn't you know it until now?' said Master Reedcoat. 'The House of Yu-yü is not equalling the House of T'ai. Our Emperor, yes, he still keeps a store of kindness to get a hold on men, and he does indeed win them, but he has never begun to draw from the source which is not man. He of the House of T'ai slept sound and woke up fresh; at one moment he deemed himself the logician's ''horse'', at the next his ''ox''; his knowledge was essential and trustworthy, the Power in him utterly genuine, and he had never begun to enter a realm which is not man.'

NOTE   Gaptooth and his friends live under the rule of the legendary Shun (whose family was the Yu-yü), one of the ideal sages of Confucians. But Shun preferred the morality which is from man to the spontaneity which is from Heaven. Chuang-tzǔ

would rather imagine a sage in the remotest past (the meaning of *T'ai* is 'ultimate')
before there was even the dichotomy of Heaven and man, long before there were
logicians distinguishing between 'X' and 'Y', 'ox' and 'horse'.

.   .   .

Chien Wu visited mad Chieh Yü.
'What did Noonbegin tell you?' asked mad Chieh Yü.
'He told me that a lord of men issues on his own authority rules, conventions, forms and regulations, and who dares refuse to obey and be reformed
by them?'
'That's a bullying sort of a Power. As far as ordering the Empire is
concerned, you might as well go wading through oceans, boring holes in
rivers, or comanding mosquitos to carry mountains on their backs. When
the sage sets in order, is he ordering the external? It is simply a matter of
straightening oneself out before one acts, of being solidly capable of doing
one's own work.
'The birds fly high to be out of danger from the stringed arrows, the field-
mice go burrowing deep under the sacred hill, where no one can trouble
them by digging down and smoking them out. Even those two creatures
know better than that.'

.   .   .

Heaven-based roamed on the south side of Mount Vast, and came to the
bank of the River Limpid. Happening to meet a man without a name, he
asked him.
'Permit me to inquire how one rules the Empire.'
'Away! You're a bumpkin! What a dreary thing to talk about! I am just in
the course of becoming fellow man with the maker of things; and when I
get bored with that, I shall ride out on the bird which fades into the sky
beyond where the six directions end, to travel the realm of Nothingwhatever
and settle in the wilds of the Boundless. What do you mean by stirring up
thoughts in my heart about such a trifle as ruling the Empire?'
He repeated the question. Said the man without a name
'Let your heart roam in the flavourless, blend your energies with the
featureless, in the spontaneity of your accord with other things leave no
room for selfishness, and the Empire will be order.'

NOTE   This is the single passage which specifically distinguishes two stages of sagehood: (1) the ecstatic roaming as 'fellow man with the maker of things', without yet
ceasing to be human, like the two mourners singing to the zither who shocked Confucius (p. 89 above); (2) the final withdrawal into the impassivity beyond life and death
of the mourner Meng-sun (p. 90 above), for whom past and present are the same, and
everyone else is as much 'I' as he is, and all the experience of the senses is

revealed as a dream. It is a curious paradox of the Taoist mockery of deliberation that the final take-off seems to depend on a choice, perhaps on the verge of death. Confucius says of the cripple Wang T'ai that he 'will pick his own day to rise out of the world (p. 77 above).

What is significant about the nameless man's remarks about government is not the content but the perspective in which the government of the Empire is seen; it is of negligible importance, yet as important as anything else in the world.

• • •

Yang Tzǔ-chü visited Old Tan.

'Suppose we have a man', he said, 'who is alert, energetic, well informed, clear-headed and untiring in learning the Way: may someone like that be ranked with the enlightened Kings?'

'To the sage this is a slave's drudgery, an artisan's bondage, wearing out the body, fretting the heart. Besides, it's the elegant markings of tiger and leopard which attract the hunter, and it's the spryest of monkeys and the dog which catches the rat that get themselves on the leash. Can someone like that be ranked with the enlightened kings?'

Yang Tzǔ-chü was taken aback.

'May I ask how an enlightened king rules?'

> 'When the enlightened king rules
> His deeds spread over the whole world
>   but seem not from himself:
> His riches are loaned to the myriad things
>   but the people do not depend on him.
> He is there, but no one mentions his name.
> He lets things find their own delight.

He is one who keeps his foothold in the immeasurable and roams where nothing is.'

2 SECOND SERIES

In Cheng there was a daemonic shaman called Chi Hsien, who knew whether a man would live or die, be ruined or saved, be lucky or unlucky, be cut off too soon or last out his term, and set the date within a year, a month, ten days, the day; it was daemonic, no less. When the people of Cheng saw him they all shunned him and fled. When Lieh-tzǔ saw him he was drunk at heart, and returned to tell Hu-tzǔ about him.

"Master, once I thought that your Way was the highest, but there is another which is higher still.'

'With you I have exhausted its scriptures but not yet exhausted its substance: have you really grasped the Way? With so many hens but no cock, what eggs can you expect from them? In matching the Way to the world you have to exert yourself too actively, and that is how you give a man the opportunity to read your face. Try bringing him here, let him take a look at me.'

Next day Lieh-tzŭ did bring him to see Hu-tzŭ. Coming out, the man said to Lieh-tzŭ

"Hmm, your master is a dead man. He won't revive, his days are not to be counted in tens. I saw a strange thing in him, saw damp ash in him.'

Lieh-tzŭ went in with tears soaking the lapels of his coat, and told Hu-tzŭ about it.

'Just now', said Hu-tzŭ, 'I showed him the formation of the ground. The shoots as they went on sprouting were without vibration but without pause. I should think he saw me as I am when I hold down the impulses of the Power. Try bringing him here again.'

Next day he brought him to see Hu-tzŭ again. Coming out, he told Lieh-tzŭ

'A lucky thing your master happened to meet me! He's recovered, the ash is aflame, he's alive. I saw him holding down the arm of the scales.'

Lieh-tzŭ went in and told Hu-tzŭ.

'Just now', said Hu-tzŭ, 'I showed him Heaven and the fertilised ground. Names and substances had not found a way in, but the impulses were coming up from my heels. I should think he saw my impulses towards the good. Try bringing him here again.'

Next day he brought him to see Hu-tzŭ again. Coming out, he told Lieh-tzŭ

'Your master does not fast, I cannot read anything in his face. Let him try fasting, I'll read his face again.'

Lieh-tzŭ went in and told Hu-tzŭ.

'Just now I showed him the absolute emptiness where there is no fore-boding of anything. I should think he saw me as I am when I level out the impulses of the breath. Try bringing him here again.'

Next day he brought him to see Hu-tzŭ again. Before the man had come to a standstill he lost his head and ran.

'Go after him,' said Hu-tzŭ.

Lieh-tzŭ went after him but failed to catch up. He returned and reported to Hu-tzŭ

'He's vanished, he's lost, I couldn't catch up.'

'Just now', said Hu-tzŭ, 'I showed him how it is before ever we come out of our Ancestor.

> With him I attenuated, wormed in and out,
> Unknowing who or what we were.
> It made him think he was fading away,
> It made him think he was carried off on the waves.

That's why he fled.'

Only then did Lieh-tzŭ conclude that he had never begun to learn, and went off home. For three years he did not leave the house.

> He cooked the dinner for his wife,
> Fed the pigs as though feeding people,
> Remained aloof in all his works.
> From the carved gem he returned to the unhewn block:
> Unique, in his own shape, he took his stand.
> Didn't tidy up the raggle-taggle.
> That's how he was to the end of his days.

NOTE Here as in chapter 1 (p. 44 above) Lieh-tzŭ is the Taoist led astray by the fascination of magical powers. His teacher Hu-tzŭ is not interested in fortune-telling, since he can withdraw beyond life and death to that serenity (with 'a heart like dead ash' and 'a frame like withered wood', cf. p. 48, which is outwardly indistinguishable from death. As elsewhere in the *Inner chapters* the only technique assumed is the control of the *ch'i* (the breath and other energies of the body) by breathing which is very deep, 'from the heels' (cf. also p. 84 above), and so even that the adept seems not to be breathing at all. For the uninitiated who cling to life, the merest glimpse of this state overwhelms with the horror of self-dissolution in ultimate solitude.

· · ·

> Don't be a medium possessed by your name,
> Don't be a stockroom for schemes.
> Don't take the weight of affairs on your shoulders,
> Don't be the man-in-charge of wisdom.

Become wholly identified with the limitless and roam where there is no foreboding of anything. Exhaust all that you draw from Heaven and never have gain in sight; simply keep yourself tenuous. The utmost man uses the heart like a mirror; he does not escort things as they go or welcome them as they come, he responds and does not store. Therefore he is able to conquer other things without suffering a wound.

· · ·

The Emperor of the South Sea was Fast, the Emperor of the North Sea was Furious, the Emperor of the centre was Hun-t'un. Fast and Furious met from time to time in the land of Hun-t'un, who treated them very generously. Fast and Furious were discussing how to repay Hun-t'un's bounty.

'All men have seven holes through which they look, listen, eat, breathe; he alone doesn't have any. Let's try boring them.'

Every day they bored one hole, and on the seventh day Hun-t'un died.

NOTE Hun-t'un is the primal blob which first divided into heaven and earth and then differentiated as the myriad things. In Chinese cosmology the primordial is not a chaos reduced to order by imposed law, it is a blend of everything rolled up together; the word is a reduplicative of the type of English 'hotchpotch' and 'rolypoly', and diners in Chinese restaurants will have met it in the form 'wuntun' as a kind of dumpling.

8

Passages related to the Inner chapters

Six of the *Mixed chapters*, chapters 23–27 and 32, include strings of miscellaneous pieces, some no more than fragments, which may come from any or all of the authors in the book. A number of them resume themes otherwise absent after the *Inner chapters* – the maker of things, the advantages of uselessness, the games Chuang-tzŭ liked to play with logic. Since he developed his philosophy in reaction against the Sophists, he had to devise a terminology of his own with which to clarify his own position. The need of it would hardly have outlasted his lifetime; in general one gets the impression that he was an enemy of logic who knew what logic is, while his successors did not. It is only in 'The sorting which evens things out' and in these *Mixed chapters* episodes that we find his idiosyncratic variations on *shih*, 'That's it' (the *shih* which deems, the *shih* which goes by circumstance, the common *shih*, the shifting *shih*), the contrasting of 'It' and 'Other', judging from a 'lodging-place', the 'whetstone of Heaven', the 'potter's wheel of Heaven'. The Syncretist editors of the second century BC must have found this material uninviting if not unintelligible, which may be why they relegated so much of it to the chapters which served as ragbags instead of incorporating it in 'The sorting which evens things out'. It will be equally unrewarding for a modern reader who is interested primarily in the literary side of *Chuang-tzŭ*, but anyone trying seriously to come to grips with the philosophy will find it very important.

Said Hui Shih to Chuang-tzŭ

'These sayings of yours are useless.'

'It is only with people who know about the useless that there is any point in talking about uses. In all the immensity of heaven and earth, a man uses no more than is room for his feet. If recognising this we were to dig away the ground round his feet all the way down to the Underworld, would it still be useful to the man?'

'It would be useless.'

'Then it is plain that the useless does serve a use.' (*Chuang-tzŭ*, chapter 26)

· · · ·

Said Chuang-tzǔ

'If archers who hit what they haven't previously specified as the target were to be called good archers, everyone in the world would be as great an archer as Yi – allowable?'

'Allowable,' said Hui Shih.

'If the world has no common ''it'' for ''That's it'', and each of us treats as ''it'' what is ''it'' for him, everyone in the world is as great a sage as Yao – allowable?'

'Allowable.'

'Then of the four doctrines of the Confucians and Mohists, Yang and Ping, which with your own make five, which is really ''it''? Perhaps you are people like Lu Chü? When a disciple of his said ''I have grasped your Way, sir; I can get a cauldron to boil in winter and can manufacture ice in summer'', Lu Chü answered: ''This is no more than using Yang to summon Yang, Yin to summon Yin, it is not what I mean by the Way. Let me show you my Way.'' Then he tuned 25-string zithers for him and put one in the hall, the other in a room: when he struck the note *kung* on one the *kung* resonated on the other, when he struck the note *chüeh* on one the *chüeh* resonated on the other, for note and pitch were the same on both. Should someone else retune one string out of place in the five notes, the twenty-five strings when he strummed would all resonate; without there ever having been a difference from the sound, the master note of the scale would have lapsed. Would you be like him?'

'At present those Confucians and Mohists, Yang and Ping, are challenging me in disputation. We formulate propositions to refute each other, we shout to browbeat each other. Are you seriously suggesting that they have never denied my position?'

'In the case of the man of Ch'i who ''blamed his son in Sung'', he had failed to make himself clear in giving orders to the gatekeeper. ''If it's the *hsing* bells he's looking for he'll get himself arrested for it, if it's a lost son he's looking for they've never left the country.'' – there was an overlooked category, don't you agree? As for the lodger from Ch'u who blamed the gatekeeper, in the middle of the night when there was no one there he got into a fight with the boatman. Without him ever having left the hill, it was enough to start a grudge.' (*Chuang-tzǔ*, chapter 24)

NOTE   Chuang-tzǔ is saying that ultimately philosophers disagree only in what they choose to name 'duty', the 'Way' and so forth, but the detail of the argument is very obscure. The point of the musical example is, I take it, that according to Lu Chü the right-thinking agree on what is meant by 'duty' as absolutely as the two zithers agree on the value of the notes, as demonstrated by their sympathetic resonance. He forgets that the notes of the scale vary in pitch with the tuning, and the resonance proves only identity in pitch. (On this interpretation, the retuning of the one string is on both zithers.)

In the last exchange Chuang-tzǔ is alluding to an otherwise unknown story. It may

be guessed that the man of Ch'i was going to visit Sung Hsing (Sung-tzŭ), a philosopher of the Chi-hsia academy in Ch'i who is mentioned elsewhere in the book (pp.
44, 278). The gatekeeper misunderstood 'Sung' as the state of that name, *hsing* as
the kind of bell so called, and *tzŭ* in its ordinary sense of 'son'. I will not hazard a
guess about the lodger from Ch'u. The point would be that the bitterest
disagreements can start from giving different meanings to words.

•   •   •

Said Chuang-tzŭ to Hui Shih

'Confucius by the age of sixty had sixty times changed his mind; whenever
he began by judging ''That's it'' he ended by judging ''That's not''. We do
not yet know of anything which we now affirm that we shall not deny it fifty-
nine times over.'

'It's that Confucius persevered in his intent, devoted himself to knowing.'

'Confucius gave up all that, and although he would say things from the
mouth he was never saying them from the heart. According to Confucius,
we go on drawing our capabilities from the ultimate root, and revert to its
magic in order to grow. To make your native note fit the pitch-tubes, your
words fit the standards, and with benefits and duties spread out before you, to
like and dislike and judge ''That's it'' and ''That's not'', this serves only to
make men submit from the mouth. But if you do cause men to submit from
the heart and not presume to take a defiant stand, you make the empire
doubly stable. Enough, enough! We have never yet succeeded in rising to his
level!' (*Chuang-tzŭ*, chapter 27)

•   •   •

Ch'ü Po-yü at the age of sixty had sixty times changed his mind; what he
began by affirming, in the end he never failed to dismiss with a denial. We do
not yet know of anything which we now affirm that we shall not deny it fifty-
nine times over. The myriad things have somewhere from which they grow
but no one sees the root, somewhere from which they come forth but no one
sees the gate. Men all honour what wit knows, but none knows how to know
by depending on what his wits do not know; may that not be called the
supreme uncertainty? Enough, enough! There is nowhere you can escape
from it; is it what one might call 'the alternative which is so together with the
alternative which is so'? (*Chuang-tzŭ*, chapter 25)

NOTE   The last sentence repeats Chuang-tzŭ's call to abolish the alternatives of
disputation by 'treating as so even what is not so' (p. 60 above).

•   •   •

In the interchange of things by the Way, their dividing is formation, their formation is dissolution. What goes on being hateful in dividing is that it makes the divisions into a completed set. The reason why the completion goes on being hateful is that it makes everything there is into a completed set. Therefore having come forth it does not go back, we see its ghost; having come forth, to 'get through' is to get through to death. The extinguished persisting as solid is a One which is a ghost; it has used the shaped to image the shapeless and has become fixed.

It has no root in it from which it comes forth and no opening for it through wich to go in, it has solidity but goes on having nothing to reside in, it has duration but never has a root or a tip. (What comes forth from somewhere but has no opening for it has solidity.) That which has solidity but goes on having nothing to reside in is the cosmos-as-spatial; that which has duration but neither root nor tip is the cosmos-as-temporal.

There is somewhere from which we are born, into which we die, from which we come forth, through which we go in; it is this that is called the Gate of Heaven. The Gate of Heaven is that which is without anything; the myriad things go on coming forth from that which is without anything. Something cannot become something by means of something, it necessarily goes on coming forth from that which is without anything; but that which is without anything is for ever without anything. The sage stores away in *it*. (*Chuang tzŭ*, chapter 23)

NOTE   Except for the later Mohists, no early Chinese thinkers are known to have fully abstracted the concepts of Space and Time; the corresponding words *yü* and *chou* seem rather to be 'cosmos-as-spatial' and 'cosmos-as-temporal'. Here Chuang-tzü has the thought, explicit nowhere else in the book, that the habit of analysing puts us in the middle of an illusory universe of rigid, static things which persists like a dead man's ghost as the process of transformation continues. In particular, by dividing off Something from Nothing, we evoke a cosmos floating in empty space and cut off from the living root out of which things grow. The sage returns to the whole which, since it has not yet divided out into separate things, is 'without anything' (and conversely 'without nothing', cf. p. 21 above).

·   ·   ·

What is ultimately fixed in the cosmos-as-spatial goes on issuing from the light of Heaven. One who goes on issuing from the light of Heaven, other men see as a man, other things see as a thing. Only the man who is on course possesses constancy. One who has constancy, man lets go of, Heaven assists. Whom man lets go of is called a subject of Heaven, whom Heaven assists is called a 'Son of Heaven'. (*Chuang-tzü*, chapter 23)

NOTE   This passage is closely related to the last. In contrast with the artificial fixity of things divided up by the intellect, the 'ultimately fixed' is what veers with the fluid course of the Way by letting itself be generated continually from the root of things (cf. p. 62 above, 'The ultimately fixed supports them'). One who can return to this course has shed the habit of analysis by which man distinguishes himself as agent from Heaven working through him, and is left with only the shape and guise of a man (cf. p. 82 above).

. . .

The men of old, their knowledge had arrived at something: at what had it arrived? There were some who thought there had not yet begun to be any things – the utmost, the exhaustive, there is no more to add. The next thought that there were things, but they preferred to think of life as the loss of something, of death as its recovery, by which dividing comes to an end. The next said: 'At first there is not anything, afterwards there is life, living we soon die. Deem ''being without anything'' to be the head, ''life'' the torso, ''death' the rump. Who knows that Something and Nothing, death and life, have a single ancestor? He shall be my friend.'

These three though different are a royal clan; they are 'Chao' and 'Ching' calling attention to positions in the succession, and the 'House of Ch'ü' calling attention to the bordered fief, they are not the One. Having 'life' is an obscuring accretion; stripping it off, say '*It* as it shifts'. Try to speak about *it* as it shifts, and it is not what you are speaking about; what it is, however, is unknowable. The Midwinter Sacrifice composed of tripes and hooves can be shared out far and wide yet cannot be shared out at all. The viewer of a house makes a full tour of rooms and shrine – and when the tour is over goes off to a latrine in it.

A 'That's it' which deems picks out by a reference *it* as it shifts. Let's see what happens now when you speak about *it* as it shifts. This is to take 'life' as the root of you and the wits as your authority, and use them to go by in charioteering 'That's it, that's not'. They really exist for you, names and substances, and using them to go by you make yourself into a hostage. You let other men judge what is honourable for yourself, and using them to go by you will die to redeem honour. People like that think of the employed as wise and the out of office as foolish, of success as glorious and failure as disgraceful. *It* as it shifts being the men of today is the cicada and the dove thinking the same as whoever thinks the same. (*Chuang-tzŭ*, chapter 23)

NOTE In distinguishing 'life', we divide into a triad like the three branches of the royal clan of Ch'u. We name the bordered thing 'living' (as the Ch'ü branch is named after the bordered land in which it is enfiefed), and the other two phases by their positions before and after (as Chao and Ching are named after ancestors in the line of the kings of Ch'u). The sage, by unlearning distinctions, reverts from the phases between which one judges 'That's it, that's not' to the '*it* as it shifts' from which they are abstracted. But the rest of us take the living phase as fundamental and let our contemporaries decide for us what is 'it' and what is not, supporting ourselves on a local and temporary unanimity which is as meaningless as the agreement of the cicada and the dove on the impossibility of long-distance flying (cf. p. 43f above).

. . .

Tzŭ-ch'i of Nan-po reclined elbow on armrest. As he looked up at the sky and exhaled, Yen-ch'eng-Tzŭ-yu entered and saw him.

'Master, you are supreme among things! Can the frame really be made to be like dry bone, the heart like dead ash?'

'I used to live in a mountain cave,' said Tzŭ-ch'i. 'During that time T'ien Ho noticed me once, and his subjects in Ch'i country congratulated him three times. I must have taken the initiative, that's how he knew; I must have offered for sale, that's how he bought. Without my taking the initiative, how would he get to know? Without my offering for sale, how could he get to buy? Alas! I lamented the man who had lost himself, then I lamented the lamenter of the man, then I lamented the lamenter of the lamenter of the man, and afterwards I withdrew further every day.' (*Chuang-tzŭ*, chapter 24)

NOTE   Tzŭ-ch'i knows that to lament is to make the mistake of distinguishing the disliked from the liked, therefore laments that he lamented and is caught up in a succession of lamenting and lamented selves. He breaks out of the dichotomy in the opening episode of chapter 2 (p. 48f above) through a trance in which he loses both 'the counterpart of himself' and 'his own self', and is declared by Yen-ch'eng Tzŭ-yu to be no longer the man who was leaning on the armrest the day before. This must be the discarded introduction of the story in chapter 2, where the editor must have revised at least the first sentence to make a new beginning.

• • •

Yen-ch'eng Tzŭ-yu said to Tzŭ-ch'i of Nan-kuo

'After I heard your words, one year and I ran wild, two years and I was tame, three years and things interchanged, four years and they were simply things, five years and the daemonic came, six years and the ghostly entered in, seven years and I was wholly Heaven's, eight years and I did not know life from death, nine years and I had the great secret.

'The "living" when its time comes we deem to be the "dead"; urging impartiality towards both is because we have been showing partiality to death. There is an origin, from which we are in the living, the Yang phase – but if there was no origin is it really so? Towards when are we proceeding, towards when not proceeding? Heaven has the numbers of the calendar, earth has the dates men count from; where would I seek an answer?

' "None knows where we shall end, how can there not be a destiny?" – None knows where we began, what destiny could there have been? "You do something to which it answers, what can it be but the spirits?" – There was nothing to be answered, how could it have been the spirits?' (*Chuang-tzŭ*, chapter 27)

NOTE   Chuang-tzŭ is playing one of his logical games with the idea of the beginning of things (as on p. 55 above). As soon as you distinguish life from death you have to give the name 'death' to the later of the phases, and therefore give it the advantage over life. You also raise the issue of why a man lives out his term or dies young, to which Confucians answer 'destiny' and Mohists 'reward or punishment by the spirits'. But to postulate an origin is to imply a time before the origin, so that the former phase (of the Yang, of life) can just as well be conceived as latter to what preceded. And how can one think of the origin either as destined (there would be nothing yet to decree the destiny) or as the work of spirits (who would have nothing to reward or punish)?

*   *   *

Archer Yi was skilled in hitting a minute target but clumsy in stopping others from praising himself. The sage is skilled in what is Heaven's but clumsy in what is man's. To be skilled in what is Heaven's and deft in what is man's, only the perfect man is capable of that. Only the animal is able to be animal, only the animal is able to be Heaven's. The perfect man hates Heaven, hates what is from Heaven in man, and above all the question 'Is it in me from Heaven or from man?' (*Chuang-tzŭ*, chapter 23)

NOTE Chuang-tzŭ generally either exalts Heaven or denies the dichotomy of Heaven and man, and to find him siding with man is so extraordinary that many try to force another meaning out of the passage. But on closer consideration one sees that to get to grips with the last and most obstinate dichotomy in his thought Chuang-tzŭ would be driven to seek an angle from which Heaven is the *wrong* one of the pair, to balance the only too familiar angle from which it is the right one. One cannot in the last resort distinguish the work of Heaven and of the man in the skilled spontaneity of the Taoist or the craftsman; if one tries, what is left as Heaven's is the purely animal, and from this point of view it is wrong to prefer Heaven.

*   *   *

'Saying from a lodging-place works nine times out of ten, weighted saying works seven times out of ten. ''Spillover'' saying is new every day, smooth it out on the whetstone of Heaven.'

'Saying from a lodging-place works nine times out of ten' – You borrow a standpoint outside in order to sort a matter out. A father does not act as marriage broker for his own son; a father praising his son does not impress as much as someone not the father. The blame for the standpoint is not on me, the blame is on the other man. If my standpoint is the same as his he responds, if it is not he turns the other way. What agrees with his standpoint he approves with a 'That's it' which deems, what disagrees he rejects with a 'That's not' which deems.

'Weighted saying works seven times out of ten' – It is what you say on your own authority. This is a matter of being venerable as a teacher. To be ahead in years, but without the warp and woof and root and tip of what is expected from the venerable in years, this isn't being ahead. To be a man without the resources to be ahead of others is to be without the

Way of Man; and a man without the Way of Man is to be called an obsolete man.

' "Spillover" ' saying is new every day, smooth it out on the whetstone of Heaven' – Use it to go by and let the stream find its own channels, this is the way to last out your years. If you refrain from saying, everything is even; the even is uneven with saying, saying is uneven with the even. Hence the aphorism 'In saying he says nothing'. If in saying you say nothing, all your life you say without ever saying, all your life you refuse to say without ever failing to say.

What from somewhere is allowable from somewhere else is unallowable, what from somewhere is so from somewhere else is not so. Why so? By being so. Why not so? By not being so. Why allowable? By being allowable. Why unallowable? By being unallowable. It is inherent in the thing that from somewhere that's so of it, that from somewhere that's allowable of it; of no thing is it not so, of no thing is it unallowable. Without ' "Spillover" ' saying is new every day, smooth it out on the whetstone of Heaven', who could ever keep going for long? The myriad things are all the seed from which they grow:

> In unlike shapes they abdicate in turn,
> With ends and starts as on a ring.
> None grasps where to mark the grades.
> Call it the 'Potter's Wheel of Heaven'.

The 'Potter's Wheel of Heaven' is the whetstone of Heaven. (*Chuang-tzŭ*, chapter 27)

NOTE The three varieties of saying are mentioned as Chuang-tzŭ's own three modes of language in the account of him at the end of the book (p. 283 below).

(1) 'Saying from a lodging-place' is traditionally taken to be the expression of ideas through imaginary conversations, a device so characteristic of *Chuang-tzŭ*. But in the terminology of 'The sorting which evens things out', which was obsolete very early but pervades this section, 'lodging-places' are the temporary standpoints between which the sage circulates as the situation changes (pp. 54, 55, 60 above). The context here implies that the lodging-place is the standpoint of the other party in debate. Although nothing can be settled by disputation, in which everyone has started from his own choice of names, it is possible to convince a man by temporarily assuming his standpoint and arguing from it – the *argumentum ad hominem* would indeed be for Chuang-tzŭ the only useful kind of debate.

(2) 'Weighted saying' is the aphorism with the weight of the speaker's experience behind it.

(3) 'Spillover' saying, the most important, is traditionally, and this time plausibly, supposed to be named after a kind of vessel designed to tip and right itself when filled too near the brim. It is speech characterised by the intelligent spontaneity of Taoist behaviour in general, a fluid language which keeps its equilibrium through changing meanings and viewpoints.

• • •

Huan, a man of Cheng, was droning and intoning his lessons in the country of Ch'iu-shih. In a mere three years Huan became a Confucian scholar. The Yellow River moistens only to three miles from its shores, Huan's bounty spread only to the clans of his father and mother and wife. It caused his younger brother to become a Mohist. When the Confucians and Mohists competed in disputation, their father gave his support to old Mo-tzŭ. Ten years later Huan killed himself. Their father dreamed that he said: 'The man who caused your son to become a Mohist was I myself.'

Why not take a look at his grave? Already he has become the cones of the autumn cypress. When the maker of things recompenses a man he recompenses not the man but what is from Heaven in the man. He treated as Other, therefore caused to treat as Other. That sort of man thinks himself somehow different from other men, to the point of putting his own parent below him; it's villagers equally humble grabbing from each other as they drink from the well. So we may say that in the present age everyone is a Huan. Thinking of one's own as the alternative that is It – one who has Power in him wouldn't know how to do that, not to mention one who has the Way. Of old this was called the punishment for retreating from Heaven. (*Chuang-tzŭ*, chapter 32)

NOTE   This is a concrete instance of the 'That's it, that's not' of Confucians and Mohists (cf. p. 52 above). In the Confucian morality the family comes first, in the Mohist love is equal for all. The man who first raises such an issue, splitting It and Other, is himself responsible for someone else choosing the alternative he rejects.

. . .

Confucius asked the historiographers Ta T'iao, Po Ch'ang-ch'ien and Hsi Wei

'Duke *Ling* of Wey was a drunkard and voluptuary, paid no heed to the government of the state, hunted to hounds and with net and stringed arrow, neglected to deal with the lords of the other states; why should he have been deemed 'the *magical* Duke'?'

'It was the 'That's it' which goes by circumstances,' said Ta T'iao.

'Duke Ling used to bathe with his three wives in the same tub,' said Po Ch'ang-ch'ien, 'yet when Shih Ch'iu was summoned to an audience he let other people carry the gift and hold him by the arm as he came towards the throne. He would be so utterly frivolous, yet so princely when he saw a man of worth; that is why he was deemed the magical Duke.'

'When Duke Ling died,' said Hsi Wei, 'they took auspices for a burial in the family graveyard, which were unlucky. They took auspices for Sandy Hill, which were lucky. They dug down a few dozen feet and found a stone coffin. They washed it and examined it, there was an inscription on it:

"No faith that my sons will put me here.
The Magical Duke will steal it and make it his tomb."

Duke Ling being deemed magical goes a long way back. What would these two know about it?' (*Chuang-tzŭ*, chapter 25)

NOTE *Ling*, 'magical', is the Duke's posthumous name, chosen as in some way descriptive of his reign. It can have a sinister sense, but Confucius takes it as an undeserved compliment to the Duke, and it does in fact have its good sense everywhere in *Chuang-tzŭ* (the sage's 'Magic Storehouse' from which he draws his capabilities, his 'Magic Watchtower' up which he climbs for wider vision). The mysterious discovery of the tomb shows that the Duke was blessed or damned by Heaven before he was born, it is by no means clear which. The point would be that the quality of Duke Ling (the sort of man who impresses as a force of nature) is in the stuff of him as Heaven generated it, and has nothing to do either with men's moral judgements or with any deliberate choice of how to live his life. 'When the maker of things recompenses a man he recompenses not the man but what is from Heaven in the man' (p. 108 above).

· · ·

When Confucius was going to Ch'u, he lodged at an inn in Yi-ch'iu. Next door everybody, husbands and wives, retainers and maids, had climbed up on the roof.

'What's all this crowd of people?' said Tzŭ-lu.

'They are the servants of a sage', said Confucius, 'who has buried himself among the people, hidden himself away in the fields. The rumour of his name has faded, but he has set himself a boundless aim. Although he says things from the mouth, at heart he has never said anything. He is in course of turning away from the world, doesn't at heart deign to have anything to do with it. He's someone who has submerged on dry land. Wouldn't it be Yi-liao of Shih-nan?'

Tzŭ-lu proposed to call him over.

'Don't bother,' said Confucius. 'He knows that I attract more attention than he does, knows that I am on my way to Ch'u, and thinks I am sure to get the King of Ch'u to summon him to court. He will regard me as a man who fawns on princes. Someone like that is embarrassed to hear a fawner's name, let alone meet one in person. What makes you think he's still there anyway?'

Tzŭ-lu went to look, and there was no one at home. (*Chuang-tzŭ*, chapter 25)

NOTE The people on the roof are presumably staring at the famous sage.

· · ·

'There are the unctuous smug ones, there are the ones who cannot see an inch in front of their faces, there are the ones with bowed shoulders.'

The ones called 'unctuous and smug', when they have studied the words of one master, so unctuously, so smugly, become privately self-satisfied and think they have no more to learn, but do not yet know that there have never yet begun to be any things. Hence the term 'unctuous smug ones'.

As for those who 'cannot see an inch in front of their faces', the louse on a pig is one of them. He picks a place where the long bristles are sparse, which he thinks is his broad mansion and spacious park, or a corner deep down in the crotch or the hoof, or in between the dugs or the hams, which he thinks is a safe home or comfortable lodging; he does not know that one morning the butcher will slap his arms and spread the tinder and lift the smoking torch, and he and the pig will both be done to a crisp. These go forward with their surroundings, these go backward with their surroundings, these are what he calls the 'ones who cannot see an inch in front of their faces'.

An example of the 'ones with bowed shoulders' would be Shun. The sheep's flesh does not hanker after the ants, the ants hanker after the sheep's flesh, because it has an appetising smell. Shun's deeds had an appetising smell which pleased the people, so that the three places where he moved to escape them turned into cities, and by the time he came to the wastes of Chih-teng there were ten times ten thousand families. Yao heard of Shun's excellence and raised him up from the barren lands, saying, 'We hope for prosperity from his coming.' When Shun was raised up from the barren lands he was already an old man, his sight and hearing were failing, but he was not allowed to end his years in peace. He was what is meant by 'one with bowed shoulders'.

This is why the daemonic man hates the coming of a crowd. If a crowd does come he stays aloof, and because he stays aloof they have nothing to gain from him. Therefore he is never too intimate with anyone, never too remote from anyone; he cherishes the Power in him, nurtures the peace in him, in order to accord with Heaven. It is this that is meant by the True Man. He casts away his knowledge to the ants, discovers how to estimate from the fish, casts away his intentions to the sheep. (*Chuang-tzŭ*, chapter 24)

NOTE   The fish in a shoal, effortlessly weaving in and out with an infallible sense of the proper distance to keep between each other, seem to fascinate Chuang-tzŭ, cf. pp. 90, 123.

• • •

Jan-hsiang found the centre of the ring where becoming veers with circumstance. Other things and he had no end nor start, no 'How long'? and no times. To be transformed day by day with other things is to be untransformed once and for all. Why not try to let them go? As for citing Heaven as your teacher yet failing to follow Heaven as your teacher, and being a fellow victim with other things, why do you have to busy yourself with them? For the sage, there has never yet begun to be Heaven, never yet begun to be man, never yet begun to be a Beginning, never yet begun to be things. If you walk the path side by side with the men of your times and do not fall away, if the source out of which you walk it is all at your disposal and does not dry up, why would you have to bother about fitting in?

When T'ang won universal dominion the Director of the Gate, T'ien Heng, tutored him in this. He followed him as tutor but was not fenced in within his school, he learned from him how becoming veers with circumstance. For the sake of this he instituted names, and for these names there were corresponding rules; he achieved the double view of it. For Confucius, his own exhaustive thinking was the tutor for this.

Jung-ch'eng said

'Subtract the days and there is no year.

What has nothing within it has nothing without.'

(*Chuang-tzŭ*, chapter 25)

Part Three

A 'School of Chuang-tzŭ' selection

1

Stories about Chuang-tzŭ

In the *Inner chapters*, at the very end of chapter 2, Chuang-tzŭ speaks once of a personal happening, his dream that he was a butterfly. Otherwise, we meet him in person only in dialogues with Hui Shih. But his school preserved or invented many tales about him, scattered over the *Outer* and *Mixed chapters*. In these he is never merely the ideal type of a Taoist sage, as Lao-tzŭ is in other stories; the humour and poetry, the irreverence for logic and for death, the scorn of worldly success, the imagery of birds, animals and trees, connect him unmistakably with the author of the *Inner chapters*. We cannot be sure that they are earlier than the third, or in most cases even the second century BC; but if they are legend, it is of the kind which accumulates round a historical person of strong personality, and is already illuminating, simplifying and disguising him within his own lifetime. They deserve the same sort of belief or suspended disbelief as unsubstantiated anecdotes about Oscar Wilde, Einstein or Churchill – 'Anyway, he was like that! (Or if he wasn't he should have been).'

Although China has a solid political history and reliable dates back to about 1000 BC, anyone not in public office remained unrecorded, and it took only a couple of generations for people to be becoming vague even about his date. If we are certain that Chuang-tzŭ lived in the late fourth century BC, it is because his friend Hui Shih did take office (under King Hui of Liang, 370–319 BC), and also because of his general place in the history of Chinese thought and literature. But the authors of these stories are not at all sure when he lived, and seldom name the rulers whom they mention. One story is plainly anachronistic, perhaps deliberately, to make an anti-Confucian joke; by crediting Chuang-tzŭ with a visit to Duke Ai of Lu (494–468 BC) it hints that an unnamed character is Confucius himself (who died in 479 BC). At the end of the second century BC the great historian Ssŭ-ma Ch'ien did try to place him chronologically. He had little to go on but the book *Chuang-tzŭ* itself (still unabridged), but adds a little more information in the opening sentences of his brief note:

'Chuang-tzŭ was a man of Meng. Personal name: Chou. He was at one time a public employee in Lacquer Garden (Ch'i-yüan). He was a contemporary of Kings Hui of Liang (370–319 BC) and Hsüan of Ch'i (319–301 BC).'

Meng was in the state of Sung, in what is now the province of Honan. Lacquer Garden may have been either the garden or the city named after it, but Chuang-tzŭ's expertise with trees and animals supports the former possibility. Ssŭ-ma Ch'ien also reproduces the full version (which we shall use) of a story mutilated in *Chuang-tzŭ*, of a mission to him from someone identified by the historian as King Wei of Ch'u (339–329 BC).

Apart from the episodes in the *Inner chapters* and one in the 'Yangist Miscellany', which we translate in their places, we assemble here all stories about Chuang-tzŭ (as distinct from dialogues in which he is merely the spokesman of his philosophy). In reading them, it should be remembered that they testify in the first place to how

There is no evidence of an organised school of Chuang-tzŭ surviving his death, and indeed very little of disciples receiving formal instruction in his lifetime.[1] However, the last six of the *Outer chapters* (chapters 17–22) are pervaded by the thought and phrasing of the *Inner chapters*, as is a great deal of material in the more miscellaneous parts of the collection. Certainly there was a tradition of thinking and writing in the manner of Chuang-tzŭ in the third and probably the second century BC, whether through personal or merely written influences.

How do we know that these documents were not written by Chuang-tzŭ himself? Both in thought and in style there is much in them which would not disgrace Chuang-tzŭ, and they often illuminate him by putting his thought more lucidly and directly. However, although it may be better not to draw too sharp a line, there is no mistaking the impression that something has changed – moderated – when one passes from the *Inner* to the *Outer chapters*, and that Chuang-tzŭ's own voice is never heard clearly again except in bits of the 'ragbag' parts of the *Mixed chapters*. The bolder, the outrageous side of Chuang-tzŭ has disappeared – the cripples, freaks and mutilated criminals, the ravings of Chieh Yü the madman of Ch'u, the extravagant praise of uselessness, the identification of waking and dreaming, the iconoclastic confrontations with death (although we do have the last in some stories about Chuang-tzŭ himself). So has the intellectual dimension of Chuang-tzŭ, the side of him which delights in playing with and challenging reason – although there is one beautiful example of it in the *Outer chapters*, the argument with Hui Shih about whether the fish are happy.[2] There is also a change in the attitude to Confucius; Chuang-tzŭ never betrayed his fundamental respect for the great moralist, but in the *Outer chapters* Old Tan (still only a minor figure for Chuang-tzŭ) has risen to such eminence that he can *condescend* to Confucius. *Lao-tzŭ*, the book ascribed to Old Tan, begins to be echoed in the *Outer chapters*, although Chuang-tzŭ never showed acquaintance with it. We meet too with philosophical terms or combinations of terms important in later Taoism but not yet found in the *Inner chapters*, such as man's 'nature' (*hsing*), the freeing of the Taoist from the world's 'ties' (*lei*), the 'Way and the Power' as concepts granted equal status and paired, and a new word for the sage's 'stillness', *ching*. On the other hand we no longer have the universe conjured up before us as 'that hugest of clumps of soil', nor do we hear again of the 'maker of things' until the account of Chuang-tzŭ himself in 'Below in the empire' at the very end of the book.

In the last six *Outer chapters* which are the heart of the 'School of Chuang-tzŭ' material one has a vague impression, widely shared by scholars, that the editor must have been trying to group his documents around the themes which he had chosen for the *Inner chapters*. Thus 'Utmost joy' (chapter 18) shares the theme of death with 'The ultimate ancestor as teacher', while 'Fathoming nature' (chapter 19) suggests 'What matters in the nurture of life'. This regrouping of passages by different writers would explain why none of the chapters shows clear evidence of coming from a single hand, and why we find material which clearly belongs together scattered over these and other chapters. (See for example the dispersal of the 'Great Man' passages, discussed on p. 143 below). We shall not attempt a complete or consecutive translation of the 'School of Chuang-tzŭ' documents. In a book where the translator is always in danger of losing his bearings and letting himself float on a stream of verbiage, it will be safer to select only passages which we can put in coherent settings, and juxtapose them so that they throw light on each other.

Chuang-tzŭ *looked* for the first half-dozen generations after his death. We can imagine even admirers having reservations, for example, about the unqualified praise of uselessness in the *Inner chapters*. They would be reassured by the story of the mountain tree,[3] where Chuang-tzŭ makes a judicious compromise between the claims of uselessness and usefulness. (This story is the earliest attested by another source; it appears complete in the *Lü-shih ch'un-ch'iu*, about 240 BC.) Of the people who delighted in tales of Chuang-tzŭ grandiosely refusing high office, some would despise worldly success on principle, others would be seeking excuses for their own failure; it would be someone of the latter sort who wrote of Chuang-tzŭ in his rags passing the King of Wei, and lamenting that the times are unfavourable to men of talent.[4]

Is there any point in trying to penetrate through the legend to the man himself? Anecdotalists and legend-mongers do not care about the thing we most want to know about a thinker, the stages and direction of his intellectual growth. The *Inner chapters*, permeated by an obsession with the life and legend of Confucius, invite the suspicion that their author must have been brought up as a Confucian,[5] but nothing in the anecdotes supports the conjecture except for a single, anomalous, reference to Chuang-tzŭ as wearing Confucian dress.[6] However, to search the stories for traces of his intellectual development may not be as futile as it appears. The alternative tradition throughout Chinese history of preferring private to public life, of which Chuang-tzŭ is the first representative who came to be classed as 'Taoist', began about 350 BC with the 'Nurture of life' school. These were the 'Yangists', the followers of the quite unmystical Yang Chu, who was content to insist that the life and health of the body are more important than worldly possessions. It is permissible to guess that Chuang-tzŭ would have started from this position. If so, stories about him may have circulated, not only among Taoists, but in the Yangist school, which survived until about 200 BC. Now the book *Chuang-tzŭ* does contain a set of four chapters representative of this tendency, which we translate under the title 'Yangist miscellany'. One of these, 'The discourse on swords', is a tale about Chuang Chou dissuading a king from encouraging swordfights, so uncharacteristic of the philosopher that many suppose it to be about someone else of the same name. The point of the story is that life is not to be sacrificed uselessly. Outside the 'Yangist miscellany', the story told to the Marquis of Chien-ho about the fish on the road[7] makes a similar point, that when a man needs help to stay alive any other help is an empty gesture. More remarkable is the eerie, anxiety-ridden story of the poaching in Tiao-ling, the only one in which Chuang-tzŭ suffers doubts.[8] Here he is unmistakably a 'Nurture of life' teacher, whose only concern is to care for his own body and avoid endangering ties. Watching the animals prey on each other, as he hunts the strange magpie and in his turn gets chased by the gamekeeper, he discovers that the whole order of nature is inimical to survival, and is thrown into confusion for three days. One might take the moral to be simply 'Be more careful in future'. But Chuang-tzŭ has made the discovery that 'it is inherent in things that they are ties to each other', which undermines the hope that one can ensure survival by renouncing external involvements. Does this story preserve a memory of Chuang-tzŭ's crisis of conversion? (I picked up this idea in conversation with Lee H. Yearley.) Perhaps it was in those three days that he took the step from self-centredness to selflessness, from the Yangist obsession with individual survival to the reconciliation with death which is the theme of 'The teacher who is the ultimate ancestor'.

The stories of the poaching at Tiao-ling and of the fish on the road are the only ones which call him by surname and given name, 'Chuang Chou' (apart from Ssŭ-ma Ch'ien's story,[9] and the butterfly episode, in which Chuang-tzŭ is talking about himself). This rather suggests a stage in his life before he earned the honorific suffix 'tzŭ'. The Tiao-ling story is unique in crediting Chuang-tzŭ with a named disciple (Lin Ch'ieh) and also with an unnamed teacher of his own. Elsewhere he is only twice mentioned as having disciples at all.[10] It is therefore tempting to essay after all a little skeleton biography of Chuang-tzǔ. His upbringing was probably Confucian, but he studied under a Yangist, and in due course became a qualified Yangist teacher with his own disciples. After a crisis which may be reflected in the Tiao-ling story he went his own way, as the irreverent drop-out of the more characteristic tales. He visited Hui Shih, and heard him use the paradoxes of space and time to prove that all things are one; but his attitude hardened against logic, and he discovered in his own ecstatic experiences the vision which dissolves all distinctions, above all the dichotomy of life and death. He never again became a formal teacher – in one story[11] he is weaving sandals for a living – and such disciples as he had were people who hung around to pick up something from his words or his mere presence, like the retinue of Wang T'ai of the chopped foot at the beginning of 'The signs of fullness of Power'. All this is speculation, but will do to make a frame on which to arrange the stories, starting from the Tiao-ling crisis and ending on his deathbed.

When Chuang Chou was roaming inside the fenced preserve at Tiao-ling, he noticed a strange magpie coming from the south, with wings seven feet wide and eyes a full inch across. It brushed against his forehead and perched in a chestnut grove.

'What bird is this?' said Chuang Chou. 'With wings so huge it doesn't fly away, with eyes so big it didn't notice.'

He hitched up his robe and quickened his step, and with crossbow at the ready waited to take aim.

He noticed a cicada, which had just found a beautiful patch of shade and had forgotten what could happen to it. A mantis hiding behind the leaves grabbed at it, forgetting at the sight of gain that it had a body of its own. The strange magpie in his turn was taking advantage of that, at the sight of profit forgetful of its truest prompting.

'Hmm!' said Chuang Chou uneasily. 'It is inherent in things that they are ties to each other, that one kind calls up another.'

As he threw down his crossbow and ran out of the grove, the gamekeeper came running behind shouting curses at him.

When Chuang Chou got home he was gloomy for three days. It made Lin Ch'ieh inquire

'Why have you been so gloomy lately, sir?'

'In caring for the body I have been forgetting what can happen to me. I have been looking at reflections in muddy water, have gone astray from the clear pool. Besides, I have heard the Master say "If it's the custom there, do as you're told." Now when I wandered in Tiao-ling I forgot what could happen to me; when the strange magpie brushed against my forehead I strayed into the chestnut grove and forgot my truest prompting, and the gamekeeper in the chestnut grove took me for a criminal. That is why I am gloomy.' (*Chuang-tzǔ*, chapter 20)

· · ·

King Wei of Ch'u, hearing of Chuang Chou's excellence, sent a messenger to greet him with rich presents, offering to make him chief minister. Chuang Chou smiled and said to the messenger from Ch'u

'A thousand pieces is a great gain indeed, to be a noble and a minister is a most honourable station. But have you never seen the ox which is sacrificed in the rites outside the city? After gorging it for several years they dress it in patterned brocades to lead it into the great ancestral hall. When that time comes, even if it should wish for no more than to be an orphaned calf, isn't it beyond all help? Get out at once, don't soil me; I would rather amuse myself swimming and playing in a filthy ditch than be made captive by the master of a state. All my life I shall refuse office and please my own fancy.' (*Chuang-tzŭ*, chapter 32, mutilated; restored from *Shih-chi*, chapter 63)

．　　．　　．

Chuang Chou's family was poor, so he went to borrow grain from the Marquis of Chien-ho.

'By all means,' said the Marquis. 'I shall soon be getting the tax-money from my lands, I'll lend you 300 pieces. Will that do?'

Chuang Chou looked furious.

'When I was coming yesterday', he said, 'there was something calling out right in the middle of the highway. I looked back into the wheel rut, and there was a perch there. I questioned it; "Hello, perch," I said, "What would you be?" "I am minister of the waves in the empire of the East Sea," it said; 'I suppose you wouldn't have a dipperful of water to keep me alive?" "By all means," I said. "I am just going on a journey south to the Kings of Wu and Yüeh, I'll have the stream of the West River diverted to where you are. Will that do?" The perch looked furious. "I've lost what I can't ever be without," it said; 'I've nowhere to live. What I need is just a dipperful of water to keep me alive; if that's all you have to say, you would do better to come looking for me first thing on the dried fish stalls".' (*Chuang-tzŭ*, chapter 26)

．　　．　　．

There was a man of Sung, Ts'ao Shang, who was sent by the King on a mission to Ch'in. When he set out he was given a few chariots; the King of Ch'in was pleased with him and gave him a hundred more. On his return to Sung he visited Chuang-tzŭ.

'To live in a cramped alley in a poor quarter,' he said, 'needy and wretched and weaving sandals for a living, scrawny in the neck and sallow in the face, I wouldn't be much good at that. To get noticed at a single stroke by a lord of ten thousand chariots, and win a hundred chariots for my retinue, that's what I can do.'

'When the King of Ch'in falls ill and calls his doctors,' said Chuang-tzŭ, 'the one who bursts a carbuncle or drains a boil gets a single chariot, the one who licks his piles gets five. The viler the treatment the more chariots one gets. You wouldn't have been treating his piles of course? What a lot of chariots you have!

'Get out!' (*Chuang-tzŭ*, chapter 32)

• • •

Someone had an audience with the King of Sung, who presented him with ten chariots. He came swaggering and bragging about his ten chariots to Chuang-tzŭ.

'There's a family by the riverside,' said Chuang-tzŭ, 'they're poor people who weave rushes for a living. A boy of theirs was diving in the deepest water, and found a pearl worth a thousand pieces. His father said to the boy: ''Fetch a stone and pound it to bits. A pearl worth a thousand pieces would surely be at the bottom of the ninefold abyss, under the chin of the black dragon. You could never have got the pearl if you hadn't caught him asleep. Supposing that the black dragon should awake, will there be the tiniest trace of you left?''

'Now the state of Sung has depths harder to plumb than the nine levels of the abyss, and the King of Sung is fiercer than the black dragon. You could never have got the chariots if you hadn't caught him asleep. Supposing that the King of Sung should awake, you'll be chopped up to a fine powder, won't you?' (*Chuang-tzŭ*, chapter 32)

• • •

Chuang-tzŭ, in a patched gown of coarse cloth and shoes tied up with string, was passing the King of Wei.

'How low you have sunk, sir!' said the King.

'It's poverty, it isn't sinking low. A man having the Way and the Power but being unable to act on them, that's sinking low. Having tattered clothes and holes in your shoes is poverty, it isn't sinking low. This is what they call being born in unlucky times. Has Your Majesty never seen a gibbon as it climbs? When it finds cedars, catalpas, camphor-trees, it goes bounding over the branches and frolics in the midst of them, and not even Yi or P'eng Meng would have time to take aim with his bow. But when it's among prickly mulberries, brambles, hawthorns, spiny citrons, it progresses warily, glances sideways, quivers and quakes and winces and shivers. It's not that bone or sinew is under more strain or is any less supple. It is dwelling in surroundings which don't suit it, don't give scope to prove how nimble it is. Now if one dwells among the unscrupulous ministers of a degenerate prince, yet desires not to sink low, how long can one expect to last? Pi-kan whose heart was cut out would be the test, wouldn't he?' (*Chuang-tzŭ*, chapter 20)

• • •

When Chuang-tzŭ was travelling in the mountains he saw a great tree with flourishing leaves and branches. A woodcutter stopped at its side but did not choose it. He asked him why, and was told

'There's nothing you can use it for.'

'This tree,' said Chuang-tzŭ, 'by its timber being good for nothing, will get to last out Heaven's term for it, wouldn't you say?'

Coming down from the mountains, he lodged at a friend's house. The friend was delighted, and ordered a boy to kill a goose in his honour. The boy had a question:

'One of them can cackle, one of them can't. Which shall I kill, please?'

'The one that can't.'

Next day a disciple asked Chuang-tzŭ

"Yesterday, because its timber was good for nothing, the tree in the mountains could last out Heaven's term for it. Today, because the stuff it's made of is good for nothing, our host's goose is dead. Which side are you going to settle for, sir?'

Chuang-tzŭ smiled.

'I should be inclined to settle midway between being good for something and being good for nothing. That seems the thing to do yet it is not, and so one still fails to shake off ties. But in roaming adrift with the Way and the Power as your chariot, that's not so.

> Without praises, without curses,
> Now a dragon, now a snake,
> You transform together with the times.
> And never consent to be one thing alone.

Now up, now down, you take as your measure the degree which is in harmony; and if roaming adrift over the Ancestor of the myriad things you treat things as things and refuse to be turned into a thing by things, how can you ever be tied? This was the rule for Shen-nung and the Yellow Emperor. But when it comes to the facts about the myriad things or the code of conduct handed down for men, that's not so.

> What you join together will part,
> What you achieve will decay.
> Honesty's hard corners will get blunted,
> If you are esteemed you are criticised,
> Do anything and there's something you leave out.

Be clever and they'll plot against you, be stupid and they'll cheat you, how can you get to be certain of anything? Sad, isn't it? Make a note of it, my disciples. Is there any direction to take except by the Way and the Power?'
(*Chuang-tzŭ*, chapter 20)

* * *

Chuang-tzŭ had an audience with Duke Ai of Lu.

'We have a lot of Confucian scholars in Lu,' said the Duke. 'Not so many study your doctrine.'

'There are not so many Confucians in Lu either.'

'The whole country is wearing teacher's garb. What do you mean, there are not so many?'

'I have heard Confucians say that the man with the round cap on his head knows the seasons of Heaven, the man with the squared shoes on his feet knows the configuration of earth, the man with the half-disc of jade on his girdle can judge decisively on one side or the other when an issue arises. But it's not so sure that gentlemen who possess their Way do wear their garb, or that wearers of their garb do know about their Way. If Your Grace really thinks otherwise, why not proclaim throughout the country "For wearing this garb without possessing this Way the punishment is death"?'

Then Duke Ai did proclaim it, and within five days there was not a man in the state of Lu who dared put on teacher's garb, except just one fellow in teacher's garb standing at the Duke's gate. The Duke summoned him at once and questioned him about affairs of state. Through a thousand, ten thousand tricks and turns he was never at a loss.

'Throughout all Lu', said Chuang-tzŭ, 'the Confucians amount to just one man. Would you call that a lot?' (*Chuang-tzŭ*, chapter 21)

.   .   .

Chuang-tzŭ was fishing in P'u river. The King of Ch'u sent two grandees to approach him with the message:

'I have a gift to tie you, my whole state.'

Chuang-tzŭ, intent on the fishing-rod, did not turn his head.

'I hear that in Ch'u there is a sacred tortoise', he said, 'which has been dead for three thousand years. His Majesty keeps it wrapped up in a box at the top of the hall in the shrine of his ancestors. Would this tortoise rather be dead, to be honoured as preserved bones? Or would it rather be alive and dragging its tail in the mud?'

'It would rather be alive and dragging its tail in the mud.'

'Away with you! I shall drag my tail in the mud.' (*Chuang-tzŭ*, chapter 17)

.   .   .

When Hui Shih was chief minister of Liang, Chuang-tzŭ went to visit him. Someone told Hui Shih

'Chuang-tzŭ is coming, he wants your place as chief minister.'

At this Hui Shih was frightened, and searched throughout the state for three days and three nights.

Chuang-tzŭ did go to visit him.

'In the South there is a bird,' he said, 'its name is the phoenix, do you know of it? The phoenix came up from the South Sea to fly to the North Sea; it would rest on no tree but the sterculia, would eat nothing but the seeds of the bamboo, would drink only from the sweetest springs. Just then an owl had found a rotting mouse. As the phoenix flew over, it looked up and glared at it, "Shoo!" Now am I to take it that for the sake of that Liang country of yours you want to shoo at me?' (*Chuang-tzŭ*, chapter 17)

 •   •   •

Chuang-tzŭ and Hui Shih were strolling on the bridge above the Hao river.

'Out swim the minnows, so free and easy,' said Chuang-tzŭ. 'That's how fish are happy.'

'You are not a fish. Whence do you know that the fish are happy?'

'You aren't me, whence do you know that I don't know the fish are happy?'

'We'll grant that not being you I don't know about you. You'll grant that you are not a fish, and that completes the case that you don't know the fish are happy.'

'Let's go back to where we started. When you said '' *Whence* do you know that the fish are happy?'', you asked me the question already knowing that I knew. I knew it from up above the Hao.' (*Chuang-tzŭ*, chapter 17)

NOTE   This is the only instance of disputation with Hui Shih in the *Outer chapters* (interest in the Sophists was already failing), and is remarkable for a playfulness which in parodying logical debate is more faithful to the detail of its structure than anything else in *Chuang-tzŭ*. When Hui Shih defended the paradoxes listed without explanation in 'Below in the Empire' (p. 283f) he must have been talking like this, as the Later Mohists do in the explanations of some of their *Canons*; what a pity we never hear what he had to say! Chuang-tzŭ's own final stroke of wit is more than a mere trick with the idiom *An chih* 'Whence do you know...?', one of the standard ways of saying 'How do you know...?' What he is saying is: 'Whatever you affirm is as relative to standpoint as how I see the fish while I stand up here on the bridge.'

 •   •   •

When Chuang-tzŭ's wife died, Hui Shih came to condole. As for Chuang-tzŭ, he was squatting with his knees out, drumming on a pot and singing.

'When you have lived with someone', said Hui Shih, 'and brought up children, and grown old together, to refuse to bewail her death would be bad enough, but to drum on a pot and sing – could there be anything more shameful?'

'Not so. When she first died, do you suppose that I was able not to feel the loss? I peered back into her beginnings; there was a time before there was a life. Not only was there no life, there was a time before there was a shape. Not only was there no shape, there was a time before there was energy. Mingled together in the amorphous, something altered, and there was the energy; by alteration in the energy there was the shape, by alteration of the shape there was the life. Now once more altered she has gone over to death. This is to be companion with spring and autumn, summer and winter, in the procession of the four seasons. When someone was about to lie down and sleep in the greatest of mansions, I with my sobbing knew no better than to bewail her. The thought came to me that I was being uncomprehending towards destiny, so I stopped.' (*Chuang-tzŭ*, chapter 18)

• • •

Chuang-tzŭ, among the mourners in a funeral procession, was passing by the grave of Hui Shih. He turned round and said to his attendants

'There was a man of Ying who, when he got a smear of plaster no thicker than a fly's wing on the tip of his nose, would make Carpenter Shih slice it off. Carpenter Shih would raise the wind whirling his hatchet, wait for the moment, and slice it; every speck of the plaster would be gone without hurt to the nose, while the man of Ying stood there perfectly composed.

'Lord Yüan of Sung heard about it, summoned Carpenter Shih and said ''Let me see you do it.'' ''As for my side of the act,'' said Carpenter Shih, ''I did use to be able to slice it off. However, my partner has been dead for a long time.''

'Since the Master died, I have had no one to use as a partner, no one with whom to talk about things.' (*Chuang-tzŭ*, chapter 24)

• • •

When Chuang-tzŭ was going to Ch'u, he saw a hollow skull, with the shape of the bone bared. He flicked it with his horse whip and took it as an occasion for questions.

'Was it by misjudgements in your greed for life that you became this thing, sir? Or was it by the troubles of a ruined state, or punishment by the headsman's axe, that you became this? Or did you commit some evil deed, and in shame of bringing disgrace on father, mother, wife and children, become this? Or did you in the miseries of cold and hunger become this? Or did you last out the span of your spring and autumn to arrive at this?'

Then at the end of the speech he pulled the skull over to him, pillowed his head on it and went to sleep. At midnight the skull appeared in a dream and said

'That talk of yours resembled a rhetorician's. Consider the things you were talking about, all belong to the ties of living men, once dead we have them no longer. Would you like to hear my exposition of death?'

'I would.'

'In death there is no lord above or subject below, nor any of the toils of the four seasons. Untrammelled we last out the spring and autumn of heaven and earth. Even the joy of a king on his south-facing throne cannot exceed it.'

Chuang-tzŭ did not believe him.

'If I were to persuade the arbiter of fate to return your body to life, make you bones and flesh and skin, restore you to father and mother, wife and children, township and neighbourhood, friends and acquaintances, would you desire it?'

The skull with a deep frown knitted its brows.

'How could I refuse the joy of a king on his throne, to suffer again the toils of humankind?' (*Chuang-tzu*, chapter 18)

. . .

When Chuang-tzŭ was dying, his disciples wanted to give him a lavish funeral. Said Chuang-tzŭ

'I have heaven and earth for my outer and inner coffin, the sun and moon for my pair of jade discs, the stars for my pearls, the myriad creatures for my farewell presents. Is anything missing in my funeral paraphernalia? What will you add to these?'

'Master, we are afraid that the crows and kites will eat you.'

'Above ground, I'll be eaten by the crows and kites; below ground, I'll be eaten by the ants and molecrickets. You rob the one of them to give to the other; how come you like them so much better?' (*Chuang-tzu*, chapter 32)

2

The dialogues of Confucius and Old Tan

The conversations between Confucius and 'Old Tan' (Lao Tan, commonly called Lao-tzŭ) are distributed over the *Outer chapters* of *Chuang-tzŭ*. The seven compose a cycle which appears to be homogeneous, although it may be noticed that they seem to have their first meeting twice over.[12] In them Confucius gratefully abandons Confucianism for the philosophy taught him, with ineffable condescension, by Old Tan. It is a version of Chuang-tzŭ's variety of Taoism, distinguished by a strong emphasis on concrete examples of natural process, physical and biological, as models for human spontaneity. There are constant echoes from the *Inner chapters* but none from *Lao-tzŭ*, the scripture ascribed to Old Tan. The seven episodes are beautifully written, in a cool, dignified yet relaxed style with a different flavour from Chuang-tzŭ's. There are some indications, not however conclusive, that the cycle belongs to a very late stratum of the book, later than the foundation of the Han dynasty in 202 BC. Confucius is represented as mentioning the 'Six Classics'.[13] The Classics were assembled and canonised very gradually in the Confucian school, and not attested as numbering six before the Han. There is also a curious reference to the 'Twelve Classics',[14] commonly identified as the six together with the six *wei-shu*, Han apocrypha which were attached to them.

In the traditional history of Chinese thought Old Tan is the founder of Taoism and the author of its greatest book, *Lao-tzŭ*. As for the book, there is no firm evidence of its existence before about 250 BC, although it had risen to prominence with extraordinary speed and sureness by the end of the century. It is frequently quoted in the Primitivist essays (*c.* 205 BC) and elsewhere in *Chuang-tzŭ*, but never in the *Inner chapters*. The story of the meeting with Confucius is a little older, and exists in a Confucian as well as in the Taoist version. The 'Questions of Tseng-tzŭ' in the Confucian *Book of Rites* has Confucius humbly consulting Old Tan on the proper conduct of funerals. Old Tan, introduced not as a philosopher but purely as a specialist in the rites, is so assured in the authority of his knowledge and venerable years that he addresses Confucius familiarly by his given name, 'Ch'iu'. The *Book of Rites* is a compilation of varied origins which took shape in the first century BC, so that there is nothing in the documentary evidence to show whether *Chuang-tzŭ* or the 'Questions of Tseng-tzŭ' is nearer to the beginnings of the story. It takes some effort of the imagination to break down the preconception that Old Tan must always have been a Taoist hero, but in fact there are strong indications that he was borrowed from the Confucians:

(1) Taoists delight in putting their own thoughts into the mouths of others, including Confucius himself. But why should Confucians put themselves at the mercy of

their rivals by gratuitously taking over a story that their own founder listened humbly to the founder of Taoism?

(2) In the *Chuang-tzŭ* dialogues Old Tan is a keeper of archives in the reduced domain of the Chou Emperor. The 'Questions of Tseng-tzŭ' gives no such details; but these particulars make Old Tan a very proper person for Confucius, who dreams of restoring the Chou tradition, to consult about the rites. His dry-as-dust occupation seems however curiously inappropriate to a Taoist sage. Chuang-tzŭ, for example, seems most himself when imagined as a carefree hermit fishing by the river.

(3) Old Tan took a long time to find himself a surname. Philosophers are generally known by the surname followed by the suffix *tzŭ*, but in his case the *tzŭ* had to be added to *Lao*, 'old', and the practice took time to establish itself. In the Chinese text of *Chuang-tzŭ* we are regularly meeting our old friends K'ung-tzŭ (Confucius), Hui-tzŭ (Hui Shih), Lieh-tzŭ, Chuang-tzŭ himself, but the name 'Lao-tzŭ' turns up only in five episodes, and of these there is only one in which he was not introduced as Old Tan. Why should Taoists fail to remember or invent a surname for their founder? A plausible answer is that he had none as a peripheral figure in a Confucian story, and when Taoists adopted him the crucial point for them was that he remain identifiable as the Old Tan who used to talk down to Confucius.

(4) Old Tan is first attested in the late fourth century in the *Inner chapters*, as one of the figures in the life or legend of Confucius whom Chuang-tzŭ uses as spokesman of his own thoughts. (Others are Chieh Yü the madman of Ch'u, Ch'ü Po-yü the wise man of Wey, and of course Confucius himself.) He is much less prominent than the madman of Ch'u, and in his three appearances only once speaks at length.[15] There is some presumption that figures whom Chuang-tzŭ constellates around Confucius would have some previous existence in his history or legend, but absolutely none that they were Taoists. In one story a friend of Old Tan is disillusioned with him because the conduct of his disciples at his funeral shows the inadequacy of their understanding of death.[16] This is a strange way for a Taoist to be talking about the revered father of his philosophy, especially on the issue of death, which for Chuang-tzŭ is the touchstone. It looks as though Chuang-tzu's Old Tan is simply the man who instructed Confucius in funeral rites.

(5) Down to about 100 BC the documented story of Old Tan is *nothing but* the story of his meeting with Confucius. The *Inner chapters* allude in passing to Confucius studying under him,[17] and the *Lü shih ch'un-ch'iu* (c. 240 BC) mentions that 'Confucius learned from Old Tan', in a context suggestive of a specialist contribution to his knowledge rather than a conversion to Taoism. In the first century BC the historian Ssŭ-ma Ch'ien fitted up Old Tan with a surname at last (Li, with given name Erh) and tried to write his biography. But, apart from a few tales and scraps of information about persons whom he recognises to be only dubiously identified with Old Tan, Ssŭ-ma Ch'ien has nothing to offer but the meeting with Confucius and one more story, of Lao-tzŭ travelling westwards through the passes, leaving his book with the 'Keeper of the Pass' (Kuan-yin), and disappearing for ever. As earlier evidence of this story we have only the name Kuan-yin, mentioned in late parts of *Chuang-tzŭ*[18] and elsewhere, but the name by itself is hardly conclusive testimony.

In all stories Old Tan has a tone of extraordinary authority, condescending to Confucius, ruthlessly criticising lesser men to their faces. It has been too easily assumed that the authority derives from being the founder of the school and the author of its scripture. But it is sufficiently explained on the assumption that Old Tan is first of all the man who even for Confucians could talk down to their master and address him as 'Ch'iu' (a familiarity reflected in the present translation by such expressions as 'Confucius, my lad'). Among all the historical or legendary persons whom Chuang-tzŭ used as his spokesmen only Old Tan has this advantage, and it would be a master-stroke to pass the anti-Confucian classic *Lao-tzŭ* under his name. As for Old Tan being founder of Taoism, philosophical schools tend to be created in retrospect. Chuang-tzŭ never knew that he was a 'Taoist', but towards 200 BC the admirers of his writings and of the little masterpiece which had recently entered into circulation as *Lao-tzŭ* were thinking of themselves as an anti-Confucian school the origins of which had better be pushed back at least as far as Confucius. Then Old Tan would present himself as the unchallengeable candidate for retrospective choice as founder.

Nowadays we are inclined to take it for granted that the hero of so confused a legend probably never existed. It is amusing to think that Old Tan might well be fully historical, but not a Taoist at all – on the contrary an archivist and instructor in the rites whom Confucius himself, it is pleasing to imagine, may have found a little too rigid, dusty, old-fashioned.

When Confucius travelled west to deposit books in the palace of Chou, Tzŭ-lu advised him

'I hear that among the keepers of archives in Chou there is a certain Old Tan who has retired and lives at home. If you wish to deposit books, sir, you might go and see what he can do for you.'

'Very well,' said Confucius, and went to see Old Tan, who would not give permission. Then he went through the Twelve Classics explaining them.

Old Tan interrupted his explanation

'Too long-winded, I would rather hear the gist of it.'

'The gist is in Goodwill and Duty.'

'May I ask whether Goodwill and Duty belong to man's nature?'

'They do. The gentleman

> If malevolent has not matured,
> If undutiful remains unborn.

Goodwill and Duty are the nature of the True Man; what more has he to do?'

'I should like to ask what you mean by Goodwill and Duty.'

'To delight from your innermost heart in loving everyone impartially is the essence of Goodwill and Duty.'

'Hmm. There's danger in that last thing you said. Isn't it after all an aberration to love everybody? Impartiality to all is a partiality. If you wish, sir, to save the world from losing its simplicity, well, it is inherent in heaven and earth to have constancies, in the sun and moon to shed light, in the stars to form constellations, in the birds and beasts to flock together, in the trees to grow upright. If you too go forward trusting to the Power in you, taking the direction which accords with the Way, you will already have attained the utmost; why be so busy proclaiming Goodwill and Duty, like the man banging the drum as he goes looking for runaways? Hmm, you are disrupting man's nature, sir.' (*Chuang-tzŭ*, chapter 13)

. . .

Confucius visited Old Tan and expounded Goodwill and Duty.

'When chaff from the winnowing blinds the eye,' said Old Tan, 'heaven and earth and the four quarters change places; when mosquitoes and gadflies sting the flesh, we lie awake all night long. Goodwill and Duty torment our hearts and keep them restless, there is no disorder worse. If you wish to save the world from losing its simplicity, may you too move as the wind stirs you, let the Power which gathers in you hold you firm; why all this urgency, like the man with the big drum on his back who goes searching for runaways? The snow goose wants no daily bath to make it white, the rook no daily inking to make it black. Simplicities of black and white are not worth arguing over; making a spectacle of oneself to be famous and praised does not make one a bigger man. When the spring dries up, and the fish are stranded together on land, they spit moisture at each other and soak each other in the foam, but they would rather forget each other in the Yangtse and the Lakes.' (*Chuang-tzŭ*, chapter 14)

·   ·   ·

When Confucius had lived fifty-one years and had not heard the Way, he went south to P'ei to visit Old Tan.

'Have you come?' said Old Tan. 'I hear that you are the best of the men of the north. Have you after all found the Way?'

'I have not found it.'

'Where did you seek it?'

'I sought it in measures and numbers, and in five years did not find it.'

'Where did you seek it then?'

'I sought it in the Yin and Yang, and in twelve years did not find it.'

'Yes. Supposing that the Way could be offered up, there is no man who would not offer it to his lord. Supposing that the Way could be presented as a gift, there is no man who would not present it to his parents. Supposing that the Way could be told to others, there is no man who would not tell it to his brothers. Supposing that the Way could be bequeathed to others, there is no man who would not bequeathe it to his sons and grandsons. That we cannot do so, much as we might wish it, is for this reason alone: unless you have an appropriator within to make it your own, it will not stay; unless you have a regulator outside to set it in the true direction, it will not transfer. If what issues from within will not be accepted outside, the sage does not let it out; if what enters from outside is not appropriated within, the sage does not rely on it.

'Names are tools for public use, one should not have too strong preferences between them. Goodwill and Duty are the grass huts of the former kings; you may put up in them for a night, but not settle in them for long, and the longer you are noticed in them the more will be demanded of you. The utmost men of old borrowed right of way through the benevolent, lodged for a night in the dutiful, to roam in the emptiness where one rambles without a destination, eat in the fields of the casual and simple, stand in the orchards where one can keep all the fruit. To ramble without a destination is Doing Nothing, to be casual and simple is to be easily nurtured, to keep all the fruit is to let nothing out from oneself. Of old they called this the roaming in which one plucks only the genuine.

'Whoever thinks what matters is to get rich is incapable of renouncing salary. Whoever thinks what matters is to get famous is incapable of renouncing reputation. Whoever is too fond of sway over others is incapable of letting another man take the controls; while he holds on to them he trembles, when he loses them he pines; and one who has no mirror in which to glimpse the source of his unease is a man punished by Heaven.

'Wrath and bounty, taking and giving, admonishing and teaching, sparing and killing – all these eight belong among the tools of ruling. Only the man who stays on course through the greatest alterations and has nothing to obstruct him anywhere may be deemed capable of employing them. As the saying goes, ''To rule is to set in the true direction''. For the man whose heart thinks otherwise, the gate of Heaven will not open.' (*Chuang-tzŭ*, chapter 14)

· · ·

Confucius visited Old Tan. Old Tan, fresh from a bath, was drying out, hair hanging down his back, so still that he seemed other than human. Confucius awaited his convenience. A little later, presenting himself, he said

'Am I in a daze? Or was it truly so? Just now, sir, your body was as motionless as withered wood, as though you had left everything behind and parted from man, to take your stand in the Unique.'

'I was letting the heart roam at the beginning of things.'

'What do you mean by that?'

'The heart is straitened by it and incapable of knowing, the mouth gapes at it and is unable to speak. But I shall try to say something which will guide you towards it.

'The utmost Yin is sombre, the utmost Yang is radiant, the sombre goes on emerging from Heaven and the radiant goes on issuing from earth; the two pervade each other, and by their perfected harmony things are generated. There is something which holds all the threads, but no one sees its shape. Reducing, increasing, filling, emptying, now shading, now lighting, renewing with the day or transforming through the month, each day it is working but no one sees a result. The living spring from something, the dying go home to something, starts and ends go on reversing along the course which had no beginning, and no one ever knows where the limit is. What else but this is the Ancestor from which we descend?'

'Let me ask about your ''roaming'' in this.'

'To grasp it is utmost beauty, utmost joy. One who grasps utmost beauty and roams in utmost joy is called the ''Utmost Man''.'

'I should like to hear the secret of it.'

'Beasts which eat grass are not irked by a change of pastures, nor creatures born in water by a change of waters, for in passing through a small alteration they do not lose the ultimately constant in them. Their pleasure or anger, sadness or joy, does not enter a halting-place inside the breast. The "world" is that in which the myriad things are one. If you grasp the whole where they are one and assimilate yourself to it, the four limbs and hundred members will become dust and grime, and death and life, end and start, will become a daytime and a night, and nothing will be able to disturb you, least of all distinctions drawn by gain and loss, good fortune or ill!

'You discard a servant as though shaking off mud, for you know that one's person is more valuable than its accessories. The value resides in oneself, and is not lost by alterations. Besides, if in a myriad transformations we shall never be nearer to a limit, why should any of them be enough to trouble the heart? The man who has cultivated the Way is free from these.'

'Sir,' said Confucius, 'by your Power you are mate to heaven and earth, yet you still depend on the most far-reaching words to train the heart. Who of all the gentlemen of old could ever dispense with them?'

'Not so. When the water murmurs it *does nothing*, the capacity is spontaneous. As for the Power in the utmost man, it does not have to be trained for other things to be unable to separate from him. It is like heaven being high of itself, earth being solid of itself, the sun and moon shining of themselves; what is there for him to train?'

After Confucius went out he spoke of it to Yen Hui.

'As far as the Way is concerned, yes, I've seen about as much as an animalcule in the vinegar! If the Master had not taken the blindfold off me, I would not have guessed the scope of heaven and earth.' (*Chuang-tzŭ*, chapter 21)

.   .   .

The Master inquired of Old Tan.

'There are men who study the Way as they would correlatives, who allow the unallowable, treat the not so as so. There is a saying of the Sophists: "Separate the hard from the white as though suspending them apart in space." Shall we call such men as these sages?'

'This is a slave's drudgery, an artisan's bondage, wearing out the body, fretting the heart. It's the dog which catches the mouse that gets itself on to the leash, and the spryest of the monkeys which is brought down from the mountain forests. Confucius my lad, I shall tell you something which you are incapable of hearing, incapable of saying. Of all that have a head and feet, the ones without a heart and ears are the majority! Of all that have shape not one endures with the Shapeless, the Featureless. Their motions and pauses, deaths and births, rises and falls, these are not the "why" of them. To study anything belongs to the realm of man. To forget all about things, forget all about Heaven, the name for that is ''forgetfulness of self'', and it is the man forgetful of self who may be said to enter the realm of Heaven.' (*Chuang-tzŭ*, chapter 12)

NOTE 'Of all that have a head and feet . . . ': all creatures except man follow the Way without thinking or being taught.

• • •

Confucius inquired of Old Tan
  'Today while you are at leisure I venture to ask about the utmost Way.'
  'Practise fasting and austerities to clear the channels of your heart, cleanse the quintessential-and-daemonic in you, smash to pieces your knowledge. The Way is profound and hard to put in words. I shall outline it roughly for you in words.

> The bright is born from the dark,
> The ordered is born from the shapeless,
> The quintessential-and-daemonic is born from the Way,
> The shaped in its origins is born from quintessence,

and reproducing their own shapes the myriad things generate. Thus the ones with nine orifices are born from the womb, the ones with eight from the egg. There are no tracks behind them when they come, no borders over which they depart, no gateway and no inner room, it's a house without walls open in the four directions. The man who hits on the same course as these grows strong in his four limbs, keen and penetrating in his thoughts, sharp in sight and hearing, effortless in employing the heart and fluid in responding to things.

> For heaven, no choice but to be high.
> For earth, no choice but to be broad.
> For sun and moon, no choice but to proceed on their courses.
> For the myriad creatures, no choice but to multiply.

Would it be of these that it is the Way?
  'Moreover, while the information which is not necessarily knowledge and the subtlety which is not necessarily wisdom are repudiated by the sage, when it comes to that which no increase increases and no reduction reduces, he guards it close. Unfathomably deep, like the ocean! Looming so high, ending but to begin again! By its cycles it measures out the myriad things without exception. Then would your ''Way of the gentleman'' be the exterior of *that* ? All the myriad things go to draw from it but it does not fail – would it be of these that it is the Way?

'In the country in the middle there is man, neither Yin nor Yang, settled between heaven and earth. He is man only for a little while, he will return to his Ancestor. Considered in its origins, the living is a puff of vapour. Though some die early or late, how much time is there between them? It is a matter of an instant. Why should it be worth bothering whether sage Yao or tyrant Chieh is right or wrong? In fruits and berries there is pattern; the ordering of men, though harder, is their means of adjusting to one another. The sage neither misses the occasion when it is present nor clings to it when it is past. He responds to it by attuning himself, that's the Power; he responds to it by matching with it, that's the Way. From this course, the emperors arose and the kings began.

'Man's life between heaven and earth is like a white colt passing a chink in a wall, in a moment it is gone. In a gush, a rush, everything issues from there; melting, merging, everything enters there. By a transformation you are born, by another you die; all that lives feels the sadness of it, man mourns over it. You shake off your bowman's kit which is Heaven's, fling down your clerk's robe which is Heaven's, a scattering! a yielding! animus and anima depart their separate ways and selfhood follows them, and you have gone to your last home. This shaping of the unshaped, unshaping of the shaped, is known to all alike, but to the man on the verge of arriving it is of no account. Its stages are ordered in sequence by all common men alike; but he when he arrives does not order and while he orders has not arrived.

> The sharpest sight will not catch a glimpse.
> Better than disputation, silence.
> No one has ever heard the Way.
> Rather than hear, stop up your ears.

It is this that is meant by grasping it absolutely.' (*Chuang-tzŭ*, chapter 22)

•　•　•

Confucius said to Old Tan

'I studied the six Classics, the *Songs, Documents, Rites, Music, Changes, Annals*, for long enough it seems to me, and know their contents thoroughly. With this knowledge I introduced myself to seventy-two princes, discoursed on the Way of the former kings and made plain the imprints of the Dukes of Chou and Shao, but not one prince saw anything he could snap up for his use. How intractable are the difficulties of making plain the Way!'

'Say rather how lucky you were born too late to meet the princes of a better ordered age! The six Classics are the worn footprints of the former kings, not what they used to imprint! What you speak of now is still the footprints, and the footprints are where the shoes passed, they are not the shoes! The white fish-hawk impregnates when the couple stare at each other with unwavering pupils, insects when the male calls from the wind above and the female answers from the wind below, the creature called Lei because in itself it is both male and female. The natures of things cannot be exchanged, destiny cannot be altered, times cannot be brought to a stop, the Way cannot be blocked up. If it coincides with the Way no course is unallowable, if it misses it no course is allowable.'

Confucius did not go out of doors for three months. When he called again he said:

'I have grasped it. Crows and magpies hatch, the fish blow out foam, the tiny-waisted metamorphose, when a younger brother is born the elder wails. Too long have I failed to be a man fellow to things in their transformations, and if one fails to be that how can one transform men?'

'Good enough,' said Old Tan. 'Confucius my lad, you've got it.' (*Chuang-tzŭ*, chapter 14)

3

The advantages of spontaneity

The episode of Cook Ting (p. 63f) is the only story about a special knack in the *Inner chapters*. But there are many more in 'Fathoming life' (chapter 19) and others among the *Outer chapters*, as well as stories about other advantages in refusing self-consciousness.

Engraver Ch'ing chipped wood to make a bellstand. When the bellstand was finished viewers were amazed, as though it were daemonic, ghostly. The Marquis of Lu paid a visit and asked him

'By what secret did you make it?'

'Your servant is a mere artisan, what secret could he have? However, there is one point. When I am going to make a bellstand I take care never to squander energy on it, I make sure to fast to still the heart. After fasting three days, I do not care to keep in mind congratulation and reward, honours and salary. After fasting five days, I do not care to keep in mind your blame or praise, my skill or clumsiness. After fasting seven days, I am so intent that I forget that I have a body and four limbs.

'During this time my lord's court does not exist for me. The dexterity for it concentrates, outside distractions melt away, and only then do I go into the mountain forest and observe the nature of the wood as Heaven makes it grow. The aptitude of the body attains its peak; and only then do I have a complete vision of the bellstand, only then do I put my hand to it. Otherwise I give the whole thing up. So I join what is Heaven's to what is Heaven's. Would this be the reason why the instrument seems daemonic?' (*Chuang-tzŭ*, chapter 19)

●   ●   ●

Chi Hsing-tzŭ trained fighting cocks for the King. After ten days the King asked

'Are the cocks ready?'

'Not yet. They go on strutting vaingloriously and working themselves into rages.'

After another ten days he asked again.

'Not yet. They still start at shadows and echoes.'

After another ten days he asked again.

'Not yet. They still glare furiously and swell with rage.'

After another ten days he asked again.

'Good enough. Even if there's a cock which crows, there's no longer any change in them. From a distance they look like cocks of wood. The Power in them is complete. A strange cock would not dare to face them, it would turn and run.' (*Chuang-tzŭ*, chapter 19)

•   •   •

Confucius looked at the view in Lü-liang. The waterfall hung down three hundred feet, it streamed foam for forty miles, it was a place where fish and turtles and crocodiles could not swim, but he saw one fellow swimming there. He took him for someone in trouble who wanted to die, and sent a disciple along the bank to pull him up. But after a few hundred paces the man came out, and strolled under the bank with his hair down his back, singing as he walked. Confucius took the opportunity to question him.

'I thought you were a ghost, but now I see you close up you're a man. May I ask whether you have a Way to stay afloat in water?'

'No, I have no Way. I began in what is native to me, grew up in what is natural to me, matured in what is destined for me. I enter with the inflow, and emerge with the outflow, follow the Way of the water and do not impose my selfishness upon it. This is how I stay afloat in it.'

'What do you mean by ''beginning in what is native to you, growing up in what is natural to you, maturing in what is destined for you''?'

'Having been born on dry land I am at home on dry land – it's native to me. Having grown up in water I am at home in water – it's natural to me. It is so without me knowing why it is so – it's destined for me.' (*Chuang-tzŭ*, chapter 19)

•   •   •

Yen Hui asked a question of Confucius.

'Once I was crossing the deep water at Shang-shen, and the ferryman handled the boat as though he were daemonic. I asked whether one can learn to handle a boat. ''Yes,'' he said. ''A good swimmer picks it up quickly; as for a diver, he would handle a boat deftly even if he had never seen one before.'' I questioned him further but that was all he had to say. May I ask what he meant?'

'A good swimmer picks it up quickly because he forgets the water. As for a diver, he would handle a boat deftly even if he had never seen one before, because he looks at the depths as at dry land, at the capsizing of a boat as at his carriage sliding backwards. Though ten thousand prospects of capsizing or sliding go on spreading out before him, they cannot intrude into the place where he dwells. Why would he be ill at ease anywhere?

'Play for tiles, and you're skilful; play for belt-buckles, and you lose confidence; play for gold, and you're flustered. Your skill is the same as ever, but if you are attaching importance to something you are giving weight to what is outside you, and whoever gives weight to what is outside him is inwardly clumsy.' (*Chuang-tzŭ*, chapter 19)

• • •

Master Lieh-tzŭ asked Kuan-yin

'The utmost man swims underwater but does not suffocate,
Treads fire but does not burn,
Walks high above the myriad things but does not tremble.

May I ask how he attains to this?'

'It is by holding fast to his purest energies, it has nothing to do with knowledge, skill, resolution, daring. Sit down, I shall tell you. Whatever has features, likeness, sound, colour, is a thing, and how can one thing put a distance between itself and other things? By what would it deserve to get ahead of them? It is mere shape and colour. Then the things which go on finding their directions in the Unshaped, or stay settled at the point where there is no transformation of anything – if someone extends his grasp to their furthest reaches, how could any thing stay settled in him? He will remain at the degree where he does not infringe upon others, and store far back along the skein without beginning where all threads meet, to roam where the myriad things end and begin; he will unify his nature, tend his energies, contain his Power, to circulate through that in which other things find their directions. In such a man as this, what is from Heaven keeps itself whole, the daemonic is without flaws; where would other things find a way in?

'When a drunken man falls from a cart, despite the speed of the fall he does not die. In his bones and joints he is the same as other men, but in encountering harm he is different, because the daemonic is whole in him. He rides without knowing it, falls without knowing it; death and life, astonishment and fear never enter his breast, so when he collides with other things he does not flinch. If this is the case even when you get your wholeness from wine, how much more when you get it from Heaven! The sage stores away in Heaven, therefore nothing is able to wound him.' (*Chuang-tzŭ*, chapter 19)

NOTE 'Storing': Ordinary men, having separated themselves off from other things, can deal with them only by hoarding them as possessions or as information stored in memory. The sage 'responds and does not store' (p. 98), there are no flaws in his wholeness through which other things can enter, settle down and immobilise him. He does not need other things because he is aware that at the root of him he is identical with them, already has them in his 'Magic storehouse' (p. 80), which is 'the world stored within the world' (p. 86). Having dissolved the barrier between self and other he has entered into the fluid interaction by which things spontaneously avoid harm from each other as fish in a shoal weave in and out without touching (cf. p. 90: 'As fish go on setting directions for each other in the water, men go on setting directions for each other in the Way').

· · ·

When Confucius was on a journey to Ch'u, taking a path through a forest he saw a hunchback catching cicadas on a sticky rod: it was as though he were picking them up off the ground. Said Confucius

'Are you just clever at it? Or do you have the Way?'

'I have the Way. When the season comes round in the fifth and sixth months, I balance balls on top of each other. If I can balance two without dropping them, I shan't miss many cicadas; if I can balance three, I'll miss one in ten; if I can balance five, it will be like picking them up off the ground. I settle my body like a rooted tree stump, I hold my arm like the branch of a withered tree; out of all the vastness of heaven and earth, the multitude of the myriad things, it is only of the wings of a cicada that I am aware. I don't let my gaze wander or waver, I would not take all the myriad things in exchange for the wings of a cicada. How could I help but succeed?'

Confucius turned and said to his disciples:

> '"Intent sustained undivided
> Will verge on the daemonic."

Wouldn't it be that venerable hunchback it is about?' (*Chuang-tzŭ*, chapter 19)

· · ·

When carpenter Ch'ui drew a figure it was true to compasses or L-square; his finger shared in the transformations of things and did not depend on the thinking of the heart to verify. Consequently his Magic Watchtower was a unity and he could go up and down it unobstructed. Shoes most suit us when we forget the feet, a belt when we forget the waist, the heart when we know how to forget "That's it, that's not", an engagement with circumstance when we neither vary inwardly nor yield to external pressures. To suit from the start and never fail to suit is to suit in forgetfulness of what it is that suits. (*Chuang-tzŭ*, chapter 19)

· · ·

Lord Yüan of Sung wanted a picture painted. All the scribes arrived, were given tablets and stood in line licking their brushes and mixing their inks; as many again were waiting outside. There was one scribe who was last to arrive, sauntered in as though he had all the time in the world, took a tablet but did not join the line, then went off to his quarters. When the Duke sent someone to have a look at him, he had taken his clothes off and was sitting there naked with his knees out.

'He'll do,' said the Duke. 'He is the true painter.' (*Chuang-tzŭ*, chapter 21)

· · ·

The Grand Marshal's forger of buckles was eighty years old, and was never out by a hair's breadth.

'Is it just that you're clever,' said the Grand Marshal, 'or do you have the Way?'

'I have the Way. Even when I was twenty I delighted in forging buckles. I might look at anything, but if it wasn't a buckle I wouldn't look close. So the man who is putting to use has depended on the man who was *not* putting to use, to get the lasting use of it, and how much more on that which puts everything to use! What thing is there that does not draw on that?' (*Chuang-tzŭ*, chapter 22)

· · ·

It is when it is to be found in a book that the world values the Way. A book is no more than sayings, but there is value in sayings; what is valuable in them is the thought. A thought is about something; what the thought is about is untransmittable in words, yet for the sake of it the world values the words and transmits the book. Even though the world values them, to me they seem valueless, because what is valued in them is not what is valuable.

The visible to sight is shape and colour, the audible to hearing is name and sound; how sad it is then that worldly people think shape and colour, name and sound, sufficient means to grasp the identity of that! If shape, colour, name, sound, are really inadequate means to grasp its identity, then, since knowers do not say and sayers do not know, how would the world recognise it?

Duke Huan was reading a book at the top of the hall, wheelwright Pien was chipping a wheel at the bottom of the hall. He put aside his mallet and chisel and went up to ask Duke Huan

'May I ask what words my lord is reading?'

'The words of a sage.'

'Is the sage alive?'

'He's dead.'

'In that case what my lord is reading is the dregs of the men of old, isn't it?'

'What business is it of a wheelwright to criticise what I read? If you can explain yourself, well and good; if not, you die.'

'Speaking for myself, I see it in terms of my own work. If I chip at a wheel too slowly, the chisel slides and does not grip; if too fast, it jams and catches in the wood. Not too slow, not too fast; I feel it in the hand and respond from the heart, the mouth cannot put it into words, there is a knack in it somewhere which I cannot convey to my son and which my son cannot learn from me. This is how through my seventy years I have grown old chipping at wheels. The men of old and their untransmittable message are dead. Then what my lord is reading is the dregs of the men of old, isn't it?' (*Chuang-tzŭ*, chapter 13

•   •   •

When King Wen was touring Tsang he saw a venerable old man fishing, but in his fishing there was nobody fishing, he was not someone fishing-rod in hand fishing for something, it was as though he had always been fishing.

King Wen would have raised him up and put the government in his hands, but feared that the great ministers and his uncles and elder brothers would be discontented with it; he would have given up and let the man be, but could not bear that the Hundred Clans should have no Heaven above them. So next morning he announced to the grandees

'Last night in a dream I saw a goodly man, dark of face and whiskered, riding a dappled horse with its hooves red down one side, who shouted, "Entrust your government to the venerable old man of Tsang, may he bring salvation to the people!"'

Said the grandees, awestruck,

'It was His Late Majesty.'

'Then let us divine it.'

'Your late father's command it is not for Your Majesty to question, what more is there to divine?'

Then he welcomed the venerable old man of Tsang and put the government in his hands.

No reforms were made in the statutes, no special decrees were issued. When three years later King Wen toured the state, the order of knights was leaderless and disunited, the senior officials did not fulfil their potentialities, traders did not venture to bring their peck-and-bushel measures over the borders. The order of knights being leaderless and disunited was because they conformed to the ruler above. Senior officials not fulfilling their potentialities was because everyone worked together. Traders not venturing to bring their peck-and-bushel measures over the borders was because other states had full confidence.

Then King Wen deemed him the greatest of teachers, and facing north as his disciple he inquired

'Can the policy be extended to the whole empire?'

The venerable old man of Tsang looked blank and did not answer, looked vague and made his excuses, set the question in the morning he had fled by the evening, and for the rest of his life he was never heard of again.

Yen Hui asked Confucius

'King Wen hadn't got there yet, had he? Why that nonsense about the dream?'

'Hush, don't say it! King Wen did all that he had to do, what is there to criticise in him? He simply adapted himself to the moment.' (*Chuang-tzŭ*, chapter 21)

•   •   •

When the sage bursts through entanglements to a comprehensive view of everything as one, without knowing what is so of it, it is his nature. He recovers his destiny and is reverberated into motion, with Heaven as his teacher; it is other men who subsequently find the names for it. If you go on worrying about knowing, and whatever you engage in is over in a moment, when it comes to a stop what are you going to do?

To those born beautiful others give a mirror; unless they are told, they do not know they are more beautiful than others. But whether they know it or not, hear of it or not, they never cease to be delightful and others never cease to enjoy them; it is their nature. To the sage's love of mankind others give the name; unless he is told, he does not know he loves mankind. But whether he knows it or not, hears of it or not, he never ceases to love mankind and others never cease to find comfort in him; it is his nature.

In your old country, your old city, as you peer at it in the distance every thing is recognisable; even supposing a maze of heaps and mounds, grass and trees has encroached into nine tenths of it, still everything is recognisable. How much more for the seer of sight and hearer of hearing! He is the man on the eighty-foot watch-tower raised high above the crowd. (*Chuang-tzŭ*, chapter 25)

•   •   •

Yang-tzŭ travelling to Sung spent a night at an inn. The innkeeper had two concubines, one of them beautiful, the other ugly. The ugly one he valued, the beautiful one he neglected. When Yang-tzŭ asked the reason, the innkeeper's boy answered

'The beautiful one thinks herself beautiful, we do not notice she is beautiful. The ugly one thinks herself ugly, we do not notice she is ugly.'

'Make a note of that, my disciples,' said Yang-tzŭ. 'If you do well but banish self-approval from your heart, will you not be loved wherever you go?' (*Chuang-tzŭ*, chapter 20)

.   .   .

When lashed boats are crossing the river, and some empty boat comes and bumps against them, even a hot-tempered man will not get angry. But if there is one man in it he will shout at him to keep clear; and if the man does not hear his first shout, or his second, then you can be sure that when he shouts the third time he will be calling him some ugly names as well. He was not angry before, now he is; it was empty before, now it has someone in it. If a man can roam in the world with emptied self, who can interfere with him? (*Chuang-tzŭ*, chapter 20)

> The skilful toil, the clever worry,
> Have no abilities and you'll have no ambitions.
> Eat your fill and stroll as you please,
> Adrift like a boat loose from its moorings.

– The emptied man who strolls as he pleases. (*Chuang-tzŭ*, chapter 32)

4

Rationalising the Way: the 'Great Man'

There are three dialogues in *Chuang-tzŭ* which share the theme of the 'Great Man' (*ta jen*) and his 'Great Scope' (*ta fang*), his breadth of vision. We shall call them the 'Autumn floods', the 'Know-little', and the 'Snail'. The first two, which are the longer and philosophically the more interesting, are so alike in phrasing as well as thought that we need not hesitate to ascribe them to one author, who probably wrote the 'Snail' dialogue as well. As for his date, he once pairs the abdications of the pre-dynastic emperor Yao and of King K'uai of Yen in 316 BC as 'former' events,[19] so that he can hardly be earlier than the late third if not the second century BC. There are several other passages related to the three dialogues – in particular three expositions of respectively the 'integrity', the 'teaching' and the 'conduct' of the Great Man – which, though scattered over different chapters, belong together and have the look of fragments broken off the end of the mutilated 'Autumn floods' dialogue. It would seem that the Great Man and his Great Scope are the slogans of a particular tendency in Taoism. The 'Snail' dialogue actually puts the Great Man above the sage.[20] In the 'Autumn floods' the river god seeking instruction from the sea god Jo expresses the fear, 'If I do not come for lessons at your gate I shall be a laughing-stock for ever in the School of Great Scope.'[21]

The most striking characteristic of these sections is a trust in the intellect which might be thought quite un-Taoist. 'Autumn floods' and 'Know-little' are sustained expositions of a coherent metaphysical system. Except at certain rhetorical climaxes there is none of the usual Taoist play with ambiguity and paradox. Remarkably, the word 'knowledge' is always used in a good sense. That this rationalising tendency made the Great Man philosophy suspect to some other Taoists is confirmed by a single example of the term outside the three dialogues and the related passages. In the exuberant attack on knowledge which introduces the chapter 'Knowledge roams north,'[22] personified Knowledge requests and receives from the Yellow Emperor a verbal exposition of the Way, in which it is declared that only the Great Man easily returns to the root of things. But the Yellow Emperor then repudiates his own account by adding that he and Knowledge are both remote from the Way precisely because they know about it. Here "Great Man" serves as a catch-phrase to identify a too intellectual type of Taoism.

The basis of the 'Great Man' metaphysic is the distinction between finite and infinite. We can count finite things, name them, sort them, and establish the 'patterns' (*li*) in which they are organised. But the whole out of which we divide them is infinite, nameless, called the 'Way' only by extending to it a name from the finite, just as we use the word *wan*, 'myriad' (in Chinese as in English primarily the number 10,000), for an indefinitely large number. Within the realm of the finite we can ask whether an event has some cause or agent or has none, but it is a mistake to extend the question to the cosmic process as a whole, since the whole transcends even the distinction between Something and Nothing.[23] (The philosophers Chi Chen and Chieh-tzŭ mentioned as rivals on this issue unfortunately left no extant writings.)

The Great Man, by identifying himself with the whole, widens his perspective to a full view of everything, with the result that he sees finite things in proportion, as only relatively great or small, good or bad. In this relativism, as in the treatment of infinity, one may suspect some influence of the Sophists. We have noticed [24] that although Chuang-tzŭ derides the Sophist Hui Shih he owes him a debt. But although Taoists might be impressed by Hui Shih's arguments for the unreality of distinctions, they must always have detested the Sophists such as Kung-sun Lung who took the opposite course, of distinguishing what to common sense is the same. This was known as 'parting the hard from the white', and the *Inner chapters* use *chien pai* 'hard and white', as a contemptuous term for logic (we translate it by 'chop-logic' [25]). It is interesting to find both the great Sophists making personal appearances in the present cycle. In the 'Snail' dialogue a Great Man who discourses on infinity is introduced to court by Hui Shih in person, from which we may infer that Hui Shih is respected, but not acknowledged as himself a Great Man. On the other hand, in another story Kung-sun Lung is turned into a laughing-stock, baffled and humiliated when he hears the teaching of Chuang-tzŭ.[26]

At the climax of 'Autumn floods', after an apparently total dismissal of all value judgements, the disoriented inquirer raises the question (never put directly anywhere else in the book) 'What is there to value in the Way?' The answer is almost disappointingly moderate and sensible. If you possess the Way you are aware of the 'patterns', the local regularities of the cosmic order, which enables you to weigh things justly against each other and avoid harm. Here a Westerner interested in moral philosophy will wonder how he is expected to weigh things except in relation to those standards of value which Taoists refuse to recognise. We touched on this issue in the Introduction.[27] The Great Man's ultimate motions are spontaneous, from Heaven and not from man. We can conceive his weighing of things not as evaluation but simply as an objective estimation of their greater or lesser effects on each other and on himself, so that he will respond to them in full awareness of their interrelations and consequences. The only value judgement assumed, therefore, is that aware reactions are better than unaware ones, which is no more than preferring truth to falsehood, reality to illusion. In Western terms it is a judgement outside moral philosophy altogether, yet it will recommend the sage to act on one kind of incipient reaction rather than another, and therefore provide him with a principle of action.

THE 'AUTUMN FLOODS' DIALOGUE

The floods of autumn came with the season, a hundred streams poured into the Yellow River, the rushing current was so great that from between the cliffs and islets of the two shores you could not tell a cow from a horse. Then the Lord of the River was exuberantly pleased with himself, thinking that everything beautiful in the world was within himself. Following the current he voyaged eastwards, until he came to the North Sea. He looked out towards the east, and did not see an end to the water. Then for the first time the Lord of the River screwed up his face. Peering into the distance towards Sea-god Jo he sighed

'There's a proverb, ''At the hundredth thing he heard about the Way he thought there was nobody like him''; it is me that's about. Then too, I used to hear men belittle the fame of Confucius and decry the dutifulness of Po Yi, and never believed them; but now that I perceive how immense you are, if I do not come for lessons at your gate it will be the worse for me, I shall be a laughing-stock for ever in the School of the Great Scope.'

'You can't talk to a frog in a well about the sea', said Jo of the North Sea, 'because it is cramped inside its hole. You can't talk to the insects of summer about ice, because they are stuck fast in their own season. You can't talk to hole-in-the-corner scholars about the Way, because they are constricted by their doctrines. Now that you have come out from your banks and have a view of the great sea, you have the good sense to be ashamed of yourself; it will be possible to talk to you about the grand pattern.

'No waters in the world are greater than the sea. Though a myriad streams end up in it, on and on till who knows when, it does not fill; though it is draining away at Wei-lü, on and on who knows how long, it does not empty. Through spring and autumn it does not alter, it knows nothing of flood or drought. How far it surpasses the streams of the Yellow River and the Yangtse is beyond measuring or counting; and, if in spite of this I have never made much of myself, it is because I recognise that, having a body sheltered by heaven and earth and energies drawn from the Yin and Yang, within the compass of heaven and earth I am no more than a pebble or a bush on a great mountain. Belonging as I do among the lesser in comparison, what excuse would I have to make much of myself?

'If you measure the Four Seas against heaven and earth, are they not like an anthill on the wide moors? If you measure the Middle Land against the Four Seas, is it not like a rice grain in a vast granary? As a term for the number of things we call them 'myriad', and mankind amounts to one of them. In the nine regions populated by men, where grain grows and ships and carriages pass, a man amounts to one of them. If you compare him to the 'myriad things', is he not like the tip of a hair on the body of a horse? What the Five Emperors abdicated, what the Three Kings fought over, what the benevolent man worries about, what the responsible man labours for, is no more than this. Po Yi by resigning it won himself a name, Confucius for talking about it was deemed a learned man; in thinking so much of themselves did not these men resemble you, when just now you thought yourself the greatest of the waters?'

'In that case, is it allowable for me to judge heaven and earth great and the tip of a hair small?'

'No. Throughout the realm of things, measuring has no limit, times have no stop, portions have no constancy, nothing whether ending or starting stays as it was. Therefore the wisest, because they have a full view of far and near, do not belittle the smaller or make much of the greater, knowing that measuring has no limit; because they have an assured comprehension of past and present, they are not disheartened by indefinite delay or on tiptoes for what is within reach, knowing that times have no stop; because they are discerning about cycles of waxing and waning, they are not pleased when they win or anxious when they lose, knowing that our portions have no constancy; because they are clear-sighted about our unvarying path, they do not rejoice in being alive or think it a calamity to die, knowing that nothing ending or starting can be kept as it was. Reckon up what a man knows; it does not compare with what he does not know. Or the time that he is alive; it does not compare with the time before he was born. He tries to use the smallest to exhaust the compass of the greatest, that is why he is lost and confused and incapable of finding himself. Seeing from this point of view, how do I know that the tip of a hair is enough to establish a standard for the most minute? Or that heaven and earth are enough to exhaust the compass of the greatest?'

'Debaters of the age all say that the most quintessential has no shape at all, the greatest cannot be encompassed. Is this the truth of the matter?'

''When the great is seen from the viewpoint of the minute, some is out of sight; when the minute is seen from the viewpoint of the great, it is invisible. The quintessential is the small as it ceases to be discernible, the outlying is the great receding out of sight, therefore their differentiation is for convenience; it is a matter of the situation from which one is seeing. The quintessential and the massive we specify in things which do have shape. What has no shape at all, number cannot divide; what cannot be encompassed, number cannot exhaust. Those which can be sorted in words are the more massive among things; those which can be conveyed through ideas are the more quintessential among things. As for what words cannot sort or ideas convey, we do not specify anything in it as quintessential or massive.'

'Beyond the realm of things, or within the realm of things, to what viewpoint must one attain if one is to find standards for noble and base, small and great?'

'If we examine them in relation to the Way, things are neither noble nor base. If we examine them in relation to other things, they see themselves as noble and each other as base. If we examine them in relation to custom, the nobility or baseness does not depend on oneself.

'Examining them in terms of degree, if assuming a standpoint from which it is great you see it as great, not one of the myriad things is not great; if assuming a standpoint from which you see it as small you see it as small, not one of the myriad things is not small. When you know that heaven and earth amount to a grain of rice, that the tip of a hair amounts to a hill or a mountain, the quantities of degree will be perceived.

'Examining them in terms of achievements, if assuming a standpoint from which it has them you see it as having, not one of the myriad things does not have them; if assuming a standpoint from which it lacks them you see it as lacking, not one of the myriad things does not lack them. When you know that east and west are opposites yet cannot do without each other, portions in achievement will be decided.

'Examining them in terms of inclinations, if assuming a standpoint from which it is right you see it as right, not one of the myriad things is not right; if assuming a standpoint from which it is wrong you see it as wrong, not one of the myriad things is not wrong. When you know that sage Yao and tyrant Chieh each thought himself right and the other wrong, the commitments behind the inclinations will be perceived.

'In former times, Shun took the throne yielded by Yao and became Emperor, Chih took the throne yielded by K'uai and was ruined. T'ang and Wu fought for a throne and reigned, Po-kung fought for a throne and perished. Judging by these cases, the propriety of contending or deferring, the conduct of a Yao or a Chieh, will be noble at one time and base at another, and is not to be taken as a constant. A battering-ram is good for smashing down a wall, but not for stopping up a hole, which is to say that it is a tool with a special use. Hua-liu the thoroughbred horse gallops a thousand miles in a day, but for catching mice is not worth a wildcat or a weasel, which is to say that it has a special accomplishment. At night the horned owl will snatch a flea and discern the tip of a hair, but when it comes out in daytime it blinks its eyes and doesn't see a mountain, which is to say that it has a special nature. If then we say ''Why not take the right as our authority and do without the wrong, take the ordered as our authority and do away with the unruly'', this is failing to understand the pattern of heaven and earth, and the myriad things as they essentially are. It is as though you were to take heaven as your authority and do without earth, take the Yin as your authority and do without the Yang; that it is impracticable is plain enough. But still they go on telling us to do so, if not foolishly then dishonestly. There were special circumstances for the abdications of the Emperors and Kings, special circumstances for the successions of the Three Dynasties. Whoever misses the time and flouts the custom is called a usurper, whoever hits on the time and accords with the custom is called a dutiful man. Hush, hush, Lord of the River! How would you know which gate is noble or base, which school is small or great?'

'If that is so, what shall I do and what shall I not do? On what final consideration am I to refuse or accept, prefer or discard?'

'If we examine them in terms of the Way,

> What shall we think noble, what shall we think base?
> This is called drifting back to the source.
> Don't fix a sphere for your intent,
> Or you'll be too lame to walk the way.

What shall we belittle, what shall we make much of?
This is called letting their turns come round.
Don't walk always on one course,
You'll be at odds and evens with the Way.

Stern!
As a lord to his state, no private favours.
Bountiful!
As the earth-god at the sacrifice, no private blessings.
Flowing everywhere!
As the infinite in the four directions, fenced in nowhere.

Embrace the myriad creatures every one,
Which of them deserves to be helped ahead?
This is called being open in every direction.
All the myriad creatures in oneness even out.
Which of them is short, which of them long?

The Way has no end and no start,
There are things which die, things which are born.
Can't be sure of a prime of life.
Now they empty, now they fill,
There's no reserved seat for their shapes.

The years cannot be warded off,
Times cannot be made to stop.
Dwindling and growing, filling and emptying,
Whatever is an end is also a start.

This is how to tell of the range of the grand summing-up and to sort out the patterns of the myriad things. A thing's life is like a stampede, a gallop, at every prompting it alters, there is never a time when it does not shift. What shall we do? What shall we not do? It is inherent in everything that it will transform of itself.'

'But in that case what is there to value in the Way?'

'Heaven and earth have supreme beauty but do not speak, the four seasons have clear standards but do not judge, the myriad things have perfect patterns but do not explain. The sage in fathoming the beauty of heaven and earth penetrates the patterns of the myriad things. Hence, in ''the utmost man does nothing, the great sage does not initiate'', what is meant is that he has a full view of heaven and earth. Now whether in that most quintessential of the daemonic and illuminated or in those hundredfold transformations, already things live and die, are round or square, and no one knows their Root. While they proliferate as the myriad things, inherently from old it is what it was. The universe though so vast has never separated from within it, an autumn hair though so tiny depends on it to be formed. While everything in the world floats or sinks and never through its lifetime stays as it was, while Yin and Yang and four seasons pass through their cycles and each keeps its place in the sequence, in the obscurity it seems lost yet it is there, in the blur it is unshaped yet daemonic, and the myriad things are nourished by it without their knowing. It is this I call the fundamental Root, from which one can have a full view of Heaven.

'Whoever knows the Way is sure of penetrating the patterns, whoever penetrates the patterns is sure to be clear-headed in weighing things, whoever is clear-headed in weighing things will not use other things to his own harm. The man of utmost Power

> Fire cannot burn,
> Water cannot drown,
> Heat and cold cannot harm,
> Beasts and birds cannot rend,

which is not to say that he ignores them, it means that since he is perspicacious about safety and danger, secure in fortune and misfortune, careful in approaching and shunning, none of them is able to harm him. As the saying goes, ''Heaven is within, man is without', and the Power goes on residing in what is from Heaven. If you know the workings of Heaven and of man, you

> Stay rooted in Heaven,
> Stay seated in the Power,
> Advance, retreat, extend, retract,
> And by returning to the crucial expound the highest.'

'What do you mean by ''Heaven''? What do you mean by ''man''?'
'That oxen and horses have four feet, this we ascribe to Heaven; haltering horses' heads and piercing oxen's noses, this we ascribe to man. Hence it is said:

> ''Don't let man extinguish Heaven,
> Don't let deliberation extinguish destiny.
> Guard it carefully, don't lose it.
> Call it 'returning to the genuine'.'''

(*Chuang-tzŭ*, chapter 17)

NOTE The 'Autumn floods' dialogue seems to be mutilated towards the end. The following three paragraphs on the integrity, teaching and conduct of the Great Man are very probably remains of the conclusion.

'Hence as the sea which accepts whatever flows east is of all things the greatest, so the sage joins together and encompasses heaven and earth and his bounty extends to the whole world, yet his identity and clan-name are unknown. Therefore alive he has no dignities, dead has no posthumous title,

his deeds are unrecorded, his name is unestablished. It is this that is meant by
the Great Man. One does not think well of a dog because it is good at barking
nor of a man because he is good at talking, still less does one deem him greatest!
Being deemed greatest is insufficient for being deemed the Great, still less for
being deemed Power! The Great is comprehensive: nothing equals heaven and
earth, but in what that we seek in them can the greatness be comprehensive?
One who knows the comprehensive in greatness does not seek anything, nor
does he lose or discard anything, for he refuses to take other things in exchange
for himself. Being inexhaustible to self-inspection, without friction in according with the ancient, this is the integrity of the Great Man.' (*Chuang-tzŭ*, chapter 24)

'The teaching of the Great Man is as shape to shadow, as sound to echo. When
asked he answers, and by drawing on everything in his own bosom he is the
counterpart of the whole world. He goes on dwelling in the echoless, travelling
in the directionless. Be finished with your restless journeying and returning,
and roam out into the infinite; have no banks between which you go in and out,
and every day renew your beginnings. In describing and sorting out shapes and
bodies, remain joined with them in ultimate sameness. In ultimate sameness
you have no self; and without a self from where would you get to have anything?
The man who perceives something is the ''gentleman'' you were yesterday,
the man who perceives Nothing is the friend of heaven and earth.' (*Chuang-
tzŭ*, chapter 11)

'Therefore the conduct of the Great Man never takes a course harmful to
others, yet he does not make much of being benevolent or generous; his
motions are not prompted by gain, yet he does not despise the gatekeeper
waiting for a tip. As for goods and possessions, he does not compete for them,
yet he does not make much of deferring and renouncing; he works for them
without relying on others, yet does not make much of living by his own efforts,
and does not despise the greedy and corrupt. In conduct he differs from the
vulgar, yet he does not make much of being eccentric and extraordinary; he
lives as one of the common people, yet he does not despise the flatterers at court.
The titles and salaries of the age are insufficient to induce him, its punishments
and disgrace are insufficient to humiliate him. He knows that there can be no
fixed portions for the right and the wrong, no fixed standards for the minute and
the great. I have heard said:

> The man of the Way is not heard of,
> The utmost Power wins no gains,
> The Great Man has no self,

which is to be at the final knot where all portions are tied up.' (*Chuang-tzŭ*,
chapter 17)

THE 'KNOW-LITTLE' DIALOGUE

Know-little asked the Grand Impartial Reconciler
  'What is meant by "ward or sector" words?'
  'A ward or sector establishes it as customary to take ten surnames, a hundred given names together. It joins together the different and treats them as similar, disperses the similar and treats them as different. Now the fact that when you point out from each other the hundred parts of a horse you do not find the horse, yet there the horse is, tethered in front of you, is because you stand the hundred parts on another level to call them "horse". For the same reason, a hill or mountain accumulates the low to become the high, the Yangtse and the Yellow River join together the small to become the big, and the Great Man joins together the partial to become impartial. This is why for influences from outside he has an appropriator which makes them his own, and he does not cling to one or another; and for outgoings from within he has a regulator which sets them in the true direction, so that others do not resist them. The four seasons have weathers proper to them; Heaven does not favour one rather than another, and so the year completes its course. The Five Bureaux have tasks proper to them; the prince is not partial to one or another, and so the state is ordered. Peace and war have abilities proper to them; the Great Man does not favour one or another, and so the Power in him is comprehensive. The myriad things have patterns proper to them; the Way is not partial to one or another, and so does not have the name of one rather than another, and so does not do one thing rather than another, and in doing nothing there is nothing it does not do.
  'Times have an end and a start, ages have their alterations and transformations. Fortune and misfortune arrive mingled inextricably, and in flouting one thing they suit something else. Each thing pursues the direction proper to it, and on its true course from one viewpoint is deviant from another. Compare them to the wide woodland, where all the hundred timbers have their own measures; or take in a full view of the great mountain, where trees and rocks share the same base. Such are what one means by "ward and sector" words.'
  'If so, is it adequate to call that the "Way"?'
  'No. Suppose you were counting off the number of things you would not stop at one myriad, yet we specify them as the "myriad things", for we use a high number as a label for what we are counting towards. Similarly, heaven and earth are the greatest of shapes, and Yin and Yang the greatest of energies, and "Way" covers both of them impartially; if we are utilising the greatest of them to label what we continue towards, that is allowable, but once we have it, can we treat it as comparable with anything else? Then if we use it in chopping to bits and disputing over alternatives, and treat it as analogous with the logician's "dog" or "horse", it will be much less adequate than they are.'

'Within the four directions, inside the six-way-oriented, from what does it arise, that from which the myriad things are born?'

'The Yin and Yang illuminate and cover over and regulate, the four seasons alternate and generate and kill. Then desire and dislike, inclination and aversion, spring up in turn; then by the coupling of male and female existence is perpetuated.

> As safety and danger change places,
> And fortune and misfortune generate each other,
> And the easy and the urgent rub against each other,
> Between cohering and dissolving each has its form.

These are the things of which names and substances can be recorded, of which even the most quintessential and least discernible can be noted.

> Their mutual patterning as they follow in sequence,
> Their mutual causation as their cycles recur,
> At its limit turns back again,
> At its end begins again.

These are the regularities which things possess, words exhaust, knowledge attains; they extend throughout but no further than the realm of things. The man who perceives the Way does not pursue them to where they vanish or explore the source from which they arise. This is the point where discussion stops.'

'Of the proposals of the two schools, of Chi Chen that ''Nothing does it'' and of Chieh-tzŭ that ''Something causes it'', which is just to the facts about them, which takes a one-sided view of their patterns?'

'That a cock has crowed or a dog barked a man knows well enough but, however great his knowledge, he cannot in words trace back to the source out of which they have transformed, or measure in thought what they will become. If you chop up into smaller and smaller divisions, you end up with something too quintessential for grading, and something too big to be encompassed. With ''Something causes it'' and ''Nothing does it'' we never escape from the realm of things, yet persist in supposing that we have passed beyond it.

> A ''something which causes'' is substance,
> A ''nothing which does'' is a void.
> There *is* a name, there *is* a substance
> – Then it occupies a place with other things.
> There is *no* name, there is *no* substance
> – Then it occupies the void between things.
> What can be said, what can be conceived,
> Recedes from it farther the more you say.

> What was before birth we could not forbid,
> What comes after death we cannot halt.
> It is not that death and life are far away
> But the pattern of them cannot be perceived.

"Something causes it" and "Nothing does it" are suppositions to which we resort in doubt. If we examine something for the root from which it grew, its past is limitless; if we search it for its offshoots, their future never stops. The limitless which never stops is nothing sayable, yet shares its pattern with things. Something having caused or nothing having done is the root of saying, but ends and begins with the things themselves.

'The Way cannot be treated as Something, or as Nothing either. "Way" as a name is what we borrow to walk it. "Something causes it" and "Nothing does it" are at single corners of the realm of things; what have they to do with the Great Scope? If you use words adequately, however much you say it is all about the Way; if inadequately, however much you say it is all about the realm of things. The ultimate both of the Way and of things neither speech nor silence is adequate to convey.

> In what is neither speech nor silence
> May discussion find its ultimate.'

(*Chuang-tzŭ*, chapter 25)

THE 'SNAIL' DIALOGUE

King Ying of Wei made a treaty with Mou, the Marquis T'ien of Ch'i. The Marquis broke the treaty, the King was angry and intended to send an assassin to stab him.

When the Minister of War, Kung-sun Yen, heard that, he was ashamed.

'Your Majesty is a lord of ten thousand chariots, yet you are using a commoner to avenge you. I request that you provide me with 200,000 armoured men; I'll attack Ch'i for you, take all its people captive, tie up all its oxen and horses, and get its lord so hot inside that boils break out on his back before we have even taken his capital. As for his general Chi, we'll wait until he makes a run for it, then we'll hit him from behind and smash his spine.'

When Chi-tzŭ heard of that, he was ashamed.

'If you are building an eighty-foot city wall, and when it is already some fifty feet high you pull it down, even the convicts would complain at the waste of their labour. We have had no war now for seven years, and have laid the foundations of the government of a True King. Kung-sun Yen is a troublemaker, don't listen to him.'

When Hua-tzŭ heard he was disgusted with them.

'The one so eloquent for invading Ch'i is a troublemaker, the one so eloquent against it is a troublemaker too, and to call them both trouble-makers is to be another troublemaker.'

'What are we to do then?' said the King of Wei.

'Simply seek out how the Way applies to it.'

When Hui Shih heard of it, he introduced Tai Chin-jen to the King.

'There is a thing called a snail,' said Tai Chin-jen. 'Does Your Majesty know about it?'

'I do.'

'There is a state on the snail's left horn called Bash, and another on its right horn called Bully. From time to time they have territorial disputes and go to war. The corpses lie on the battlefield in tens of thousands, and when the victors harry the retreat they do not turn back for fifteen days.'

'Hmm. Aren't you trying to make a fool of me?'

'Allow me to substantiate it for Your Majesty. Do you think there are limits in the four directions and above and below?'

'There are no limits.'

'Do you know how to let the heart roam in the limitless, so that when it returns among the lands within our ken they seem hardly to exist?'

'I do.'

'Among the lands within our ken is Wei. Inside Wei is the city of Liang. Inside the city of Liang is Your Majesty. Between you and Bash and Bully, is there any distinction for disputation to make?'

'No distinction.'

When the guest went out the King was in a daze, as though he had lost his wits. Hui Shih presented himself.

'He's a Great Man,' said the King. '"Sage" is inadequate to describe him.'

'A puff into a flute', said Hui Shih, 'is like a scream, a puff into the ring on the hilt of your sword is no more than a wheeze. Yao and Shun are praised by everyone; but to cite Yao and Shun in front of Tai Chin-jen would be like uttering a single wheeze.' (*Chuang-tzŭ*, chapter 25)

• • •

Kung-sun Lung inquired of Prince Mou of Wei

'I learned as a child the Way of the former kings, and grew up enlightened about the conduct of Goodwill and Duty. I joined together the same and the different, parted the hard from the white, found the not so to be so and the unallowable allowable, frustrated the cleverness of the hundred schools and wore out the eloquence of one speaker after another; I seemed to myself peerless in understanding. Now I have heard the words of Chuang-tzŭ, and am dazed with wonder at them. I don't know whether it's that I don't think as coherently as he does or that I don't know as much as he does. At present there isn't a theme on which I would let a squawk out of my beak. May I ask the secret of it?'

Prince Mou, reclining elbow on armrest, took a long breath, looked up at the sky and smiled.

'Did you never hear about the frog in the deep-down well? He said to the turtle of the East Sea "A happy life I have! I go out and hop up on to the well-rail, come in and rest on the wall where there's a cracked tile. I have water to plunge in which comes right up to my armpits and holds up my chin, mud to wade in which submerges my feet so deep that you can't see the heels. Look round at the mosquito larvae and crabs and the tadpoles, not one of them compares with me. And to have the water of an entire hole at your command, the joy of a deep-down well where you can do as you please, is the highest of distinctions. Why don't you call now and then, sir, come in and see the view?"

'Before the turtle of the East Sea got his left foot in, his right foot was already jammed. Then as he shuffled backwards he told him about the sea. "A distance of 1,000 miles gives no idea of its size, a height of 8,000 feet gives no impression of its depth. In the time of Yü there were nine floods in ten years, but its water was not swelled by them; in the time of T'ang, there were seven droughts in eight years, but its shores were not shrunk by them. Not to be pushed into shifting when durations are too short or long, not to be driven forward or backward when the water is too much or little, this is the great joy of living in the East Sea."' Then the frog of the deep-down well was stunned with amazement to hear it, beside himself with bewilderment.

'To resume, if, without the wit even to know the border between the right and the wrong, you wish to have a full view of what Chuang-tzŭ talks about, it's like making a mosquito carry a mountain on its back, or a millipede gallop through the Yellow River; most certainly you are unequal to the burden. And someone who, without the wit to know how to evaluate supremely subtle words, makes the best of the advantages of his own time, is he not the frog in the deep down well?

'Moreover, that man treads the Yellow Springs and mounts the heights of the sky, has no north, no south, free to range in every direction, to merge in the immeasurable; he has no east, no west, begins in the black abyss, returns to the universal thoroughfare. But you in your bewilderment seek by scrutiny, grope by disputation, which is simply to use a tube to peer at the breadth of the sky, use an awl to poke into the depths of the earth; isn't the means after all too petty? You had better be gone.

'One thing more. Did you never hear of the boy of Shou-ling who mimicked the walk of Han-tan? He failed to catch on to the local knack, but lost his original gait too; all he could do was crawl home on his hands and knees. You had better be off now, or you will forget what you could originally do, lose your art.'

Kung-sun Lung's mouth gaped and would not shut, his tongue lifted and would not come down, then he broke away and ran. (*Chuang-tzŭ*, chapter 17)

• • •

In the ultimate Beginning there is nothing, without anything, without a name. It is that from which the One arises; there is the One, but not yet shaped. When things get it as the means by which they are generated, we call it the 'Power'.

In the not yet shaped there is division. The about to be so without anything intervening, this we call 'destined'. By halts in its motions it generates things. Things completing the patterns of their generation, this we call 'shaping'. Each shaped body, for the protection of the daemonic in it, has its own norm or rule; this we call its 'nature'.

By the training of our nature we recover the Power. When Power is at its utmost, we accord with the Beginning. In according we attenuate, in attenuating we become Great, and blend together the twitters of the beaks. When the twitters of the beaks blend, we are blended with heaven and earth.

> Their blending is a blurring,
> You seem a fool, you seem obscure.
> It is this one calls the Power from the depths.
> In accord with the ultimate course.

(*Chuang-tzŭ*, chapter 12)

NOTE   Except for a string of definitions in chapter 23 (translated p. 190 below) this is the most comprehensive attempt in *Chuang-tzŭ* to organise basic concepts in a cosmological scheme. It shares two traditional Chinese assumptions: (1) the generation of things from the ultimate root is not an event at the beginning of time but a continuing process; (2) the substantial condenses out of and dissolves into the insubstantial, the *ch'i* (for which our English equivalent is 'energy') which has the place in Chinese cosmology occupied by matter in ours. The basic metaphor behind the word 'matter' is of timber (Latin *materia*), inert and chopped up and put together by the carpenter; *ch'i* on the other hand is in the first place the breath, alternating between motion and stillness, extended in space but insubstantial, although condensing to become visible on a frosty day. The *ch'i* is conceived as becoming solider the more slowly it moves, with the more tenuous circulating within and energising the inert, for example as the *ching* 'quintessence', the vitalising fluid in the living body. In its ultimate degree of fineness we could think of it in Western terms as pure energy. Here this pure energy is identified, on the one hand with the Nothing in which things originate, on the other with the Power at the centre of the man which generates him and all those of his motions which are not chosen but 'destined', those which are on the point of coming about unless thought intervenes. By identifying himself with his most tenuous energies he assumes the larger view of the Great Man, and sees the utterances of philosophers (which Chuang-tzŭ compared to the twittering of birds, p. 52 above) as equally valid and invalid from their different viewpoints; his own language blends them all and seems nonsensical.

The identification of the ultimate with Nothing, although common in later Taoism, is surprising in *Chuang-tzŭ*, which generally seems to put the Way beyond the dichotomy of something and nothing, as both 'without anything' and 'without nothing' (cf. pp. 55, 103, 104, 153, 163f). Some scholars therefore prefer a different punctuation of the first sentence, which becomes ''In the ultimate Beginning there is that which is without nothing, which is without a name.''

5

Irrationalising the Way: 'Knowledge roams north'

In strong contrast with the rationalising approach of the 'Autumn floods' and 'Know-little' dialogues is a cycle of stories in 'Knowledge roams north' (chapter 22) and neighbouring chapters. In these to speak articulately about the Way is enough to show that one has not grasped it; the proof of insight is that you refuse to speak, or try but forget what you meant to say, or fall into a trance while you are being told, or see in a flash stimulated by some aphorism which on reflection seems meaningless, or burst into improvising song, or are moved by music without understanding what it is doing to you. In one of these stories Confucius propounds something very like the *kōans* ('What is the sound of one hand clapping?') with which Zen Buddhists set out to smash the frame of conceptual thinking a thousand years later. He asks, in the style of the debates of the sophists, whether it is 'allowable' that 'there is no past and no present, no start and no end, before you have children and grandchildren you do have children and grandchildren'. The question does not invite a 'Yes' but stirs some inkling which tongue-ties the disciple before he can answer 'No', and the point is made: 'Enough, that you failed to answer!' [28]

Chuang-tzŭ had declared that the man who has unlearned all distinctions and refuses to formulate a preferred alternative has no right even to say that 'Everything is one'. [29] Here too we find the Yellow Emperor admitting that he must be ignorant of the Way because he *knows* that everything is one. [30] To know is to have formulated verbally, which only the ignorant would be so inept as to do – more extravagant games are played with the word 'know' than Chuang-tzŭ himself ever ventured. The rationalising 'Great Man' philosopher, for whom knowledge is an unquestioned good, is revealed as the target when the Yellow Emperor, in his role of unenlightened wordmonger, actually uses his slogan, the 'Great Man'. [31]

In this cycle we may notice the fondness for allegorical figures (such as 'Knowledge'), for the legendary Yellow Emperor (a villain for the Primitivist and the Yangist), and for Confucius, who is treated as a pure spokesman of Taoism. The cycle seems homogeneous and probably belongs to the late third or second century BC, when the Yellow Emperor and the Lao-tzŭ of the book which bears his name have become the acknowledged representatives of Taoism. The 'Knowledge roams north' story quotes extensively from *Lao-tzŭ*, as do other Primitivist and 'School of Chuang-tzŭ' passages, but never the *Inner chapters*.

Knowledge roamed north to the banks of Black Water, climbed the hill of Loom-in-the-gloom, and met with Donothing Saynothing there. Said Knowledge to Donothing Saynothing

'I have questions I wish to put to you. What should I ponder, what should I plan, if I am to know the Way? What should I settle on, what should I work at, if I am to be firm in the Way? What course should I follow, what guide should I take, if I am to grasp the Way?'

Three things he asked, but Donothing Saynothing wouldn't reply. No, it wasn't that he wouldn't reply, he didn't know how to reply. Knowledge with his questions unanswered returned to the south of White Water, climbed to the top of Desert-of-doubts, and noticed Scatterbrain there. Knowledge repeated his questions to Scatterbrain.

'Ahaa!' said Scatterbrain, 'I know it, I'll tell you!'

Half-way through what he wanted to say he forgot what he wanted to say. Knowledge with his questions unanswered returned to the Imperial Palace, saw the Yellow Emperor, and put the questions to him.

'Don't ponder, don't plan,' said the Yellow Emperor, 'only then will you know the Way. Settle on nothing, work at nothing, only then will you be firm in the Way. Follow no course, take no guide, only then will you grasp the way.'

'You and I know it. The other two do not know it. Which of us are on to it?'

'That Donothing Saynothing is truly on to it, Scatterbrain seems to be, you and I have never been anywhere near it. The knower does not say, the sayer does not know, so the sage conducts a wordless teaching.

> The Way is incommunicable,
> The Power is impenetrable,
> Goodwill can be contrived,
> Duty can be left undone.
> The Rites are a shared pretence.

Hence it is said

"The Way lost, only then Power: Power lost, only then Goodwill: Goodwill lost, only then Duty: Duty lost, only then the Rites. The Rites are the Way's decorations and disorder's head."

And also

"The doer of the Way every day does less, less and less until he does nothing at all, and in doing nothing there is nothing that he does not do."

Now that we are things already, if we wish to revert and go home to the root, will it not be hard for us? Is it easy for any except the Great Man? Life is an adjunct of death, death is the origin of life, who knows where their threads go back? Man's life is the gathering of energy; when it gathers he's deemed alive, when it disperses he's deemed dead, and if even death and life are deemed adjuncts, is there anything I could still see as a misfortune?

'Therefore the myriad things are the One. As much of it as we find beautiful is deemed daemonic and precious, as much of it as we find ugly is deemed foul and rotten. The foul and rotten is transformed back into the daemonic and precious, the daemonic and precious is transformed back into the foul and rotten. Hence it is said: ''Pervading the world there is only the one energy.'' That is why the sage values the One.'

'When I asked Donothing Saynothing,' said Knowledge to the Yellow Emperor, 'he wouldn't reply to me. No, it wasn't that he wouldn't reply to me, he didn't know how to reply to me. When I asked Scatterbrain, half-way through what he wanted to tell me he wouldn't tell me. No, it wasn't that he wouldn't tell me, half-way through what he wanted to tell me he forgot. Now I ask you, and you do know, so why are we nowhere near it?'

'That the first of them was truly on to it was because he didn't know. That the next one seemed to be was because he forgot. That you and I have never been anywhere near it is because we do know it.'

When Scatterbrain heard about it he judged the Yellow Emperor knowledgeable about words. (*Chuang-tzŭ*, chapter 22)

NOTE   The explicit quotations are from *Lao-tzŭ* 38, 48. There are also phrases from *Lao-tzŭ* 56 and 2.

*   *   *

Gaptooth asked Reedcoat about the Way. Said Reedcoat

'If you adjust your body right and unify your vision, the harmony from Heaven will arrive. If you put together your knowledge and unify your measurements, the daemonic will come to lodge in you. The Power will be your glory, the Way will be your home. Have an innocent eye like a newborn calf and never go looking for precedents.'

Before he finished speaking Gaptooth had fallen asleep. Reedcoat was delighted, and departed singing as he walked

> 'A body like dry bone,
> A heart like dead ash.
> Genuine, the solid knowledge in him:
> He needs no precedents to hold himself up.
> Dim, dim, drowsy, drowsy,
> Hasn't a heart, you'll get no advice from him.

What man is that?' (*Chuang-tzŭ*, chapter 22)

. . .

Shun put a question to Ch'eng

'Can one succeed in possessing the Way?'

'Your own body is not your possession, how can you ever possess the Way?'

'If my own body is not my possession, who does possess it?'

'It is the shape lent to you by heaven and earth. Your life is not your possession; it is harmony between your forces, granted for a time by heaven and earth. Your nature and destiny are not your possessions; they are the course laid down for you by heaven and earth. Your sons and grandsons are not your possessions; heaven and earth lend them to you to cast off from your body as an insect sheds its skin. Therefore you travel without knowing where you go, stay without knowing what you cling to, are fed without knowing how. You are the breath of heaven and earth which goes to and fro, how can you ever possess it?' (*Chuang-tzŭ*, chapter 22)

. . .

Tung-kuo-tzŭ inquired of Chuang-tzŭ

'Where is it, that which we call the Way?'

'There is nowhere it is not.'

'Unallowable unless you specify.'

'It is in molecrickets and ants.'

'What, so low?'

'It is in the weeds of the ricefields.'

'What, still lower?'

'It is in tiles and shards.'

'What, worse than ever!'

'It is in shit and piss.'

Tung-kuo-tzŭ did not reply.

'Your questions, sir', said Chuang-tzŭ, 'miss the whole point. When Director Huo asks the Superintendent of the Market about assessing the pigs, the lower down in the pig he tests with his foot the more likely that if it is fat the whole pig is fat. You deal only in ''in no case'' and ''necessarily'', you have nowhere into which to escape from things. What is so of the ultimate Way is so too of the most comprehensive words. ''Universal'', ''everywhere'', ''all'', these three are different names for the same substance, what they point to is one.

'Suppose you come roaming with me in the palace where there is nothing at all, where you put things in their places by joining them as the same, without anywhere an end or limit? Suppose you come with me to *do* nothing at all? To be calm and still! Vacant and pure! In tune and at ease! To diffuse away our intents, to set out in no direction and arrive not knowing where, to come and go without knowing where it will stop. I have already been there and back but do not know where it ends, I have loitered in its immensities, but the greatest knowledge which enters it will not find its limits.

'What makes things things has no border between it and things; it is the borders which are between things which we mean by the borders of things. It is the unbordered borderer, the unbordered which borders. When we say "fill" and "empty", "decline" and "prime", what is deemed the filling or the emptying is not the filling-and-emptying, what is deemed the decline or the prime is not the decline-and-prime, what is deemed the root or the tips is not the root-and-tips, what is deemed the accumulating or the dispersing is not the accumulating-and-dispersing.' (*Chuang-tzŭ*, chapter 22)

. . .

Ah Ho-kan studied with Shen-nung under Old Dragon Lucky. Shen-nung was sleeping, elbow on armrest, in the daytime behind closed doors. Ah Ho-kan at noon flung wide the door and entered to say

'Old Dragon is dead!'

Shen-nung, leaning on the armrest, gripped his staff and rose to his feet, threw down the staff with a clatter on the floor and laughed.

'He that was Heaven to me knew that I am coarse and rude, that is why he abandoned me and died. Enough! Having no mad words to burst me open he died, wasn't that it?'

Yen Kang-tiao hearing of it said:

'The man who identifies himself with the Way has gentlemen from all over the world attaching themselves to him. Now of as much of the Way as the tip of an autumn hair he had not yet succeeded in settling on one part in ten thousand, yet he knew enough to keep back his mad words till he died – not to speak of the man who does identify himself with the Way!

> Look, it has no shape.
> Listen, it has no sound.
> In the discourse of men
> It is called the Mystery.

That's how one discourses about the Way, but it is not the Way.'

Then Translucence put a question to Infinity

'Do you know the Way?'

'I am ignorant.'

He put the same question to Donothing. Said Donothing

'I know the Way.'

'In your knowledge of the Way is there number?'
'There is.'
'What sort of number?'
'I know that the Way

> Can ennoble,
> Can demean,
> Can knot together,
> Can disperse.

This is how I know of number in the Way.'
Translucence asked Neverbegan about these words:
'Then of Infinity's not knowing it and Donothing's knowing, which is on to it and which is not?'
'Ignorance is profound, knowing it is superficial. Not knowing it is inward, knowing it is outward.'
Then Translucence looked upward and sighed.
'Is it by not knowing it that you know? Is it that if you do know you are ignorant? Who knows the knowing which is ignorance?'
'The Way is inaudible,' said Neverbegan, 'whatever you hear is something else. The Way is invisible, whatever you see is something else. The Way is ineffable, whatever you talk about is something else. Do you know that the shaper of shapes is unshaped? The Way does not fit a name.
'To answer any question about the Way is to be ignorant of the Way,' said Neverbegan. 'Even the asker about the Way never heard about the Way. In the Way there is nothing to ask about, in the question there is nothing to answer. To raise questions about the unquestionable is to ask about the finite, to offer answers to the unanswerable is to lack the inward. As for someone who lacks the inward and awaits questions about the finite, a man like that outwardly never has a full view of Space and Time, inwardly remains ignorant of the ultimate beginning. This is why he will never rise higher than Mount K'un-lun, never roam in the ultimate void.' (*Chuang-tzŭ*, chapter 22)

* * *

Lightflash put a question to Nothing's-there
'Are you something, sir? Or isn't there anything there?'
Getting no answer, Lightflash looked intently at his countenance. It was an unfathomable blank: looking at it all day he did not see, listening to it all day he did not hear, groping at it all day he did not touch.
'The utmost!' said Lightflash, 'which of us can attain to this? The most you can say about me is that something isn't there, but not yet that nothing

isn't there. He has got so far that there isn't anything there; by what road does one attain to this?' (*Chuang-tzŭ*, chapter 22)

. . .

Jan Ch'iu asked Confucius:
   'Is what preceded heaven and earth knowable?'
   'It is. Whether past or present makes no difference.'
   Jan Ch'iu was at a loss for a question and withdrew. Next day he presented himself again.
   'Yesterday I asked whether what preceded heaven and earth is knowable and you said, sir, that it is. Yesterday that came to me as an illumination, today it is obscure to me. May I ask what you meant?'
   'Yesterday when you were illuminated the daemonic caught on to it ahead of you. If today it is obscure to you, is that because you are seeking it for the undaemonic as well? There is no past and no present, no start and no end, before you have children and grandchildren you do have children and grandchildren – allowable?'
   Jan Ch'iu failed to reply.
   'Enough, that you failed to answer. One does not by being alive turn death into life, does not by being dead turn life into death. Is it that death and life depend on something else? There is something in which both of them count as one. Would whatever is born before heaven and earth be a thing? What makes things things is not a thing; the emergence of a thing cannot have preceded things. It was as when there are things in it, and being as when there are things in it will never cease. That ''the sage never ceases to love mankind'' takes its analogy from this.' (*Chuang-tzŭ*, chapter 22)

NOTE   The quotation in the last sentence is from p. 141 above.

. . .

Ch'eng of North Gate inquired of the Yellow Emperor
   'When Your Majesty performed the music of the Hsien-ch'ih in the wilds of Lake Tung-t'ing, the first time I heard it I was afraid, the next time I idled through it, the last time I was confused. I was overwhelmed, dumbfounded, could not get my bearings.'
   'I was afraid you might find it like that!' said the Yellow Emperor. 'First I played it as a work of man, but attuned to Heaven; I made it march in accord with Rites and Duty, but founded in the ultimate clarity.

> See the four seasons take their turns,
> The myriad things in sequence come to birth,
> Now it's glory, now decline,
> Peaceful and martial each in its proper place.

> Now the clear notes, now the dull,
> The Yin and Yang by tuning harmonised:
> Make their notes flow, make them spread,
> When first the hibernating insects stir
> *I* startle them awake with a clap of thunder!
> No conclusion rounds it off,
> There was no overture when it began,
> Now they're dying, now they're living,
> Now they're falling, now they're rising,
> To the norm that it proclaims there is no end. –

Yet nothing can be depended on to last. That is why you were afraid.

'Next I played it as the harmony of Yin and Yang, illumined by the torch-light of sun and moon. Its notes

> Can shorten, can lengthen,
> Can weaken, can harden,
> Altering and transforming it evens out in oneness,
> Does not submit to precedents and norms.
> In a valley it fills the valley,
> In a pit it fills the pit.
> It stops up the leaks, holds fast to the daemonic,
> And takes its measure from the things themselves.
> Its notes are vibrant and fluid,
> The names of its pieces radiant and sublime.

This is what makes the ghosts and daemons stay in the dark, and the sun, moon and stars proceed on their courses. I let it stop at the borders of the finite, but flow in the stream which has no stop. You tried to think about your destination but could not know it, peer after it but could not see it, pursue it but could not reach it. You stood baffled in the Way which has emptiness all around it, you "mumbled lolling on withered sterculia", eye and knowledge remained limited by what you wanted to see, effort remained constricted by what you wanted to pursue. We had failed to get anywhere, hadn't we? Shapes were solid, the gaps were empty; then a point came when you veered with the line of least resistance. You were veering with the line of least resistance, that is why you idled through it.

'Next I played it with notes which never idled, and tuned it to the spontaneous course of destiny. So it was as though

> Mingled and merged, densely sprouting,
> In the primaeval mass there is no shape.
> Spreading and scattering, leaving no trail behind,
> In the darkness of its depths there is no sound.
> It moves without direction,
> Resides in mystery.

> Some call it death,
> Some call it life,
> Some call it the fruit,
> Some call it the flower.
> Flowing onwards, dispersing outwards,
> It does not submit to any note as norm.

The world does not trust it, seeks confirmation from the sage. To be a 'sage' is to penetrate to the essential and follow destiny through. To have the impulses from Heaven unreleased but the five senses all ready at our disposal, it is this that is called the 'music from Heaven'. Wordlessly the heart delights in it. Therefore the House of Yu-yen composed a eulogy of it:

> "Listen, and you do not hear its sound.
> Look, and you do not see its shape.
> It fills up heaven and earth,
> And wraps round the limits in the six directions."

You were trying to listen to it, but there is nothing to perceive in it; that is why you were confused.

'The "joy" begins in fear; you were afraid, so saw the world as terrible. Next I played it idling along; you idled through it, so escaped from the world. I concluded it in confusion; you were confused, and so a fool; you were a fool, and so on the Way, the Way which can be carried around with you as your baggage.' (*Chuang-tzŭ*, chapter 14)

NOTE The Confucians immensely valued the ancient ceremonial music as a moral influence of the same order as the rites themselves (cf. the pairing of 'Rites and Music', as on p. 92 above). With the loss of all early Chinese music the present episode is inevitably obscure; but we can see that the three performances advance in a dialectical progression.

(1) A strict formal performance inspiring the Confucian virtues. Its structure is imposed on nature, artificially harmonising Yin and Yang, decreeing the reawakening of life in spring. In treating the listener as a member of society with moral duties, it also terrifies him with a sense of his transience in the relentless succession of life and death.

(2) A free spontaneous performance in which nature rebels against art. The listener is still trying to impose a human sense of purpose on to the music, and when he abandons the fruitless effort and surrenders to the flow thinks of himself as idling. ('Mumbled lolling on withered sterculia' alludes to Chuang-tzŭ's taunt at the sophist Hui Shih exhausting himself on intellectual problems, cf. p. 82 above.)

(3) The final perfect performance (and it is indeed the proof of your spiritual development as a Taoist if you can imagine this one) which breaks out of the dichotomy of order and licence. The listener is drawn into a whole in which he no longer distinguishes melody and rhythm, towards the quiescence in which all the senses are prepared to function but he does not yet hear, the ultimate silence out of which music emerges. As he returns to the source out of which things have not yet divided, he ceases to analyse and is content to be a fool. But only if he dares this surrender of rational and moral judgement; most of us want sages to tell us what to do.

The end of the episode alludes to the etymology of the word *yüeh*, 'music', which in spite of a very early divergence in pronunciation is cognate with *lo*, 'joy', and continued to be written with the same graph.

•   •   •

When Confucius was beleaguered between Ch'en and Ts'ai, and for seven days did not eat cooked food, he rested his left hand on a withered tree, with his right hand tapped a withered branch, and sang the air of the House of Yen. He had the instrument but did not beat in time, had the voice but did not keep to the notes of the scale; the sound of the wood and the voice of the man by their licence touched men's hearts.

Yen Hui, standing stiff with folded hands, rolled his eyes round to peep at him. Confucius was afraid that out of admiration he might incline to over-estimate him, out of love might incline to be sorry for him.

'Hui,' he said,

> 'Not to be affected by losses from Heaven is easy.
> – Not to be affected by gains from man is hard.
> —There is no start which is not an end.
> ——What is man's is one with what is Heaven's.

Who was it, the singer just now?'

'I venture to ask about "Not to be affected by losses from Heaven is easy".'

'Hunger and thirst, cold and heat, being pent in and stopped up and failing to advance, are heaven and earth proceeding on their courses, the off-flow from things as they turn in their cycles; the point is to let oneself flow on with them. As minister of a man you would not presume to desert him, and would you deny the fidelity with which you uphold even the Way of the Minister to the service with which we wait on Heaven?'

'What do you mean by "Not to be affected by gains from man is hard"?'

'If from my first employment everything goes easily for me, if titles and salary are mine for the asking and nothing stands in my way, I am being profited by other things, they do not derive from myself; my destiny, yes, is something external to me. A gentleman does not rob, a man of excellence does not steal; who am I to claim these things as my own?

'As the saying goes, "There is no wiser bird than the swallow." Where its eye ought not to alight it will not as much as look; even if it drops its berry it will abandon it and make off. When for all its dread of man it will pounce for it in the midst of men, it's simply that the altars of its homeland are located there.'

'What do you mean by "There is no start which is not an end"?'

'That which transforms the myriad things within it, yet does not know them as abdicating their places in it, how would it know when they finish, how would it know when they start? We have only to set our course straight and await them as they come.'

'What do you mean by ''What is man's is one with what is Heaven's''?'

'That something is man's is of Heaven, that something is Heaven's is also of Heaven. That man is unable to take as his own what is Heaven's is his nature. The sage by calmly identifying himself with the onflow lasts out his time.' (*Chuang-tzǔ*, chapter 20)

NOTE The song on which Confucius improvises is presumably the quatrain ascribed to the House of Yu-yen in the last episode (p. 166 above). He is displaying an admirable serenity in the face of the enemies who beset him. But he refuses to be admired, on the grounds that it is easier to be indifferent to misfortunes which are not one's own fault than to strokes of luck which are equally independent of merit.

The last item is another attempt to solve the obstinate dichotomy of Heaven and man. In the last resort not only the spontaneous in man, but the deliberate actions for which he takes credit, derive from Heaven. The opposite position, that the man is author even of his spontaneous reactions, is repudiated.

Political divisions are the work not of Heaven but of man, and the swallow knows nothing about them. May not some spot where swallows venture in spite of the throngs of people be the equivalent of their state capital?

The answer to the question 'Who was the singer?' is of course not the man Confucius but Heaven speaking through him.

. . .

Yen Hui asked of Confucius:

'When you step slow, sir, I too step slow; when you trot I trot too; when you gallop I gallop too. When you are off so fast that you are gone before the dust has settled, I am left staring after you.'

'Hui, what are you talking about?'

'When you step slow I too step slow – what you say I say too. When you trot I trot too – What you argue I argue too. When you gallop I gallop too – what you say about the Way I say too. As for ''When you are off so fast that you are gone before the dust has settled, I am left staring after you'', it is simply that without having to give your word you are trusted, that instead of joining a gang you have room for everyone, that although you have no regalia the people come swarming to pay court to you, and you do not know how it happens.'

'Oh, this does need to be looked into! There is no greater sorrow than the death of the heart, the death of the man is after all second to it. From the rising of the sun in the east to its setting in the far west, all the myriad things take their direction from it; whatever has eyes and feet cannot do its work without this, is present while this is out, absent when this goes in. It is like that with all things; there is something on whch they depend to die, and depend to live. Having once received man's finished shape, I remain untransformed as I wait for extinction, I move on the course set for me by other things, day and night without an interval, ignorant where it will end. What is fermenting in the finished shape, even a knower of destiny can never spy out in advance; this is how from day to day I become as I was about to be.

'You and I have been shoulder to shoulder all our lives, how sad that you should fail! I am afraid that you have gone on paying attention to what I used to attract attention. That is already extinct but you seek it supposing that it exists, it's seeking a horse in the market after everyone has gone. While I am being attentive to you I forget absolutely, while you are being attentive to me forget absolutely too. In any case, why be bothered by it? Even if I do go on forgetting the ''I'' which is past, there is something unforgetting which remains in me.' (*Chuang-tzŭ*, chapter 21)

6

Utopia and the decline of government

The Taoist idealisation of a spontaneity not disrupted by rational control becomes in political terms a faith in the spontaneously cohesive forces in society rather than in order deliberately imposed from above. *Lao-tzŭ*, which is written from the viewpoint of the prince, is pervaded by an awareness of the uselessness of trying to control political forces, which however the ruler can guide by locating the crucial points and moments and exerting the minimum pressure to the maximum effect. In most of *Chuang-tzŭ*, on the other hand, the viewpoint is that of the subject, who thinks things run better the less they are interfered with from above. Throughout the book we find sketches of Utopias flourishing in distant times or regions, and skeleton histories of the decline of government.[32] Here we assemble the few examples not translated elsewhere in this selection.

It was at one time popular in the West to think of the political philosophy of Taoism, even that of *Lao-tzŭ*, as anarchism. But most although not all Taoism accepts one basic premise of ancient Chinese thinking, that social order centres on a ruler, and depends on influences emanating from the *te*, the 'Power' in him, which moves men to follow him even without the backing of armed force, until it fades with the decline of the dynasty. Chuang-tzŭ himself gives the doctrine an unusual twist by hinting that the influences sustaining the social order may have nothing to do with the Emperor, and be emanating from some unnoticed sage in private life.[33] We do however find genuinely anarchistic Utopias, 'without ruler and subject', in the Taoist revival about AD 300, in *Lieh-tzŭ*, and most remarkably in Pao Ching-yen, who goes so far as to say that rulers were instituted not by Heaven but by the strong to oppress the weak.[34] Pao Ching-yen is known only by lengthy extracts in a suspiciously tame and conventional refutation of him by the great alchemist Ko Hung of the fourth century AD, who may well have invented him as a spokesman of subversive thoughts of his own. This suspicion is a reminder that any literary traces of such dangerous ideas would only be the top of what might be a considerable iceberg.

The essay with which we start this section is a complete chapter, 'Menders of nature' (chapter 16). It is an apology for the hermit's life by an author of uncertain date, not recognisable anywhere else in the book. His style is pedestrian but he is interesting as the first documented instance of a true anarchist in China, in the sense that he conceives the ideal community as living in a spontaneous oneness without any ruler at all. He dates the decline of the social order from the very first rulers, Sui-jen and Fu-hsi, and is explicit that the sage is a hermit except in the Utopian age, when he enters the world not to take office but to submerge in the primordial oneness. This anarchism is rooted in what looks like a Taoistic variation on the doctrine of the goodness of human nature preached by the Confucian Mencius. The author surprises us by recommending the Confucian moral virtues, which like Mencius he sees as inherent in human nature. He holds that if we still the passions and achieve the equilibrium in which tranquillity and awareness support and enhance each other, Goodwill and Duty become natural to us, and so do Music (which otherwise excites the passions) and Rites (which otherwise are empty formalities).

MENDERS OF NATURE

Menders of their nature by vulgar learning, trying to recover what they originally were; muddlers of the desires by vulgar thinking, trying to perfect their enlightenment – we may call them the blinkered and benighted people.

The men of old who cultivated the Way used calm to nurture knowing. They knew how to live but did not use knowing to *do* anything; one may say that they used knowing to nurture calm. When knowing and calm nurture each other, harmony and pattern issue from our nature. The Power is the harmony, the Way is the pattern. The Power harmonising everything is Goodwill, the Way patterning everything is Duty. Fellow-feeling with others when duty to them is understood is Loyalty; . . . . is Trustworthiness. When loyalty is pure and solid, return to the essential emotions is Music; when trustworthiness is activating expression and gesture, compliance with the forms is the Rites. When rites or music are practised without the rest, the world falls into disorder. If something else lays down the direction for you, you blinker your own Power. As for the Power, it will not venture blindly; and things which do venture blindly are sure to lose their natures.

The men of old lived in the midst of the merged and featureless, and found tranquillity and mildness with those of their own time. At this era the Yin and Yang were harmonious and peaceful, ghosts and daemons did no mischief, the four seasons were properly proportioned, the myriad creatures were unharmed, all that live escaped untimely death. Even if men did have knowledge, they had nothing to use it on. It is this that is called being in utmost oneness. At this era things were *done* by nobody, and were constantly so of themselves.

A time came when the Power declined, until Sui-jen and Fu-hsi began their rule over the world. The consequence was that there was compliance but not oneness. The Power declined a stage further, until Shen-nung and the Yellow Emperor began their rule over the world. The consequence was that there was control without compliance. The Power declined a stage further, until Yao and Shun began their rule over the world. It was only after they started the fashion of reforming through government, and rinsed the clean and broke up the unhewn, parted from the Way in order to become good, endangered the Power in order to act, that we relinquished our nature to follow after the heart. And it was only after hearts became perceptive and knowing, yet proved inadequate to settle the world, that we tacked culture on to them, added information to them. And it was only after culture obliterated substance, and information swamped the heart, that the people for the first time fell into perplexity and disorder, and had no means to return to the natural and essential in them and recover what they originally were.

Observing from this point of view, the age has abandoned the Way, the Way has abandoned the age. When the age and the Way have abandoned each other, from where would men of the Way rise up in the age, from where would the age be resurrected by the Way? As long as there is no means for the Way to rise up in the age or the age to be resurrected by the Way, even if a sage is not living in the mountain forests the Power in him has been obscured. It has been obscured, therefore it is not that he has chosen his obscurity.

As for what of old was meant by 'living in obscurity', it was not that someone was lying low and refusing to show himself, or keeping his words to himself and refusing to make them public, or hoarding his knowledge and refusing to let it out. It was that the fate of the times was too much awry. If he was lucky in his times and there was full scope for him in the world, he would return to the oneness and leave no trace behind. If he was unlucky in his times and there was no scope for him in the world, he would deepen his roots, secure the ultimate in him, and wait. This is the Way to save your life.

Those who of old guarded their lives did not use disputation to ornament knowing, did not use knowing to get the most out of the world, did not use knowing to get the most out of the Power. They stayed undaunted in their places and returned to their nature, what more would they have to do? It is inherent in the Way not to be trivially active, inherent in the Power not to be trivially perceptive. Trivial perceptions injure the Power, trivial actions injure the Way. Hence it is said, 'Simply set yourself in the true direction.' It is the happiness of being whole which is meant by success.

As for what of old was called 'success', it was not a matter of the caps and carriages of high office, it meant simply that nothing could add to their happiness. But what is called 'success' nowadays *is* a matter of caps and carriages. Caps and carriages do not belong to one's person by its nature and destiny. A thing which comes to us by chance is a lodger with us, and we who give it lodging can neither ward off its coming nor stop it going away. The men of old did not for the sake of caps and carriages indulge ambitions, did not on account of failure and need conform to the vulgar. It was simply that they were as happy in one condition as the other, and therefore had no worries. Nowadays when our lodgers depart we are unhappy, from which it can be seen that we never fail to lay waste even such happiness as we have. Hence it is said, 'Those who abandon their own selves to other things, and lose their nature to the vulgar are to be called "the wrong-way-round people".' (*Chuang-tzu*, chapter 16)

·   ·   ·

When Yi-liao of Shih-nan visited the Marquis of Lu, the Marquis looked careworn.

'Why that careworn look?' said the master from Shih-nan.

'I have studied the Way of the former kings and trained myself for the task inherited from my forebears, I revere the spirits and honour excellence, do everything myself and never rest for a moment, yet there is no escape from trouble. That is why I am so careworn.'

'My lord has a shallow method of ridding himself of troubles. The fox with his rich fur and the leopard with his spotted coat settle in the mountain forest and lurk in caves of the cliffs, to be left in peace. They go abroad at night and rest by day, to be on the alert. Even in hunger, thirst, hardship, they still go only one at a time to riverside or lakeside for food, that's how disciplined they are. If none the less they still do not escape trouble from the nets and traps, what fault is it of theirs? It's that their hides are a disaster to them. Now in your case isn't it the state of Lu which is your hide? I would wish my lord to strip his body and rid it of its hide, wash his heart and rid it of desires, and roam in the wilds where there is no other man.

'In South Yüeh there is a city, the name of the state is Steadfast Power. Its people are foolish and simple, are rarely selfish and have few desires. They know how to work but not how to store, and give without thought of a return. They do not know what a duty fits or a rite accompanies. Heedlessly, carelessly, they tread the path which opens out in every direction. They enjoy their lives and there's a fine funeral for them when they die. I would wish my lord to leave the state, abandon the customary, and go on a journey with the Way as his helper.'

'The Way there is long and perilous, and there are mountains and rivers between; I have no boat and carriage, what could I do?'

> 'Not to be stiff-necked,
> Not to be hidebound,
> Is all the carriage that you need.'

'The way there is dark and long, where no one dwells; whom would I have for a neighbour? I have no provisions, I have no food, how could I ever arrive there?'

'Reduce your expenditures, lessen your desires, and even unprovided you will have enough. May my lord ford the river and drift out over the ocean, gaze into the distance beyond sight of shores, go farther and farther in ignorance where there is an end. Those who come to see you off will all turn back from the shore. You will be far indeed from here.

'As owner of others you have ties, owned by others you have cares, which is why Yao neither owned nor was owned by other men. Therefore I would wish to free my lord from his ties, rid him of his cares, to wander alone in the kingdom of the ultimate void.' (*Chuang-tzŭ*, chapter 20)

•   •   •

Men Wu-kuei and Ch'ih-chang Man-chi were viewing the army of King Wu.

'He isn't up to the House of Yu-yü!' said Ch'ih-chang Man-chi; 'that's why we have run into these troubles.'

'If the world were equitably ordered, would the House of Yu-yü have been putting it in order? Or did it have to be disordered before he put it in order?'

'If it's an equitably ordered world that you want, why take the Yu-yü into account at all? When the Yu-yü medicined the sores, it was putting a wig on a head already bald, fetching a doctor for a man already sick. A filial son carrying the medicine to treat his compassionate father looks haggard in the face; to the sage it is an embarrassment.

'In an age when Power is at its utmost, they don't ''promote excellence'', don't ''employ ability''. The man above is like a treetop, the people are like wild deer. They are upright but do not know how to think of it as Duty, love each other but do not know how to think of it as Goodwill, are genuine but do not know how to think of it as Loyalty, keep their word but do not know how to think of it as Good Faith. Moved like the insects in spring their employers are each other, they do not think of government as a gift from above. Therefore their steps leave no footprints, their deeds leave no records behind them.' (*Chuang-tzŭ*, chapter 12)

NOTE   'Promoting excellence' and 'employing ability' are Mohist slogans for the reform of government, which became widely accepted even in the Confucian school as the old hereditary fiefs developed into bureaucratised states. The following displaced fragment may continue the same story. It explains that there need be no righteous wars (like King Wu's) if the people follow the Heaven which moves them spontaneously, not the Heaven which men invent as the authority for their own doctrines.

'An avenger does not smash Excalibur, even the most hot-tempered man does not resent a tile blown by the wind. That is why the world is peaceful and equitable. Therefore that there are no disorders from invasion and battle, no punishments by execution and extermination, is because they follow this Way. They throw open not man's Heaven but Heaven's Heaven. In whoever throws open Heaven the Power is born, in whoever throws open man violence is born.

> Not suppressing the Heaven in them,
> Not deluded by the man in them,
> The people are near to acting on their true promptings.'

(*Chuang-tzŭ*, chapter 19)

·   ·   ·

When Yao ruled the empire, Po-ch'eng Tzŭ-kao was set up as lord of a fief.

After Yao passed the throne to Shun, and Shun to Yü, Po-ch'eng Tzü-kao resigned his fief and took up the plough.

Yü went to visit him and found him in the fields ploughing. Yü approached briskly, obeying the etiquette for an inferior, stood before him, and asked:

'Sir, formerly when Yao ruled the empire, you were set up as lord of a fief. After Yao passed the throne to Shun, and Shun to myself, you resigned your fief to take up the plough. May I ask why?'

'Formerly when Yao ruled the empire, the people were willing without being rewarded, were in awe without being punished. Nowadays you do reward and punish, yet the people have become malevolent. From now on the Power will deteriorate, from now on punishment will prevail; the misrule of coming ages has its beginning now. Why don't you leave me alone? Don't interrupt my work.'

Busy with his ploughing, he did not turn his head.

(*Chuang-tzü*, chapter 12)

NOTE There is evidence of a wide variety of hermits with different philosophies and objections to the existing order (for example, the 'Tillers', cf. p. 169), and this story is unlikely to be Taoist in origin. Yü was the first ruler to hand the throne to his own son instead of the best available man, thus founding the first dynasty, the Hsia. In a longer version of this story, preserved in chapter 7 of the *Hsin-hsü* (a miscellany of the first century BC), Po-ch'eng Tzü-kao's main objection is to the introduction of hereditary succession.

7

The cult of immortality

The emperor Shih-huang-ti (221–210 BC), the reunifier of China under the Ch'in dynasty, is the first firmly dated Chinese who pursued the elixir of life. The hope of physical immortality soon became an obsession, to a degree unequalled up to the present in any other civilisation. The methods tried included life-prolonging herbs, mineral drugs concocted by alchemists, abstention from cereals, meditative techniques with controlled breathing, sexual and other physical exercises, magical or religious rites. Those who first introduced these arts at court were magicians (*fang-shih*) from the north-eastern states of Ch'i and Yen, centres of the Yin-Yang school. With the decline of the Hundred Schools of ancient philosophy and the polarisation of all trends of thought as either official, respectable and therefore 'Confucian' or unofficial, disreputable and therefore 'Taoist', the promoters of the elixir had to gravitate to the latter. From the first century AD at the latest, the salesmen of immortality classed themselves as Taoist, and soon afterwards the Taoist religion founded by Chang Tao-ling (*c.* AD 142) extended the promise of immortality from the elite patrons of magicians and alchemists to the common man. It is a fascinating irony of intellectual history that the label 'Taoism' came to apply both to a philosophy which demands before anything else reconciliation to the natural cycle of life and death, to the decay of the body and the loss of personal identity (in *Lieh-tzŭ*, *c.* AD 300, just as much as in *Chuang-tzŭ*), and to magical, religious or proto-scientific measures for reversing the spontaneous course of biological process to fulfil the most unrealistic of our hopes, to live for ever.[35]

The *Inner chapters* have a couple of possible references to legendary figures who lived for ever. The daemonic man in the mountains of Ku-yi who 'does not eat the Five Grains'[36] is certainly dieting himself like an immortal, although Chuang-tzŭ does not call attention to the matter. Chuang-tzŭ also mentions the ascension of the Yellow Emperor;[37] in later legend at least, he did not die but rose into the sky on the back of a dragon. However, the dissolution of the body and the loss of personal identity are affirmed or assumed not only in the *Inner chapters* but in the Primitivist essays (which use the slogan 'fathoming what our nature and destiny essentially is'),[38] and the Yangist, the Syncretist and most of the 'School of Chuang-tzŭ' episodes. In the whole of this heterogeneous collection, in which we can expect to find any tendency of the fourth, third, or second centuries BC which came to be classable as Taoist, there are only two passages which recommend the pursuit of immortality. They appear among the miscellaneous stories in chapters 11 and 12 of the *Outer chapters*, and are interesting as the earliest evidence of interaction between philosophical Taoism and the cult of immortality.

In spite of their diametrically opposed attitudes to the problem of death, the two movements did converge at one place, the technique of meditation. In Taoism, as in Indian Yoga, the stilling of the mind by controlled breathing and posture is among other things good for health. It enables one to live out man's natural term as well as reconcile oneself to living no longer. The reconciliation is in any case to destruction as a separate self; if you can fully identify yourself with the cosmic process within which personal death is a trivial episode, in becoming one with the universe you do achieve a kind of immortality. On the other side too, there is no firm dividing line between the eater of elixirs of immortality and the health freak who wants only to live out his term, indeed none throughout Chinese history between the proto-sciences of medicine and of alchemy. Thus the Syncretistic chapter 'Finicky notions', translated below,[39] recommends the cultivation of the 'daemonic' and 'quintessential' energies as a means to reconciliation with death ('In his death he transforms with other things ... His dying is like going to rest'), but also to living out one's term, and declares that no more is needed to achieve the ends of the physical exercises called *tao-yin*, 'guiding (the breath) and pulling (the limbs)'; evidently the practitioners of these had a more modest aim than immortality.

Of the two stories translated below, the tale of Kuang-ch'eng tzŭ is a curious adaptation of philosophical Taoism. Kuang-ch'eng-tzŭ lives to the age of 1,200 years by closing the senses to the outside world; he thus prevents the escape of the daemonic and quintessential energies, which remain in the body and continue to vitalise it. However, this is only a temporary solution. He will win his final escape by the philosophical Taoist union with the cosmic process, conceived not as a flight beyond life and death but as actual immortality. At the end of the story the apparently outrageous claim to live for ever while everyone else dies means presumably that by expanding himself to become the universe he escapes the death which is the fate of mere individual selves.

The other story, of Yao and the frontier guard, has nothing in common with philosophical Taoism. Presumably it comes from the magicians of the early Han, not yet Taoist even in name. Far from preaching renunciation, it promises, through prayers or rites, the blessings of wealth, numerous progeny, and immortality in a paradise, the 'realm of Ti (God)'.

When the Yellow Emperor had reigned as Son of Heaven for nineteen years, and his writ ran throughout the empire, he heard that Kuang-ch'eng-tzŭ was living on Mount K'ung-t'ung, so he went to visit him.

'Sir, I hear that you have attained the utmost Way, and venture to ask about the utmost Way's quintessence. I wish to pick out the quintessences of heaven and earth and use them to assist the Five Grains and nurture the people. I wish too to put the Yin and Yang to service in order to perfect the growth of everything that lives. What would you advise?'

'What you wish to ask about', said Kuang-ch'eng-tzŭ, 'is the substance of things, but it is the ruins you have made of them that you are trying to put to service. Ever since you have been ruling the empire, it has rained before the clouds even gathered, the plants and trees have shed their leaves before they were even yellow, the light of sun and moon has got dimmer and dimmer. You of the shallow fawner's heart, why should you deserve to be told about the utmost Way?'

When the Yellow Emperor withdrew, he relinquished the empire, built a special house, matted it with white reeds, and lived in retirement for three months.

He went again to request an audience. Kuang-ch'eng-tzŭ was asleep with his face turned south. The Yellow Emperor approached on his knees, north-ward like a subject before the throne, kowtowed twice and asked

'Sir, I hear you have attained the utmost Way, and venture a question. How shall I rule the body to make it long-lasting?'

Kuang-ch'eng-tzŭ rose with a start.

'A good question! Come, I shall tell you about the utmost Way.

> The quintessence of the utmost Way
> Is dark, dark, secret, secret:
> The apex of the utmost Way
> Is mystery, mystery, silence, silence.
> Look at nothing, listen to nothing,
> Cling to the daemon and be still,
> The body will correct itself,
> Always be still, always be pure,
> Don't put your body under strain,
> Don't let your quintessence waver,
> And then it will be possible to live on and on.
>
> When the eye has nothing that it sees,
> The ear nothing that it hears,
> The heart nothing that it knows,
> Your daemon will abide in the body,
> And then the body lives on and on.
> Take care of the inside of you,
> Shut up the outside of you,
> To know too much is to decay.

For you I shall ascend above the supremely bright, as far as the source of the utmost Yang; for you I shall enter the gate of the dark and secret, as far as the source of the utmost Yin.

> Heaven and earth have their own offices,
> The Yin and Yang their own treasuries.
> Take care to abide in your own self,
> And other things will flourish of themselves.

I abide where they are one, in order to settle where they harmonise, and so I have been training myself for 1,200 years and my body has never decayed.'

The Yellow Emperor kowtowed twice.

'It is Kuang-ch'eng-tzŭ whom I declare my "Heaven".'

'Come,' said Kuang-ch'eng-tzŭ, 'I shall tell you. The things which belong to That are boundless, but all men think they have an end; the things which belong to That are immeasurable, but all men think they have a limit. Who-ever grasps my Way is of the emperors that were and the kings that shall be, whoever misses my Way begins in the light of day and afterwards is earth. Now everything that springs forth is born from earth and returns to earth.

Therefore I shall leave you to enter the gate of the boundless and roam in the fields of the limitless.

> I shall be a third luminary with the sun and moon,
> I shall share the constancy of heaven and earth.
> Close up to me, a blur!
> Far away from me, a blank!
> Yes, the rest of men die every one,
> And I alone remain!'

(*Chuang-tzŭ*, chapter 11)

.   .   .

Yao was touring Hua. Said a border guard of Hua:
'Hmm, a sage. Let me pray for the sage. I promise you a long life, sage.'
'Don't want that,' said Yao.
'I'll make you rich, sage.'
'Don't want that.'
'I'll see you have many sons, sage.'
'Don't want that.'
'Long life, wealth, many sons, other men desire, why not you?'
'The more sons the more fears, the more wealth the more bother, the longer the life the more humiliations. These three are no use in nurturing Power, so I don't want them.'
'At first I thought "Is he a sage?", now that's how you are, a "gentleman". When Heaven breeds the myriads of the people it makes sure that they have jobs to do; however many sons you have, if you find jobs for them why should you fear for them? However rich you are, if you give others their shares, why should you be bothered by them? As for the sage,

> A quail as he perches, a chick as he eats,
> On his bird's voyage he leaves no track.
> When the empire has the Way,
> He's companion to all things as they thrive.

> When the empire lacks the Way
> He cultivates the Power in the comfort of retirement.
> A thousand years and he's weary of the world,
> Departs and rises up as an immortal.

> He rides upon those white clouds
> All the way to the realm of God.
> None of the three misfortunes comes to him,
> Never does disaster strike his body.

Then why should he get humiliated?'

The border guard made off, Yao went after him.
'Permit me a question.'
Said the border guard
'Stand back!' (*Chuang-tzŭ*, chapter 12)

8

'The essentials of our nature and destiny'

'The essentials of our nature and destiny' is a phrase which attracts attention especially in the Primitivist essays, where it seems to operate as a slogan. It is explained in a brief essay preserved at the head of chapter 19, 'Fathoming nature'. Its basic principle is to allow life to follow the natural course laid down for it by Heaven, and accept death when it comes. To pursue worldly ambitions involves us in anxieties about external things, and wears out the 'quintessence', the vitalising seminal fluid which sustains health, growth and generation. Nor is there any point in fussing about health; the way to live long is not to worry about it. The phrase may be seen as a slogan against worldliness on the one hand and on the other the cult of prolonging life which obsessed some of the unworldly.

The word *hsing*, 'nature', is derived from *sheng*, 'be born, live', and written with the same graph distinguished by a radical. A thing's nature is seen as the course which its life must follow if it is to grow to completion and last out its term. In many cases at least the radical was supplied only in a later graphic standardisation of the text, and in 'essentials of nature and destiny', as in such phrases as 'tend nature', 'injure nature', where the choice between 'nature' and 'life' makes no difference to the sense, the scribal tradition was hesitant and inconsistent in adding it. In the present translation we shall stick consistently to 'nature'.

The continuity of the thought is twice interrupted by what look like hostile comments by an irritated reader; we print them between the lines in italics.

Whoever fathoms the essentials of our nature will not busy himself with anything irrelevant to life. Whoever fathoms the essentials of our destiny will not busy himself with what knowledge can do nothing about.

To nurture the body, one in the first place becomes dependent on other things; but sometimes the things are more than enough yet the body remains unnourished. To stay alive, the precondition is not to part from the body; but sometimes without parting from the body one has ceased to be alive. Life's coming cannot be resisted, its going cannot be stopped Alas! the worldly think nurture of the body is sufficient to preserve life; and if really it is insufficient to preserve life, why should worldly things be worth doing?

(Even if they aren't worth doing, there's no escape from doing what has to be done.)

For one who wishes to escape from concern with the body, the best course is to abandon worldly ambitions. Abandoning them, he will be without ties; without ties, his course will be straight and smooth; if it is straight and smooth, he renews life side by side with what is other than himself; and to be renewing life is to be almost there.

If we abandon affairs the body will not be worn out, if we forget about life the quintessence will be unimpaired. When the body is intact and the

(Are affairs so unimportant that we can abandon them, is life so unimportant that we can forget about it?)

quintessence restored, we become one with Heaven. Heaven and earth are the father and mother of the myriad things.

> Cohering we become separate,
> Dissolving become what first we were.
> To have body and quintessence unimpaired,
> It is this that is called 'being able to move on'.

Through the quintessential to the still more quintessential, we return to becoming the helpers of Heaven.

(Chuang-tzŭ, chapter 19)

. . .

Who fathoms the essentials of our nature is sublime, who fathoms how to know is petty. Who fathoms the universal destiny follows where it takes him, who fathoms a little destiny is the creature of his luck.

(Chuang-tzŭ, chapter 32)

9

Stray ideas

When in an ancient text we stumble on what looks like a modern idea, we are always faced with the question whether thinkers within different conceptual schemes can be saying the same thing. It is pointless to exclaim in wonder 'So they knew that thousands of years ago!', but stimulating to explore these unexpected points of contact as critical places where ancient thinkers reveal both their nearness and their remoteness from ourselves.

Here we assemble four examples.

1 EVOLUTION

A story about Lieh-tzǔ talking to a skull (as Chuang-tzǔ himself does elsewhere)[40] leads on to a remarkable passage which describes how all living things, including man, develop out of each other and ultimately from primeval germs in the water. This may or may not be the continuation of Lieh-tzǔ's address to the skull. (Our translation assumes that it is.) In any case its background is the Taoist thesis that death does not matter since personal identity is illusory; my birth and death are no more than moments in the universal process of transformation.

This passage, repeated with modifications in chapter 1 of *Lieh tzǔ* (*c.* AD 300), has long attracted the attention of Western readers as an early example of evolutionary thinking. Certainly the Taoist agrees with Darwin on some of the issues on which Westerners found him most challenging; he thinks of species as mutable and metamorphosing into or generating each other, sets no limits to their fluidity, and includes man himself in the process. Within the Taoist scheme of things none of this is strange or shocking, as it was to nineteenth-century Christians. Further, he has the new, simple and beautiful thought that one might, by stringing together observed metamorphoses of plants and insects, and reported prodigies such as human children being born of horses, show how a man could evolve from the simplest forms of life. But he sees this only as a striking illustration of the continuity of man with the rest of nature, with a bearing on the problem of reconciliation with death; he is not trying to explain the origin of species.

The chain from the primordial germs to man has some breaks in the standard text of *Chuang-tzǔ*, but they are certainly due to textual mutilation. In the present translation we fill them from the *Lieh-tzǔ* parallel (which has only one break, stuffed with metamorphoses from other sources), and from the *Chuang-tzǔ* passage as quoted in chapter 887 of the tenth-century encyclopedia *T'ai-p'ing yü-lan* (which fills this gap as well). But it is not a true evolutionary chain. What matters for the Taoist is not the chronological sequence but the possibility at any time of one thing turning into or generating another. Thus he has two lines of descent from the *yang-hsi*, and two leading to the *yi-lu*.[41]

The identification of much of the fauna and flora, including some for which I have ventured English equivalents, remains problematic. But the one word which is crucial to the understanding of the whole is *chi*, here translated 'germ'. *Chi* is a word applied generally to the ultimate source of movement, growth or change in a thing or situation. In a machine it is 'the thing which makes it go' (we use this equivalent on p. 186 below), for example the trigger of a crossbow. When Chuang-tzŭ asks whether the cycles of the heavenly bodies have something which 'triggers them off',[42] he is using the same Chinese word.

Lieh-tzŭ on a journey took a meal by the roadside, and saw a hundred-year-old skull. He plucked a stalk and said, pointing at it,

Only you and I know that you have never died, have never lived. Is it really you who are miserable, I who am happy?

'In seed there is a germ. When it gets to water it becomes the water-plantain, when it gets to the border between water and land it becomes the "frog's coat", when it breeds on dry land it becomes the plantain. When the plantain gets to rich soil it becomes the "crow's foot". The root of the "crow's foot" becomes ground-beetles, its leaves become butterflies. The butterfly in a short while metamorphoses into an insect which breeds under the stove and looks as though it has sloughed its skin, named the *ch'ü-to*. The *ch'ü-to* after 1,000 days becomes a bird named the *kan-yü-ku*. The saliva of the *kan-yü-ku* becomes the *ssü-mi*, which becomes the vinegar animalcule *yi-lu*.

'The animalcule *yi-lu* goes on being born from the animalcule *huang-k'uang*, which goes on being born from the *chiu-yu*, which goes on being born from the gnat, which goes on being born from the firefly, which goes on being born from the *yang-hsi*. The *yang-hsi* staying alongside a bamboo which for a long time has not sprouted gives birth to the *ch'ing-ning*, which gives birth to the leopard, which gives birth to the horse, which gives birth to man. Man in due course goes back into the germs. The myriad things all come out from the germs, all go into the germs.' (*Chuang-tzŭ*, chapter 18)

2 SELF-ALIENATION

In a passage known only by quotation, said to be from the *Inner chapters*,[43] Chuang-tzŭ (if he is indeed the author) plays boldly with the noun *wu*, 'thing', using it verbally as 'to thing' (make into or treat as a thing), to mark off as a thing separate from other things and from oneself. He is writing about the Way:

'It is shapeless, therefore shapes everything; it is thingless, therefore *things* everything. The unthinged is able to thing things, the unshaped is able to shape shapes. Therefore the shaper of shapes and thinger of things is not a shape and is not a thing. Is it not after all a delusion to go looking among shapes and things for what is neither shape nor thing?'

We have elsewhere translated the phrase *wu wu*, 'thinging things', expanding it to 'treating things as things' or 'making things into things'.[44] In one of the passages it is not the Way but the sage who 'things things and is not thinged by things', and the marking off is primarily of other things from himself. He sees all things as external to him, and refuses to let them turn him into one more thing dragged along by its involvements with the rest:

'If you treat things as things and are not made into a thing by things, how can you be tied by involvements?'[45]

Like Hegel's 'alienation', which it calls to mind, this very abstract idea has a practical application. When Taoists contrast things with self, they are generally thinking in the first place of property. As will be seen from the passage below, the sage is able to recognise his possessions as mere things, external and dispensable, and to 'exist alone' in perfect detachment from them. Others, however, turn themselves into things by becoming identified with their possessions, cannot exist without them. The Confucian Hsün-tzǔ similarly speaks of the superiority of the gentleman to the farmer, merchant or craftsman who, expert in one thing, is identified with his profession:

'Whoever is expert in a thing is by means of the thing made into a thing; whoever is expert in the Way treats every thing as a thing.' (*Hsün-tzǔ*, chapter 21)

When Chinese speak of being 'thinged', and Marxists and others in the West of 'alienation' (equally difficult and slippery terms originating in metaphysics), to what extent have we the right to say they are expressing the same idea?

Alas for the ignorance of owners of lands! To own a land is to own a great thing, and the owner of a great thing cannot treat as a thing. In treating as things one is not made into a thing, that is how one treats things as things. If it is clear to you that 'what makes things things is not a thing', you can do better than merely reign over the hundred clans of the empire!

> Go in, go out of the Six-way-oriented,
> Go roaming over the Nine Regions.
> Depart without anything, come without anything,
> It is this that is meant by 'exist without anything.'

The man who exists without anything – his is the rank which is to be judged supreme. (*Chuang-tzǔ*, chapter 11)

3 DOWN WITH TECHNOLOGY!

Chuang-tzǔ's kind of Taoist, with his assumption of decline from a primeval state of perfection, and antipathy to such civilised artificialities as morality, logic and organised government, might be expected to look askance at the rather hectic pace of technological progress after the belated start of the Iron Age in China in the sixth century BC. However, although Taoist writers in *Chuang-tzǔ* show no gratitude for technological advances, ignoring Sui-jen's discovery of fire, Fu-hsi's of hunting and Shen-nung's of agriculture even when mentioning them as sages, they seldom positively disapprove. The 'Primitivist' writer is unrepresentative, as we imply by giving him that name. He does speak of such cunning devices as stringed arrows, basket-nets and pitfalls as disordering the fish, birds as animals, and may even be showing some awareness of ecological damage when he says that we 'dissipate the quintessences in the mountains and rivers' and 'interrupt the round of the four seasons'.[46]

However, even the Primitivist uses technological examples primarily as metaphors; he objects to people wanting to manipulate human nature as the potter moulds clay rather than to the potter himself. Such remarks as 'damaging the unhewn block to make vessels is the crime of the craftsman'[47] can hardly be taken literally. His criticisms centre not on practically useful devices but on moralism, ritualism, logical disputation, arts and luxuries.

But there is one famous episode in the *Outer chapters* in which a hermit coldly rejects a labour-saving device proposed by a disciple of Confucius. His objection is not to social or ecological effects but to the deliberate calculation of benefit and harm, disruptive of Taoist spontaneity, which motivates the search for new inventions. It would evidently be pointless to reply that in tilling and irrigating he is himself benefiting from past discoveries; these are already customary exercises which do not start off that weighing of prospects which divorces the reasoning man from nature.

The story concludes with a comment by Confucius which many understand as qualifying the criticism of technology. They read an ambiguous sentence, as 'He [the hermit] perceives one side of the matter but does not know about the other'; but in chapter 7 of *Huai-nan-tzŭ* (*c*. 120 BC) the sentence reappears in a plainer context, where it can only be understood as 'He perceives the oneness of everything, does not know about duality in it'. Our translation follows the second alternative. It explains why the hermit is said to preserve the tradition of Hun-t'un, the mythical emperor who in the very last episode of the *Inner chapters* represents the primal blob out of which the myriad things have not yet begun to divide.

Tzŭ-kung travelled south to Ch'u, turned back towards Chin, and while passing along the south bank of the Han river saw an old man looking after his vegetable garden. He had dug out a passage down into the well, from which he emerged with a pitcher in his arms to water the soil. Splash, splash! it was costing him a lot of effort with the poorest of results to show for it.

'Suppose you had a contrivance', said Tzŭ-lung, 'which in one day would irrigate a hundred fields. You would have plentiful results to show for very little effort; wouldn't you prefer that?'

The gardener lifted his head and looked at him.

'How does it work?'

'The thing which makes it go is a piece of wood chiselled to make it heavier at the back end than at the front. It pulls up the water as though you were plucking it straight out of the well, as fast as bubbles in a boiling pot. It's called a well-sweep.'

The gardener made an angry face and said with a sneer:

'I heard from my teacher that whoever has contrivances with tricks to make them go is sure to have activities with tricks to make them go. Whoever has activities with tricks to make them go is sure to have a heart with tricks to make things go. If a heart with tricks to make things go is lodged inside your breast, the pure and simple will not be at your disposal. If the pure and simple is not at your disposal, the daemonic and vital will be unsettled. Anyone in whom the daemonic and vital is unsettled, the Way will not sustain. It isn't that I don't know, it's that I would be ashamed to make it.'

Tzŭ-kung, too embarrassed to meet his eye, looked down at the ground without answering.

After a while the gardener said:

'What sort would you be?'

'A disciple of Confucius.'

'Aren't you those people who make themselves so learned to get to be like the sages, go in for fancy talk so that they can look down on the crowd, and sing sadly to their lonely zithers to attract attention from the world? If you would forget about your daemonic energies and let your bodies fall away from you, there might be hope for you. When you can't put even your own selves in order, what time have you to waste on putting the world in order? Go away, don't interrupt my work.'

Tzŭ-kung was shocked out of countenance, in too much of a dither to pull himself together. He had travelled another thirty miles before he recovered.

'That man just now,' said a disciple, 'what would he be, sir? Why was it that when you saw him you looked so upset, you weren't yourself for the rest of the day?'

'I used to think there was just one man in all the world, I never knew there was anyone like that. I heard the Master say "In enterprises seek the practicable, in results the successful; to show the most results for the least effort is the Way of the Sage." Now it turns out to be otherwise. Abide by the Way and the Power stays whole, where the Power stays whole the body stays whole, where the body stays whole the daemon stays whole; and the daemon staying whole is the Way of the Sage. Leaving life to take its course, he moves on side by side with the people, and does not know his destination, unthinking, perfect in innocence! Results, profit, tricks to make things go, cunning, must be absent from the heart of such a man. Such a man goes only where he himself intends, does nothing which is not from his own heart. Even if the whole world praises him, and he wins acceptance for his opinions, he is too proud to notice: even if the whole world blames him, and he is alone in his opinions, he is too indifferent to care. One for whom there is neither gain nor loss in the world's praise or blame may be pronounced a 'man in whom Power is whole'! It is we ourselves who deserve to be called drifters of the wind and waves.'

When he was back in Lu he told Confucius about it.

'He is a follower and practitioner of the tradition of the House of Hun-t'un,' said Confucius. 'He perceives the oneness of everything, does not know about duality in it; he orders it as inward, does not order it as outward. Someone who by illumination enters into simplicity, by Doing Nothing reverts to the unhewn, who identifies himself with his nature and protects his daemon, as he roams among the vulgar, is he really so astonishing to you? In any case, when it comes to the tradition of the House of Hun-t'un, how would you and I be adequate to understand it?' (*Chuang-tzŭ*, chapter 12)

4 IT ISN'T HIS FAULT, IT'S SOCIETY

That crime is inevitable unless people are decently fed was widely understood in ancient China. The Confucian Mencius, Chuang-tzŭ's contemporary, observed that banditry increases with bad harvests, and declared that a ruler who merely punishes crime, without taking steps to ensure an adequate food supply, is setting a trap for his own people.[48] But the next episode is unusual in tracing the origin of crime directly to the institution of rank and property (not, as the Primitivist does, simply to the institution of codified morality, cf. pp. 207–10 below), and also for its intensity of moral passion, unexpected in a Taoist.

Po Chü had been studying under Old Tan.
'Let me go and see something of the world,' he said.
'Enough of that! Anywhere in the world it's the same as here.'
But he persisted.
'Where will you start?' said Old Tan.
'I shall start from Ch'i.'
Arriving in Ch'i, he saw the corpse of a criminal exposed in the market-place. He pushed it over onto its back, took off his court robe and shrouded it. Crying out to Heaven he bewailed it:
'Alas, alas! The whole world shares a great calamity, and you are the one to suffer it ahead of us. They say, "Let no one rob, let no one murder." But it was only after grades of esteem were instituted that men noticed they had grievances, only after property was accumulated that they noticed things to quarrel over. Now that we have instituted what stirs up grievances and accumulated what stirs up quarrels, and so impoverished and distressed their lives that they never have time to rest, how can we be surprised if it ends in this?
'Of old those who were lords of men ascribed successes to the people and took failures on themselves, thought the credit for someone's honesty belonged to the people and the discredit for someone's crookedness belonged to themselves. Therefore if a single body was disfigured by punishment they retired and blamed themselves. Nowadays it is otherwise. They keep things more secret yet fault you for being unaware, make difficulties greater yet condemn you for hanging back, make responsibilities heavier yet punish you for being unequal to them, set the destination farther off yet execute you for failing to arrive. When the people are at the end of their wits and their strength, the next stage is to lie; every day there is more lying, how can knights or people do without lying? If their strength is insufficient they lie, if their wit is insufficient they bully, if their property is insufficient they rob. For the deeds of the thief and the robber, whom shall we call to account?'
(*Chuang-tzŭ*, chapter 25)

10

Miscellaneous

When Yen Hui went east to Ch'i, Confucius looked worried. Tzǔ-kung left his mat to inquire

'Your disciple ventures to ask, sir, why you look so worried about Hui going east to Ch'i?'

'A good question of yours, that! Formerly Kuan-tzǔ said something which I think very good: "A bag too small cannot hold something big, a well-rope too short cannot draw from deep down." Such a man recognises that one is destined to accomplish only so much, is shaped to be fit only for so much; no matter how, it cannot be increased or reduced. I am afraid that Hui will speak with the Marquis of Ch'i about the Way of Yao, Shun and the Yellow Emperor, and emphasise his points with sayings of Sui-jen and Shen-nung. The Marquis will search within himself for something he will not find. Not finding it, he will be perplexed; and when the man you are advising is perplexed, you die.

'Besides, don't tell me that you haven't heard the story? – Once a seabird came down in the suburbs of Lu. The Marquis of Lu welcomed and banqueted it in the shrine of his ancestors, performed the music of the Nine Shao to entertain it, provided the meats of the T'ai-lao sacrifice as delicacies for it. Then the bird stared with dazed eyes and worried and pined, did not dare to eat one slice, did not dare to drink one cup, and within three days it died. This was caring for a bird with the cares proper to oneself, not to a bird. Someone who cared for it with the cares proper to a bird would let it perch in the deep woods, play on the shoals, float in the Yangtse and the Lakes, eat loaches and minnows, come down with the column as it flies in formation to veer with the line of least resistance and settle. There was nothing that bird hated more to hear than a human voice, what would it make of all our hubbub? Perform the music of the Hsien-ch'ih and the Nine Shao in the wilds of Lake Tung-t'ing, and when the birds hear it they fly up, when the beasts hear it they run off, when the fish hear it they plunge deep, when humans hear it they gather in a circle to watch. A fish by staying in the water lives, a man by staying in the water dies; that they necessarily differ from each other is because their needs are inherently different.

Therefore the former sages

> Did not expect people to be one in their abilities,
> Did not set them the same tasks.
> The name stayed confined to the substance,
> The duty was fitted to the occasion.

It is this that is meant by "as branches reaching all the way out, as spokes held firm at the centre".' (*Chuang-tzŭ*, chapter 18)

•   •   •

The bait is the means to get the fish where you want it, catch the fish and you forget the bait. The snare is the means to get the rabbit where you want it, catch the rabbit and you forget the snare. Words are the means to get the idea where you want it, catch on to the idea and you forget about the words. Where shall I find a man who forgets about words, and have a word with him? (*Chuang-tzŭ*, chapter 26)

•   •   •

The 'Way' is the Power's arranging in a layout. 'Life' is the emanation from the Power. The 'nature' of something is its resources for life. The motions from our nature are called 'doing'. Doing becoming contrived is called 'failing'.

'Knowing' is being in touch with something, 'knowledge' is a representation of it. As for what knowledge does not know, it is as though you were peering in one direction.

It is what sets moving on the course which is inevitable that is called the 'Power'. It is the motions being from nowhere but yourself that is called being in 'order'. The names contrast but the substances take their courses from each other. (*Chuang-tzŭ*, chapter 23)

NOTE   To organise basic concepts in a system of definitions may seem an un-Taoistic enterprise, but we have already noticed one instance (p. 156 above). Here the model seems to be Mohist. The later Mohists developed chains of definitions, deriving the circle from the concept of similarity and the moral virtues from the opposites 'desire' and 'dislike'.[50] From a couple of references to 'what the sage desires and dislikes *beforehand* on behalf of men' and to the circle as 'known *beforehand*',[51] it seems that they thought of the definitions as establishing what we would call 'a priori' knowledge. The Taoist attempts to construct a similar chain deriving his concepts, not from 'desire' and 'dislike', but from the 'inevitable', the unchosen, the motion in which thought does not intervene.

The sentences about knowledge are outside the chain. 'Knowing' (which is a good thing) is being in touch with things as they come and go, 'knowledge' (which is a bad thing) is preserving fixed representations of them. When Taoists speak of 'what knowledge does not know'[51] the point, we are told, is that knowledge immobilises as though we remained peering in one direction. This section is directly related to the definitions and illustrations in the Mohist *Canons* A 3-6: 'The "wits" are the

capability.... Like the eyesight.' ' "Knowing" is being in touch with something...
Like seeing.' ' "Thinking" is seeking it... Like peering. ' "Understanding" is
being clear about it.... Like seeing clearly.'

•   •   •

The conductor of the sacrifice to the ancestors donned his black square-cut
vestments and looked down through the bars of the pen to give advice to the
pigs:

'What is your objection to dying? For three months I shall fatten you up,
for ten days do austerities, for three days fast; I shall spread white reeds and
lay out your shoulders and rumps on an engraved stand. Will you agree to it
then?'

Giving counsel on the pigs' behalf you would say: 'The best thing for
them is to feed them husks and dregs and keep them inside the bars of the
pen.' But when you take counsel on your own behalf, if alive you will be
honoured with a carriage and cap of office, and dead you can get to be on top
of a painted hearse inside a richly ornamented coffin, you'll agree to it. What
on the pigs' behalf you would refuse, on your own behalf you will accept.
Where's the difference between you and the pigs? (*Chuang-tzŭ*, chapter 19)

•   •   •

Duke Huan went hunting in the lowlands with Kuan Chung as his chariot-
eer, and saw a sprite there. The Duke clutched Kuan Chung's hand.

'Did you see that?'

'I didn't see anything.'

When the Duke got back he was raving and fell ill, and did not come out
for several days. One of the knights of Ch'i, Huang-tzŭ Kao-ao, said to him

'It is Your Grace who is wounding himself, how could a sprite wound
Your Grace? If energies which have congested blow away and do not return
to the body, one is enfeebled; if they rise high and won't come down, it
makes one irritable; if they sink low and won't go up, it makes one forgetful;
if they settle mid-way, at the heart, one falls ill.'

'If that's so, do sprites exist at all?'

'They do. In the ditch there's Li, in the stove there's Chi. In the rubbish-
heap inside the door lives Lei-t'ing. Under the north-east corner Pei-a and
Kuei-lung go hopping about, and, as for the north-west corner, Yi-yang lives
down below there. In the water there's Wang-hsiang, in the hills Hsin, in the
mountains K'uei, in the moors P'ang-huang, and in the lowlands Wei-yi.'

'May I ask what Wei-yi looks like?'

'Wei-yi is in girth no bigger than a wheel-hub but is as long as a carriage-
shaft, he wears a purple coat and scarlet hat. He's an ugly-looking thing, and
when he hears the noise of a thundering carriage he supports his head with

both hands and stands straight up. The man who sees him is on the verge of becoming overlord of the empire.'

Duke Huan smiled with delight.

'That's the one I saw.'

Then straightening coat and cap he sat down beside Huang-tzŭ, and before the day was out had not noticed that his sickness was gone. (*Chuang-tzŭ*, chapter 19)

NOTE   In case the reader wishes to search for these creatures round the house, here are descriptions by commentators, from between the third and seventh centuries AD. 'The daemon of the stove looks like a beautiful girl, wears a red dress, its name is Chi.' 'Kuei-lung looks like a small boy, 1 foot 4 inches high, in a black coat, red head-scarf, and big cap, wears a sword and grasps a spear.' 'Yi-yang has a leopard's head and horse's tail – some say a dog's head.' 'Wang-hsiang: it looks like a small boy, red and black in colour, with red claws, big ears, long arms.' 'Hsin: it looks like a dog with horns, body tattooed in the five colours.' 'K'uei: as big as an ox, looks like a drum, walks on one foot.' 'P'ang-huang: it looks like a snake, with two heads, tattooed in the five colours.'

When Confucius travelled west to Wey, Yen Hui asked Music-master Chin:

'What do you think of our master's travels?'

'A pity! Such trouble he'll be getting into!'

'Why so?'

'Before the straw dogs are laid out for the sacrifice, they are packed in bamboo boxes wrapped in patterned brocades, and the medium and the priest fast and do austerities before escorting them. But once the sacrifice is over, nothing remains for them but to have their heads and spines trampled by the passers-by, or be gathered as fuel for the kitchen stove. If you were to pick them up again, put them in the boxes, wrap them in the brocades, should some traveller or townsman doze in their shade, even if he did not dream he would surely be often troubled in his sleep. Now your master has indeed picked up the straw dogs once laid out by the former kings, and gathered disciples who on his travels and at home doze in their shade. So when a tree was chopped down over him in Sung, and he had to hide his tracks in Wey, and was in such straits in Shang and Chou, weren't these his dreams? When he was besieged between Ch'en and Ts'ai and for seven days did not eat cooked food, and death and life were next-door neighbours, wasn't that his troubled sleep?

'On water it is most convenient to travel by boat, on dry land in a carriage; if you were to try to push a boat on land because it goes so well on water, you could last out the age without travelling an inch. Are not the past and the present his water and his dry land? And Chou and Lu his boat and carriage? At the present day, to have an urge to get the institutions of Chou running in Lu is like pushing a boat on dry land, there's no result for all your labour, you're certain to bring disaster on yourself. He has never known about the turns which have no fixed direction, about being unrestricted in responding to things. Besides, don't tell me that you have never seen a well-sweep? Pull and it points down, let go and it points up. The pulling is by the man, it isn't it that pulls the man, so whether up or down it cannot be blamed by the man.

'Therefore in the rites and duties, laws and measures, of the Three Highnesses and the Five Emperors, what mattered was not having them the same but having things in order. So if you want an analogy for their rites and duties, laws and measures, aren't they like the cherry-apple, pear, orange and pumelo? The flavours contrast but all are approved by the mouth. Just so a rite, duty, law or measure is something which alters in response to the times.

'Now suppose you take an ape and dress him in the robes of the Duke of Chou, he will surely bite and gnaw, tug and tear, restless until he has ripped everything off. When you observe the differences between past and present, they are as different as an ape and the Duke of Chou. Just so when Hsi Shih had heartburn and was scowling at the neighbours, the ugliest woman in the neighbourhood saw it and thought she looked beautiful, and after getting home she too pounded herself on the breast and scowled at the neighbours. When the rich men of the neighbourhood saw her they shut their doors tight and would not go out, when poor men saw her they snatched their wives and children by the hand and hurried away. She knew the scowl was beautiful but not why it was beautiful. A pity! Such trouble he'll be getting into!' (*Chuang-tzŭ*, chapter 14)

NOTES TO PART THREE

1 cf. p. 117 above.
2 cf. p. 123 above.
3 cf. p. 121 above.
4 cf. p. 120 above.
5 cf. p. 17f above.
6 cf. p. 244f below.
7 cf. p. 119 above.
8 cf. p. 118 above.
9 cf. p. 118f above.
10 cf. pp. 121, 125 above.
11 cf. p. 119 above.
12 cf. pp. 128, 129 above.
13 cf. p. 133 above.
14 cf. p. 128 above.
15 cf. p. 96 above, also pp. 65, 78f.
16 cf. p. 65 above.
17 cf. p. 79 above.
18 cf. pp. 137 above, 281 below.
19 cf. p. 147 above.
20 cf. p. 154 above.
21 cf. p. 145 above.
22 cf. p. 160 above.

23 cf. p. 152f above.
24 cf. p. 9 above.
25 cf. pp. 55, 82 above.
26 The dialogue of Chuang-tzŭ and Hui Shih on the bridge (p. 123 above), which concludes the chapter 'Autumn floods' (chapter 17), may well be from the 'Great Man' writer. One hesitates to credit him with the whole chapter, but the 'Autumn floods' and Kung-sun Lung episodes occupy the greater part of it.
27 cf. p. 13f above.
28 cf. p. 164 above.
29 cf. p. 56 above.
30 cf. p. 160 above.
31 cf. p. 160 above.
32 cf. pp. 204, 206, 209, 212f, 215, 237 below.
33 cf. p. 45f above.
34 cf. Kung-chuan Hsiao, *History of Chinese Political Thought*, translated F. W.

Mote (Princeton, 1979), vol. 1, pp. 619–30. Pao Ching-yen is translated in Étienne Balazs, *Chinese Civilization and Bureaucracy*, translated H. M. Wright (New Haven, 1964), pp. 242–6.

35 For the varieties of later Taoism, see Holmes Welch, *The Parting of the Way* (London, 1958) and Holmes Welch and Anna Seidel (eds), *Facets of Taoism* (New Haven, 1979). For contemporary religious Taoism in Taiwan, see Michael Saso, *Teachings of Taoist Master Chuang* (New Haven and London, 1978). For Taoist alchemy, see Joseph Needham, *Science and Civilization in China* (Cambridge, 1974), vol. 5/2, and Nathan Sivin, *Chinese Alchemy: preliminary studies* (Harvard, 1968).

36 cf. p. 46 above.

37 cf. p. 86 above.

38 cf. p. 181 above.

39 cf. p. 265 below.

40 cf. p. 124 above.

41 The sequence can be treated as chronological by the single expedient of taking the recurring *sheng-hu X*, 'go on breeding from X', as though it were *sheng X*, 'breed X'. The fit is then so neat that one is tempted to delete the *hu* or assume some special idiom, and I succombed to the temptation when translating the parallel passage in *Book of Lieh-tzŭ* (London, 1960) (p. 21). But this time I follow the example of Burton Watson (Chuang-tzŭ, p. 196) in letting the text mean what it says.

42 cf. p. 49 above.

43 *Chih-kuan fu-hsing ch'uan-hung chüeh*, ch. 10/2 (*Taishō Tripitaka* no. 19120), p. 440 C/20–3).

44 cf. pp. 121, 162, 164 above.

45 cf. p. 121 above.

46 cf. pp. 210, 215 below.

47 cf. p. 205 below.

48 cf. *Mencius*, translated D. C. Lau, 1A/7, 6A/7, pp. 58f and 164.

50 *Later Mohist Logic*, pp. 47–9 and 57f.

51 ibid., pp. 247 and 342.

Part Four

The essays of the Primitivist
and episodes related to them

Within the medley of a book called *Chuang-tzŭ*, there is one other writer with an identity as distinctive as that of the Chuang-tzŭ who wrote the *Inner Chapters*. He is the author who wrote the first three *Outer chapters* (Chapters 8–10) and the introductory essay of the fourth, whom we shall call the 'Primitivist'. He shares certain ideas (the primal Utopia which ended with Shen-nung and was disrupted by the Yellow Emperor, the equal harmfulness of the moralist and the criminal, the usurpation of the state as a crime which puts morality in the service of the victor) with the Yangist author of 'Robber Chih' (chapter 29), who however differs from him both in thought and in style. Since 'Robber Chih' and the Primitivist 'Rifling trunks' are two of the most famous chapters in the book, and are among those which have come through best in previous translations, we must try to place them in their proper contexts.

We have seen that Chinese philosophy was most active at the time when the empire of the Chou had broken up into competing states. Chuang-tzŭ lived towards the end of the fourth century BC; during the next century the state of Ch'in in the far north-west steadily advanced towards the conquest of the rest. As the struggle for political power approached its climax the moralistic teachings of Confucians and Mohists seemed less and less persuasive. The only philosophers patronised by the Ch'in were the Legalists such as Han Fei (died 233 BC), who undertook an amoral analysis of the conditions of political power comparable with Machiavelli's. During this period one notices, in the Legalists, in the Primitivist and the 'Robber Chih' writer, something of that vicious contempt for moralists which emerges in periods when the contrast between moral pretensions and political realities has become insupportable.

In 221 BC the King of Ch'in conquered the last surviving state, Ch'i in the northeast, and proclaimed himself the Emperor Shih-huang-ti. In 213 BC he banned the philosophical schools and burned their books, so that the Ch'in dynasty is conveniently taken as the end of the great period of Chinese thought which began with Confucius (551–479 BC). However, as with all such historical conveniences, history itself was not so tidy. The first stage of the reunification barely outlasted the death of Shih-huang-ti in 210 BC. During the interval of civil war (209–202 BC), when it must have seemed that the Ch'in had been only a brief interruption in the age of the 'Warring Kingdoms', the philosophical schools, suppressed for only four years, no doubt emerged from hiding to compete for influence over the rival contenders for the throne. In the case of the Confucians, it is known that they joined up with the peasant rebel Ch'en Sheng (209–208 BC), and that K'ung Fu, head of the family of Confucius, took office under him. The reunification was finally consolidated by the Han dynasty (206 BC–AD 220), which was at first inclined to a syncretism centred on Taoism, but committed itself to Confucianism under the Emperor Wu (140–87 BC).

The Primitivist probably wrote in the time of civil war, within a few years of 205 BC, when the future was still undecipherable. Admittedly one of his anecdotes, of Robber Chih discoursing on morality[1] is found earlier, in the *Lü-shih ch'un-ch'iu* (*c.* 240 BC); but the parallelism is of the sort without verbal identity except in the more pungent sayings, suggesting independent borrowings from oral tradition. The essays assume that the empire is still a battleground of contending states, yet are later than the Ch'in unification, for there is a specific reference to the fall of the T'ien family which reigned in Ch'i right down to 221 BC.[2] They mention that the earlier moralism has degenerated into the naked reliance on punishment which we know to have characterised the Ch'in[3] but the main targets are the schools which the Ch'in suppressed, the Confucians, Mohists and Yangists. The Primitivist implies a recent revival of the schools when he says that 'Yang and Mo are starting to put on airs and think they are getting somewhere',[4] and still more clearly when, at the end of a historical sketch in which the origins of Confucianism and Mohism have been mentioned much earlier, he says: 'In the present age the condemned to death lie back to back, the shackled in cangues and stocks are elbow to elbow, there is always a mutilated man somewhere in sight, yet it is just now that the Confucians and Mohists start putting on airs and come flipping back their sleeves among the fettered and manacled.'[5] The Primitivist essays are political polemics which defend a Taoist conception of society against the other reviving schools, in particular the Confucians, who in the next century will be the victors.

Unlike the *Inner chapters* the Primitivist chapters are consecutive essays, in a uniform prose which is repetitive but vivid, idiosyncratic, egotistical, pugnacious. The ideas may be Taoist but the temperament is not; the Primitivist thinks in elaborately parallelised sentences and in those patterns of concepts (the 'Five Colours', 'Five Notes', 'Five Smells', 'Five Tastes', 'Five Organs') which came to dominate Chinese thinking during the Han dynasty but which Chuang-tzŭ himself dissolves in the fluid, unpredictable motions of his thought. In spite of this intellectual rigidity the language lives because it is informed by un-Taoistic passions, scorn and anger. For the Primitivist, the meaning of Taoism is essentially social and political, the defence of human spontaneity against a state which suppresses by punishments and beguiles by moral appeals. Now that the Ch'in have fallen, he wants nothing more of government than to be left alone; in particular he does not want to be managed by moralists, the reviving Confucians and Mohists.

The Primitivist is an extremist who despises the whole of moral and aesthetic culture. He wants to revert to the simplest mode of life, undisturbed by the temptations of luxury and sophistication, intellectual abstraction, above all by Confucian and Mohist moralism. We noticed earlier a little 'School of Chuang-tzŭ' essay on the 'essentials of our nature and destiny', which recommends allowing the biological process of life to take its course, neither shortening it by worldly ambitions which wear out the vital energies nor trying vainly to prolong it.[6] The Primitivist adopts the 'essentials of our nature and destiny' as his slogan. He demands that we remain true to the 'Nature' by which the body passes through its stages from birth to death, and to the 'Power' in us, which is in the first place the bodily powers such as eyesight and hearing. Unfortunately man's nature can be tempted to excess, so that he grows out of shape, as some bodies grow webbed toes; and his powers can be distorted by the artificialities of art and music, diverted in a wrong direction like a sixth finger growing from a hand. When cosmological schematists associate the five moral constants (Goodwill, Duty, Rites, Wisdom, Trustworthiness) with the Five Organs (liver, lungs, heart, kidneys, stomach), they turn moral convention into a second nature, as painful to renounce as webbed toes being ripped apart or a sixth finger being bitten off. Although the ruler should leave people to organise their collective life spontaneously, he retains one function, to 'keep in place and within bounds', to shut us off from temptations to 'indulge our nature to excess' and 'displace our powers'.[7]

By the bad habit of reasoning and moralising mankind has disrupted the spontaneous harmony, not only of his own society but of the cosmos itself, so that now even the seasons come irregularly and the animals live distorted lives. The decline began with the Yellow Emperor; previously, down to the time of Shen-nung ('Daemonic Farmer', the inventor of the plough), men lived in spontaneous community united by the Power shared by all men. Here there is an implicit contrast with the traditional idea that society is held together by influences emanating from the Power in the ruler, which is renewed and wanes with each succeeding dynasty. The Primitivist seems even to identify the Power with the powers of ordinary people to feed and clothe themselves:

> 'By their weaving clothed, by their ploughing fed –
> This is called "sharing in the Power".
> In oneness and without faction –
> The name for it is "free as the air".'[8]

Here we can discern an influence from outside Taoism. Throughout the literature of the third and second centuries BC the reign of Shen-nung represents a distinctive political ideal, unlike those of Confucians, Taoists or any other well documented school. It has the look of a peasant Utopia; everyone is required to support himself by his own labour, the ruler ploughs side by side with his people and does not raise taxes, issue decrees, punish or go to war, and government, which is decentralised in small fiefs, has no apparent function except to foster agriculture and keep the price of grain constant by storing in good years and issuing in bad. In the Legalist *Book of Lord Shang* (*c*. 250 BC)[9] and in 'Robber Chih',[10] as in the Primitivist writings, the regime of Shen-nung is ended by the Yellow Emperor, inventor of the state and of war. It may be identified as the ideal of the obscure 'School of the Tillers' (*Nung-chia*), whose lost classic was a manual of agriculture called *Shen-nung*.[11] Their only known spokesman is Hsü Hsing, who about 315 BC was leading a small community of farmers and craftsmen which professed the doctrine of Shen-nung, required the ruler to plough with his own hands, and talked about keeping prices constant.[12] There is one story in the Yangist 'Yielding the throne' which must come from the Tillers; it has the hermits Po Yi and Shu Ch'i protesting against the uprising of the Chou on purely pacifist grounds and comparing King Wu unfavourably with Shen-nung.[13] It may be guessed that some of the verse about the Golden Age in the Primitivist 'Horses' hooves' and in 'Robber Chih' is also of Tiller origin.

The Chinese text of the Primitivist chapters is four times interrupted by aphorisms headed 'Therefore it is said . . . ', three of which are direct quotations from *Lao-tzŭ*, a text of which there is no trace in the *Inner chapters*, and which is unattested until late in the third century BC. It happens that these fit so badly into their contexts that we dismiss all four as glosses and omit them from this translation, but there is sufficient evidence throughout of a strong influence from *Lao-tzŭ*. However, *Lao-tzŭ* is written from the viewpoint of the ruler, and presents Doing Nothing as a strategy for achieving the maximum effect by the least interference in the natural course of events; the Primitivist on the other hand, like Chuang-tzŭ, writes as a private citizen who wants to be left alone. His own programme of government by Doing Nothing is introduced by the preamble 'So if the gentleman is left with no choice but to preside over the world . . . '.[14] Did it have much to do with the real politics of the time? More perhaps than readers of the last two thousand years have suspected. If we read his essays as pamphlets circulating during a specific crisis, the breakdown of the uniquely repressive Ch'in dynasty, we can see his Utopia less as a nostalgic dream than as a political myth which could be effective in focusing tendencies towards minimalised government in the present.

1

Webbed toes

Webbed toes or a sixth finger are issuing from the man's nature, yes! but are superfluous to his powers. An obstinate wart or dangling wen are issuing from the man's body, yes! but are superfluous to his nature. One who goes on inflating and diverging into Goodwill and Duty and assigns functions to them, classifies them as belonging to his Five Organs, yes! but they are not the true course of the Way and the Power. To be webbed on the foot, then, is to tack on functionless flesh; to have an offshoot on the hand is to sprout a functionless finger; and to inflate and diverge into webbings and offshoots on the essential Five Organs is, by the excess and aberration of practising Goodwill and Duty, to inflate and diverge from the functions of eyesight and hearing.

Thus to web the eyesight deranges the Five Colours, vitiates emblems and designs by excess, by the dazzle of greens and yellows and multicoloured vestments, do you deny it? – but Li Chu did that. To inflate the hearing deranges the Five Notes, vitiates the Six Pitch-tubes by excess, by instruments of bronze and stone and silken strings and bamboo, and the Huang-chung and Ta-lü modes, do you deny it? – but Music-master K'uang did that. To grow Goodwill as an offshoot stretches the powers and blocks up our nature in order to harvest repute and renown, and make the world celebrate with pipe and drum their submission to inapplicable laws, do you deny it? – but Tseng and Shih did that. To diverge into disputation balances tile on tile and ties the cord in knots, chiselling phrases and hammering sentences to make the heart stray among questions about 'the hard and the white', 'the same and the different', and fatuously admire useless propositions, do you deny it? – but Yang and Mo did that. All these then are Ways which inflate into webbings and diverge into offshoots; they are not the absolutely true course of the world.

The man on that absolutely true course does not lose the essentials of our nature and destiny. So his joins are not webbings, his forkings are not offshoots; the long in him does not constitute a surplus, the short in him does not constitute an insufficiency. Just so, though the duck's legs are short, if you added more on he would worry; though the crane's legs are long, if you lopped some off he would pine. Then what by nature is long is not to be lopped off, what by nature is short is not to be added to; there is nothing to get rid of or to worry over. May I suggest that Goodwill and Duty do not belong to the essentials of man? Why is it that those benevolent people worry so much?

Moreover even someone with webbed toes will weep when they are ripped apart; even someone with a sixth finger will scream when it is bitten off. Of the pair of them, one has a surplus in the number, the other an insufficiency; but when it comes to the worrying, they are as one. The benevolent people of the present age get bleary-eyed worrying about the age's troubles, the malevolent rip apart the essentials of their nature and destiny by gluttony for honours and riches. So may I suggest that Goodwill and Duty do not belong to the essentials of man? Why is it that ever since the Three Dynasties there has been all this fuss in the world?

To depend on the carpenter's curve and line, compasses, L-square, to straighten you out, is to pare away your nature; to depend on cords, knots, glue, lacquer, to hold you together, is to violate your powers; and to bow and crouch for Rites and Music, and smirk and simper over Goodwill and Duty, in order to soothe the hearts of the world, is to lose the constant in you. There *is* such a thing as constancy in the world. But in whatever is constant, being bent is not by the use of the carpenter's curve, being straight is not by the use of his line, being round is not by the use of compasses, being square is not by the use of the L-square, being stuck is not by the use of glue and lacquer, being tied is not by the use of rope or cord. Thus everything in the world springs into life without knowing how it is born, attains unthinkingly without knowing how it attains. Hence the present is no different from the past, and nothing can be missing from its place. Why then do the benevolent and dutiful in an unending procession, as though glued and lacquered and tethered and roped, come straying out into the realm of the Way and the Power, bringing delusion to the world?

The slightly deluded take a wrong turning, the utterly deluded barter away their nature. How would we know that this is so? Ever since the House of Yu-yü called in the benevolent and the dutiful to bother the world, everyone in the world has been stampeding as though for his life after Goodwill and Duty; is this not bartering one's nature for Goodwill and Duty? So let us try to sort the matter out. Since the Three Dynasties everyone in the world has been bartering his nature for some other thing. In the case of the knave, he sacrifices himself for profit; of the knight, for reputation; of the noble, for family; of the sage, for the world. So these various sorts of men, whose occupations are so dissimilar, whose reputations are so differently rated, are as one when it comes to injuring one's nature and making a sacrifice of oneself.

Two boys, Tsang and Ku, were together minding the flock, and both lost their sheep. When they were asked what happened, it turned out that Tsang had brought a book to study, Ku had been idling away the time tossing dice.

The two boys had dissimilar occupations, but in losing their sheep there was nothing to choose between them. Po Yi died for reputation at the foot of Mount Shou-yang, Robber Chih for profit on the top of East Ridge. What the two men died for was not the same, but in damaging life and injuring nature there was nothing to choose between them. Why must it be Po Yi that we judge right, Robber Chih that we judge wrong? Everyone in the world is a human sacrifice. When the sacrifice is for Goodwill and Duty, the vulgar call you a gentleman; when it is for riches, they call you a knave. Though in their sacrifice they were as one, one of them was a gentleman, the other was a knave; but in the damage to life and harm to nature Robber Chih was another Po Yi, and what does it matter which was the gentleman and which was the knave? Century-old wood is broken to make a libation vessel; you decorate it in yellow and green, its chips lie in the gutter. If you compare the libation vessel with the chips in the gutter, in beauty and ugliness they are wide apart, but in losing the nature of wood they are as one. Chieh or Chih, Tseng or Shih, in the doing of duty are wide apart, but in the losing of man's nature there is nothing to choose between them.

Then again, there are five ways to lose one's nature. Firstly, the Five Colours derange the eye and impair its sight. Secondly, the Five Notes derange the ear and impair its hearing. Thirdly, the Five Smells fume in the nostrils and cause congestion between the brows. Fourthly, the Five Tastes dirty the mouth and make it sickly. Fifthly, inclinations and aversions disturb the heart and make one's nature volatile. These five are all harmful to life; and if Yang and Mo are just now starting to put on airs and think they are getting somewhere, it is not what I would call getting somewhere. If the man who gets somewhere is caught where he can't get out, is that what you think is getting somewhere? Then the pigeons and doves in a cage must be supposed to have got somewhere too. And to have inclinations and aversions, sounds and colours, blocking up the inside of you, and leather cap or snipe-feather hat, memorandum tablet in belt and trailing sash, constricting the outside of you, to be inwardly squeezed inside the bars of your pen, outwardly lashed by coil on coil of rope, and complacently in the middle of the ropes suppose that you have got somewhere, amounts to claiming that the condemned man with his chained arms and manacled fingers, or a tiger or a leopard in its cage, has got somewhere too.

Moreover whoever keeps his nature subordinate to Goodwill and Duty, though as intelligent as Tseng and Shih, is not what I would call a fine man; and whoever keeps his nature subordinate to the Five Tastes, though as intelligent as Yü Erh, is not what I would call a fine man either. Whoever keeps his nature subordinate to the Five Notes, though as intelligent as Music-master K'uang, does not have what I would call good hearing; and whoever keeps his nature subordinate to the Five Colours, though as intelligent as Li Chu, does not have what I would call good eyesight. When I call someone a fine man, it is not Goodwill and Duty that I am talking about, but simply the fineness in his powers; nor when I call someone a fine man is it the Five Tastes that I am talking about, but simply a trust in the essentials of our nature and destiny. When I say someone has good hearing, I mean not that he hears that, but simply that he hears with his own ears; and when I say someone has good eyesight, I mean not that he sees that, but simply that he sees with his own eyes.

To see something, but not with your own eyes, to gain something, but not by your own grasp, this is gaining what is gain for other people, not gaining by your own grasp what is gain for yourself; it is being suited by what suits other people, not suiting yourself with what is suitable to yourself. Those suited by what suits other people, not suiting themselves with what is suitable to themselves, even Robber Chih on the one hand and Po Yi on the other, are the same in being vitiated by excess and aberration. I remain humble before the Way and the Power, and that is why I would not venture either to act on the elevated principles of Goodwill and Duty or to perform the debased deeds of excess and aberration.

2

Horses' hooves

The horse has hooves to tread the frost and snow, and hair to ward off wind and cold, it champs the grass and drinks the waters, lifts the knee high and prances. Such is the true nature of the horse, and even if it had lofty terraces and great halls it would have no use for them.

Then came Po Lo and said, 'I'm good at managing horses.' He singed them, shaved them, clipped them, branded them, tied them with martingale and crupper, cramped them in stable and stall, and the horses which died of it were two or three out of ten. He starved them, parched them, made them trot, made them gallop, in formation or neck to neck, tormented by bit and reins in front and threatened from behind by whip and goad; and the horses that died before he finished were more than half.

The potter says, 'I'm good at managing clay; my circles are true to the compasses, my squares to the L-square.' The carpenter says, 'I'm good at managing wood; my bends are true to the curve, my straight edges correspond to the line.' Do you suppose that it is in the nature of clay and wood to want to be true to compasses and L-square and the carpenter's curve and line? But still generation after generation cites them as models for us, 'Po Lo was good at managing horses, potters and carpenters are good at managing clay and wood'. This too is the error of those who manage the world.

In my opinion being good at governing the world is not like this. The people have a nature which is constant:

> By their weaving clothed, by their ploughing fed –
> This is called 'sharing in the Power'.
> In oneness and without faction, –
> The name for it is 'free as the air'.

Therefore in the age when Power was at its utmost

> Their step was unfaltering,
> Their gaze was unwavering.

During that time

The mountains had no paths nor trails,
The marshes had no boats nor bridges.
The myriad creatures, all that lives,
Let their territories merge together.
The beasts and birds had undepleted flocks,
The grass and trees grew to their full height.

So one could tie up a bird or animal on a lead and take it for a walk, or pull down a branch and peep into a crow's or magpie's nest. In the age when Power was at its utmost, men lived in sameness with the birds and animals, side by side as fellow clansmen with the myriad creatures; how would they know a gentleman from a knave?

In sameness, knowing nothing!
Not parted from their Power.
In sameness, desiring nothing! –
Call it 'the simple and unhewn'.

In the simple and unhewn the nature of the people is found.

Then came the sages, trudging along after Goodwill, straining on tiptoe after Duty, and for the first time the world was in doubt; immersing in the flood to make Music, or picking to pieces to make Rites, and for the first time the world was divided. Then, unless the simple unhewn block were damaged, who would make libation vessels? Unless the white jade were broken, who would make the halved emblem tablet? Unless the Way and Power were discarded, where would we find Goodwill and Duty? Unless we had parted from the natural and essential, on what would we use Rites and Music? Unless the Five Colours were deranged, who would make designs and decorations? Unless the Five Notes were deranged, who would tune to the Six Pitch-tubes? Damaging the unhewn block to make vessels is the crime of the craftsman, ruining the Way and the Power to make Goodwill and Duty is the error of the sage.

As for horses, when they live out on the plains they eat grass and drink the water, when pleased they cross necks and stroke each other, when angry swing round and kick at each other. That is as far as a horse's knowledge goes. If you put yokes on their necks and hold them level with a crossbar, the horses will know how to smash the crossbar, wriggle out of the yokes, butt the carriage hood, spit out the bit and gnaw through the reins. So if even a horse's wits can learn to do mischief, it's the fault of Po Lo.

In the time of the House of Ho-hsü, the people when at home were unaware of what they were doing, when travelling did not know where they were going, basked in the sun chewing a morsel or strolled drumming on their bellies. This was as far as the people's capabilities went. Then came the sages, bowing and crouching to Rites and Music, in order to square off the shapes of everything in the world, groping in the air for Goodwill and Duty, in order to soothe the hearts of the world, and for the first time the people were on tiptoes in their eagerness for knowledge. Their competition became centred on profit, it could not have been otherwise. This too is the error of the sages.

3

Rifling trunks

If you intend to take safe precautions against the thieves who rifle trunks, grope in bags, break open cupboards, you must wind round with straps and cords, fasten with bolts and hasps – this is what conventional opinion calls wisdom. However, if a big enough thief comes he will put the cupboard on his back, hoist up the trunk, sling the bag on his shoulders, and make off, and fear only that the straps, cords, bolts and hasps will not hold. That being so, isn't the man we were calling wise on the contrary a man who is piling up a store for the sake of a big enough thief?

So let's try to sort the matter out. Are there any whom conventional opinion calls wise who are not piling up a store for the sake of the great thieves? Are there any whom it calls sages who are not guarding the store for the sake of the great thieves? How would we know that this is so? Formerly in the state of Ch'i one city was within sight of the next, the cries of cocks and dogs in one village could be heard in the next, the water spread with fishnets and the land tilled with hoe or plough was some 2,000 *li* square. In the manner in which everywhere within its four borders it instituted ancestral shrines and altars to the soil and the grain, or organised provinces, districts, cities, villages, hamlets, when did it ever fail to take the sages as models? However in one morning T'ien Ch'eng killed the lord of Ch'i and stole his state. Nor was it only the state he stole; he stole it complete with all its wise and sagely laws. So T'ien Ch'eng has gone on having the reputation of a thief and bandit, yet the man himself lived as secure as Yao or Shun; small states did not dare to condemn, great states did not dare to punish, and for twelve generations his house possessed the state of Ch'i. Then isn't it on the contrary that he stole the state of Ch'i complete with all its wise and sagely laws and used them to keep safe his robbing, thieving self?

So when one of Robber Chih's band asked him 'Do robbers too have the Way?', Chih answered

'Where can you go unless you have the Way? A shrewd guess at where the things are hidden in the house is the intuitiveness of the sage. Being first man in is courage. Being last man out is Duty. Knowing whether or not you can bring it off is wisdom. Giving everyone fair shares is Goodwill.

Without the five at his disposal, no one in the world could ever make a great robber.'

Judging by this, without the Way of the sage the good man would not stand, without the Way of the sage Robber Chih would not walk. If the good men in the world are fewer than the bad, the sages have benefited the world less than they have harmed it. With the birth of the sages the great robbers arise. Smash the sages, turn the thieves and bandits loose, and for the first time the world will be in order.

> When the river dries up the valley is depopulated,
> By the levelling of the hills the deeps are filled.

Once the sages are dead the great robbers will not arise, the world will be at peace and there will be no more trouble.

Until the sages die the great robbers will not stop. Even if we had twice as many sages to bring order to the world, the result would be to double the benefit to Robber Chih. If you institute pecks and bushels to measure things by, he'll steal them and the pecks and bushels with them. If you institute scales to weigh things by, he'll steal them and the scales with them. If you institute tallies and seals to guarantee things, he'll steal them and the tallies and seals with them. If you institute Goodwill and Duty to bend things straight, he'll steal them and Goodwill and Duty with them. How would we know that this is so? The man who steals a buckle is put to death, the man who steals a state becomes a prince, and at the gates of a prince you'll see the benevolent and the dutiful. Then isn't this stealing the Goodwill and Duty, the sagehood and wisdom? So the man who, succeeding as a great robber, wins the throne of a state, and steals Goodwill and Duty, and annexes the pecks and bushels, scales, tallies and seals for his own benefit, even the rewards of high-fronted carriage and cap of office cannot induce, the terror of the executioner's axe cannot deter. This redoubling of the benefit to Robber Chih which puts him beyond the reach of prohibitions is the fault of the sage. The sage is the sharpest tool of empire, he is not a means of bringing light to the empire.

So be rid of the sages, discard the wise, and then the great robbers will stop. Fling away the jades, crush the pearls, and the petty thieves will not arise. Burn the tallies, burst the seals, and the people will be rustic and simple. Split the peck-measures, snap the scales, and the people will not wrangle. Utterly demolish the laws of the sages throughout the world, and for the first time it will be possible to sort out and discuss things with the people.

Pull the Six Pitch-tubes out of sequence, melt down the organ-pipes and snap the zither-strings, stuff up blind Music-master K'uang's ears, and at last throughout the world men will contain their hearing where it belongs. Obliterate emblems and designs, scatter the Five Hues, gum up Li Chu's eyes, and at last throughout the world men will contain their eyesight where it belongs. Smash and snap the carpenter's curve and line, throw away compasses and L-square, shackle Craftsman Ch'ui's fingers, and at last throughout the world men will be in possession of their skills. Scrape away the tracks of Tseng and Shih, gag the mouths of Yang and Mo, cast away Goodwill and Duty, and at last Power throughout the world will be the same from its profoundest depths.

If men contain their eyesight where it belongs, there will be no more dazzle in the world. If men contain their hearing where it belongs, there will be no more involvements in the world. If men contain their knowledge where it belongs, there will be no more perplexities in the world. If men contain their powers where they belong, there will be no more aberration in the world. Tseng and Shih, Yang and Mo, Music-master K'uang and Craftsman Ch'ui and Li Chu were all men who situated their powers outside themselves, and so dazed and confused the world. These are matters for which laws are useless.

Don't tell me that you do not know about the age when Power was at its utmost? Formerly, under the Houses of Jung-ch'eng, Ta-t'ing, Po-huang, Chung-yang, Li-lu, Li-hsü, Hsien-yüan, Ho-hsü, Tsun-lu, Chu-jung, Fu-hsi and Shen-nung, throughout that time the people made use of knotted cords, * found their own food sweet enough, their own dress beautiful enough, were happy in their own customs, content in their own abode. Neighbouring countries saw each other in the distance, heard the sounds of each others' cocks and dogs, but the people grew old and died without ever coming and going. Such is a time of utmost order.

Nowadays things have gone so far that the people lift their heels and crane their necks, tell each other 'In such-and-such a place there's a good one', and pack up provisions and head for him, so that inside the family they desert their parents and outside leave the service of their lords, their footprints go on meeting at the borders of the princes' states, their wheel-ruts go on mingling a thousand miles from home. This then is the fault of the ruler's lust for knowledge.

If the ruler does lust after knowledge and lacks the Way, the empire is in utter disorder. How would we know that this is so? If there is too much knowledge of bows, crossbows, bird-snares, stringed arrows, triggered traps, the birds are disordered in the sky. If there is too much knowledge of hooks, baits, nets and basket-traps, the fish are disordered in the water. When there is too much knowledge of pitfalls, springes, snares, traps, gins, the animals are disordered in the woodlands. When we have too much of the vagaries of cunning and deception, of wrenching apart 'the hard and the white' and jumbling together 'the same and the different', the vulgar are perplexed by disputation. Therefore, if the world is benighted in utter confusion, the blame rests on the lusters after knowledge.

---

* The device for record-keeping which preceded the invention of writing. This whole passage is parallel with Lao-tzŭ, 80.

Thus everyone in the world has enough sense to inquire into what he does not know, yet we do not have the sense to inquire into what we already do know. Everyone knows how to condemn what he judges to be bad, yet we do not know how to condemn what we have already judged good. This is why we are in utter disorder. So we disturb the brightness of the sun and moon above, dissipate the quintessences in the mountains and rivers below, interrupt the round of the four seasons in between; of the very insects which creep on the ground or flit above it, not one is not losing its nature. How utterly the lust for knowledge has disordered the world! Since as far back as the Three Dynasties this has been happening; they neglect the plain people and delight in bustling sycophants, abandon calm and mildness and Doing Nothing, and delight in noisy ideas. All that noise has thrown the world into disorder.

4

Keep it in place and within bounds

I have heard something about keeping the world in place and within bounds, I have heard nothing about governing the world. You 'keep it in place', because you fear that everyone may indulge man's nature to excess; you 'keep it within bounds', because you fear that everyone may displace man's powers. If everyone refused to indulge his nature to excess and displace his powers, would there be any such thing as governing the world?

Formerly when Yao governed the world he made everyone exultantly delight in his nature, which is excitement; and when Chieh governed the world he made everyone suffer miserably in his nature, which is discontent. To be excited or discontented is to go counter to the Power; and nothing in the whole world which goes counter to the Power can last for long.

Is it that people were too pleased? That unbalances in favour of the Yang. Too angry? That unbalances in favour of the Yin. When Yin and Yang were both off balance, the seasons came at the wrong times, the proportions of heat and cold were imperfect, and does not that injure rather than benefit the bodies of men? It caused men's joy and anger to miss their occasions, they had no constant home in which to settle, however much they pondered they remained unsatisfied, and broke off half-way without finishing what they started. It was then that for the first time the world was agitated by restless ambitions, and only after that that you had the conduct of Robber Chih on one hand and of Tseng and Shih on the other. The result is that though you mobilise the whole world to reward the good among us it is insufficient, though you mobilise the whole world to punish the wicked among us it remains inadequate. So the world itself is not big enough to do the rewarding and punishing. Since the Three Dynasties we have ended up in fussing over this business of rewarding and punishing; what chance do they give themselves of finding security in the essentials of our nature and destiny?

Or would you rather indulge the eyesight? That's to be led into excess by spectacle. Or hearing? That's to be led into excess by sounds. Or Goodwill?

That's to disorder your own powers. Or Duty? That's to upset the patterns of other things. Or Rites? That's to encourage artifice. Or Music? That's to encourage letting yourself go in excess. Or sagehood? That's to encourage the polite accomplishments. Or knowledge? That's to encourage fault-finders. When the world is ready to find security in the essentials of our nature and destiny, it does not matter whether these eight are retained or not; it is when the world is not so inclined that these eight start to warp and derange and disorder the world, that the world starts to honour them and finds it cannot do without them. How utterly deluded the world is! Nonsense to say they are simply obsolete things we have got rid of! On the contrary, people prepare with fasts and austerities before speaking about them, kneel before the throne to present them, mime them in dance to drums and song. It leaves me at my wits' end!

So if the gentleman is left with no choice but to preside over the world, his best policy is Doing Nothing. Only by Doing Nothing will he find security in the essentials of his nature and destiny. So if you value regard for your own person more than governing the world, you are fit to be entrusted with the world; if you love the care of your own person more than governing the world, you deserve to have the world delivered to you. If then a gentleman does prove able not to dislocate his Five Organs and stretch his eyesight and hearing, then sitting as still as a corpse he will look majestic as a dragon, from the silence of the abyss he will speak with a voice of thunder, he will have the promptings which are daemonic and the veerings which are from Heaven, he will have an unforced air and *do nothing*, and the myriad things will be smoke piling higher and higher. Why after all should I bother about governing the empire?

Ts'ui Chu asked Old Tan

'Without governing the empire, how are we to improve men's hearts?'

'Be very careful not to meddle with man's heart. Man's heart when spurned goes down, when promoted goes up, when down is the prisoner and when up is the executioner. Gently it goes on yielding to the harder and stronger, yet it has corners and it jabs, it is engraved, it is polished. When hot it is a scorching flame, when cold it is congealed ice, it is so swift that between a glance up and a glance down it has twice gone right round the four seas. At rest it is still from the depths, in motion it takes to the air on the course laid down by Heaven. Is there anything as eager and proud and impossible to tie down as the heart of man?'

In former times the Yellow Emperor was the first to use Goodwill and Duty to meddle with the hearts of men. After that Yao and Shun worked the fat off their thighs and the hairs off their shins to nourish the bodies of everyone in the world, tormented their Five Organs using them to make Goodwill and Duty, tired out the energies in their blood estimating laws and measures, but still there were some they failed to conquer. Yao thereupon banished Huan Tou to Mount Ch'ung, expelled the San-miao to San-wei, exiled

Kung-kung to Yu-tu; this is failing to conquer the world, is it not? By the time of the Three Kings the whole world was in utter panic. At worst there were tyrant Chieh and robber Chih, at best there were Tseng and Shih, and the Confucians and Mohists sprung up in all their variety. From that time on, becoming friendly or hostile they doubted each other, becoming stupid or clever they cheated each other, becoming good or bad they blamed each other, becoming trustworthy or faithless they vilified each other, and the world fell into decay. Ultimate Power ceased to be shared, and our nature and destiny were frayed and smudged. The whole world lusted after knowledge and the Hundred Clans were in turmoil. From that time on we have hatcheted and sawed to get things in shape, inked the carpenter's line to trim them, hammered and chiselled to sunder them, and the world has been jumbled in utter chaos. The fault was in meddling with men's hearts.

The result is that men of worth hide away under the great mountains and craggy cliffs, while the lords of 10,000 chariots go on trembling with anxiety up in the shrines of their ancestors. In the present age the condemned to death lie back to back, the shackled in cangues and stocks are elbow to elbow, there is always a mutilated man somewhere in sight, yet it is just now that the Confucians and Mohists start putting on airs and come flipping back their sleeves among the fettered and manacled. Alas, it passes belief, their impudence and shamelessness passes belief! I am inclined to think that sagehood and knowledge are the wedges of the stocks and the cangue, that Goodwill and Duty are the pin and hole of fetters and manacles. How do I know that Tseng and Shih are not the whistling arrows which signal the attack of tyrant Chieh and robber Chih?

5

Episodes related to the Primitivist essays

Of the following passages, the dialogue of Old Tan and Tzŭ-kung is certainly by the Primitivist or some follower of his. Not only does it share his slogan 'the essentials of nature and destiny' and the theory of a historical decline starting with the Yellow Emperor, it repeats a passage from 'Keep it in place and within bounds' ('sitting as still as a corpse . . . ')[15] and another from 'Rifling trunks' ('So we disturb the brightness of the sun and moon above . . . ').[16] In this dialogue it may be noticed that the positions credited to Yao and to Yü in far antiquity are those of the Confucian and Mohist schools respectively (the Mohists originated disputation, and 'Robbers are people but killing robbers is not killing people' was a thesis which they defended, cf. *Later Mohist logic* pp. 487–9).

The second passage is put together from fragments in chapters 12 and 11 which dovetail neatly. Here the evidence of authorship is weak, and I must confess to being guided mainly by a subjective but persistent feeling that I can hear the Primitivist's indignant crotchety voice.

When Confucius returned from his visit to Old Tan he did not talk for three days.

'Now that you have seen Old Tan, sir', asked a disciple, 'how would you assess him?'

'For the first time in my life I have seen the dragon. The dragon

> Cohering, becomes a solid presence;
> When most elusive makes its best effects.
> It rides upon the breath of the clouds,
> And soars above the Yin and Yang.

My mouth gaped so wide I could not get it shut. Who am I to assess Old Tan?'

Said Tzŭ-kung:

'Then there really is a man who "sitting as still as a corpse looks as majestic as a dragon, and from the silence of the abyss speaks with a voice of thunder", who is prompted into motion like heaven and earth? Can I get to see him too?'

Then introducing himself as a disciple of Confucius he called on Old Tan. Old Tan, who was sitting cross-legged in the hall, answered in a faint voice:

'The cycle of my years is fulfilled and I depart. What lesson have you come to teach me?'

'In the ruling of the empire the Five Emperors and the Three Kings were not the same, but in the glory of their renown they are as one; why is it that you alone, sir, think that they were not sages?'

'Young man, come a little nearer. Why do you say they were not the same?'

'Yao gave up the throne and Shun took it, Yü worked with his hands and T'ang made war, King Wen obeyed Chow and did not venture to rebel but King Wu rebelled against Chow and disdained to obey. That is why I say they were not the same.'

'Young man, a little nearer, and I shall tell you how the Five Emperors and the Three Kings ruled the empire. When the Yellow Emperor ruled the empire, he unified the hearts of the people; if someone failed to weep at the death of his own parents, the people saw nothing wrong. When Yao ruled the empire, he differentiated the hearts of the people by the sense of kinship; if someone for the sake of the nearer reduced by degrees his duties to the farther, the people saw nothing wrong. When Shun ruled the empire he made the hearts of the people competitive; pregnant women gave birth by the tenth month, children by their fifth month were able to talk, before their first smile they were starting to tell who from who, and then for the first time there were premature deaths among men. When Yü ruled the empire he made the hearts of the people disputatious; the more men used their hearts for thinking the more there was for weapons to do, killing robbers wasn't killing people, each man became a breed of his own and the empire came to be as it is.

'This is why the empire was in utter panic, and the Confucians and Mohists both sprang up. When they first started there were rules of conduct, but by now men are using their own daughters as their wives, unspeakable! I tell you, when the Five Emperors and Three Kings ruled the empire, in name they "ruled" it, but misrule was never worse. The knowledge of the Three Kings disturbed the brightness of the sun and moon above, dissipated the quintessences in the mountains and rivers below, interrupted the rounds of the four seasons in between. That knowledge of theirs has a sting crueller than a scorpion's tail, no beast however rarely spied is left secure in the essentials of its nature and destiny, yet still they think they are sages. Is it not shameful, that shamelessness of theirs!'

Tzŭ-kung, much taken aback, did not know where to put his feet. (*Chuang-tzŭ*, chapter 14)

·   ·   ·

The filial son does not flatter his parents, the loyal minister does not fawn on his lord: there is no higher excellence in minister or son. If you affirm whatever your parents say, approve whatever they do, even the vulgar will call you an inadequate son; if you affirm whatever your lord says, approve whatever he does, even the vulgar will call you an inadequate minister. But don't they understand that the same necessarily applies to themselves? If you affirm whatever the vulgar affirm, approve whatever the vulgar approve, you don't find them calling you a fawner and flatterer. Then do the vulgar really have more authority than one's parents, more majesty than one's lord?

Call one of them a flatterer and he looks offended, call him a fawner and he looks angry, yet he is a flatterer all his life, a fawner all his life. When he gathers a throng around him by apt illustrations and elegant phrases, there is a contradiction between start and end, motive and outcome. He chooses the hang of his dress, the colours which adorn it, his mannerisms of expression and gesture, to appeal to the taste of his times, yet denies that he is a flatterer or fawner; it is to ordinary people that he is attaching himself, he shares their judgements of right and wrong, yet he denies that he is one of the crowd. It is the last word in foolishness.

One aware of being a fool is not the biggest fool, one aware of being deluded is not the most deluded. The most deluded is never disabused, the biggest fool is for ever unaware. If of three travellers there is one who is deluded, they can still be directed to the destination, for the deluded is in a minority; but if two are deluded, they will fail to get there however hard they try, for the deluded are the majority. Is it not sad that now, when the whole world is deluded, even when I do signal the direction it doesn't do any good?

Great music does not get an entrance into villagers' ears, but if it's 'Snap the willow' or 'The pretty flowers' they burst into gleeful laughter. Just so, lofty words do not lodge in the hearts of the crowd; the most sublime do not stand out, because the words of the vulgar are in the majority. When at every fork in the road you are all the more deluded, you will never reach your destination; and now, when the whole world is deluded, even when I do signal the direction what good can it do? To persist in what one knows can do no good is one more delusion, so it's best to let things be and refrain from pushing. If I don't push who is going to worry?

A leper, when in the middle of the night a child is born to him, hurries torch in hand to look at it, for there is nothing that in his suspense he fears more than that it will resemble himself. But vulgar people are all pleased if others go on thinking the same as themselves, and hate others to disagree with them. To wish others to agree with you, and be displeased if they do not, is to have the aim of becoming superior to the many; and how can anyone who makes superiority to the many his aim ever be superior to the many? Rather than have the support of the many to confirm what you were taught, it is better that the many arts of ruling be as many as possible; yet the people who so desire to run somebody's state for him are the ones who go on contemplating the benefits of the rule of the Three Kings without noticing its disadvantages. This is to trust the man's state to luck, and how long can you trust it to luck without losing it? Your chances of saving his state are not one in 10,000, the odds that you will lose it are more than 10,000 to one. (*Chuang-tzŭ*, chapters 12 and 11)

NOTES TO PART FOUR

1   cf. p. 207f above.
2   cf. p. 207 above.
3   cf. pp. 211, 213 above.
4   cf. p. 202 above.
5   cf. p. 213 above.
6   cf. p. 181f above.
7   cf. p. 211 above.
8   cf. p. 204 above.
9   *The book of the Lord Shang*, translated J. J. L. Duyvendak (London, 1928), pp. 284f.
10   cf. p. 237 below.

11   A. C. Graham, *The NUNG-CHIA 'School of the Tillers' and the origins of peasant Utopianism in China*, Bulletin of the School of Oriental and African Studies, London, 42/1 (1979), 66–100.
12   *Mencius*, translated D. C. Lau (Penguin Classics, 1970), 3A/4.
13   cf. p. 232f. below.
14   cf. p. 212 above.
15   cf. pp. 212, 215 above.
16   cf. pp. 210, 215 above.

Part Five

The Yangist miscellany

There is a block of four chapters distinguished by titles which sum up their themes (chapters 28–31, 'Yielding the throne', 'Robber Chih', 'The discourse on swords', and 'The old fisherman'); since the rest of the *Outer* and *Mixed chapters* have titles taken from their opening words, these must have composed a single collection before they entered the book. They seem not to be Taoist at all, but to come from late representatives of the Yangist school, towards the end of the third century BC. Its traditionally recognised founder, Yang Chu (*c*. 350 BC), is not known to have left any writings, but his tenets are summed up in chapter 13 of *Huai-nan-tzŭ* (*c*. 120 BC) as 'keeping one's nature intact, protecting one's genuineness, and not tying the body by involvements with other things'. The philosophical encyclopedia *Lü-shih ch'un-ch'iu* (*c*. 240 BC) includes him in a list of ten philosophers as the advocate of 'valuing self'; it also has five chapters which expound the doctrines which we have noticed ascribed to him,[1] although without naming him. Similarly in *Chuang-tzŭ* the Primitivist mentions the disputation of 'Yang and Mo',[2] but Yang Chu is not named in the present chapters, which seem to be actual documents of Yangist disputation contemporary with the Primitivist. It may be guessed that the Yangists, unlike the Confucians and Mohists, did not look back to a founder or depend on a book, and that Yang Chu was no more than an early representative of the movement whom it was convenient to pick out when a name was needed to identify it.

The 'Yangist miscellany' had already been incorporated in *Chuang-tzŭ* by the time of the great historian Ssŭ-ma Ch'ien (145–*c*. 86 BC), who in his biographical note on Chuang-tzŭ mentions both 'Robber Chih' and 'The old fisherman' among his writings. As for 'Robber Chih', we shall offer when we introduce the chapter evidence that it comes from the same period as the Primitivist, the interregnum between the Ch'in and Han dynasties (209–202 BC). 'The old fisherman' implies a time of settled government, presumably under the Han, but is not necessarily much later; one can imagine that with the reunification of China under a relatively benign government in 202 BC the political atmosphere would change from the cynicism of 'Robber Chih' to the contentment of 'The old fisherman' almost overnight. Of the other two chapters there is little to say except that 'Yielding the throne' is later than the *Lü-shih ch'un-ch'iu* (*c*. 240 BC), with which it shares not only many stories but comments on them characteristic of that book.

Yangism is the oldest Chinese philosophy of life which caters for the person of some means who prefers the comforts and limitations of private life to the prospects and dangers of office. So does the Taoism of Chuang-tzŭ and his school (and from the early centuries AD so does Buddhism); but it differs from these philosophies in having nothing mystical about it, in posing only the question 'What are my true interests?' These interests are weighed with as much calculation as the benefits and harms of mankind in general are weighed by the rival Mohist school; we are not yet in the antirational world of Taoism, for which calculations of prudence and of morality are seen as equally disruptive of spontaneity. There is only one place in all the four chapters where we seem for a moment to be making the jump from rational self-interest to Taoist mysticism, in the second of the three 'Robber Chih' dialogues.[3] Here a debate between advocates of Confucian morality and of worldly success is referred to a third party, who begins his reply with a Taoist-sounding verse culminating in the advice: 'In accord with the Way walk your meandering path.' But in the late third and second centuries the didactic verse even of a Legalist such as Han Fei tends to use Taoist imagery, and as soon as the arbiter descends to prose he talks like a Yangist, judiciously advising both parties not to endanger their lives by being either too moral or too greedy.

The Primitivist's pairing of the disputation of the Yangists with that of the Mohists is by no means arbitrary, for although the latter asked 'What benefits the world?' and the former 'What benefits me?', they have points in common in the terminology and technique of debate. For example, the later Mohist dialectical chapters, the Yangist chapter *Shen wei* ('Be aware of what you are for') in the *Lü-shih ch'un-ch'iu*, and the second and third dialogues of 'Robber Chih' all share a technical use of falling-tone *wei*, 'for the sake of', to pose the question of what one is *for*, one's end in life, the final criterion by which all actions are to be judged. But there are also significant differences. Mohist disputation had become by the third century BC purely logical, a sustained effort, comparable with the Greek, to settle problems definitively by reason alone. But the less philosophical applied the word *pien*, 'disputation', to the art of political persuasion, and used it adjectivally ('subtle, eloquent') of rhetorical skill in advising a prince or negotiating an alliance. The Yangist disputation is of this sort. The dialogues in 'Robber Chih', 'The discourse on swords' and 'The old fisherman' are demonstrations of virtuosity in the art of persuasion, in which both Confucius and Chih are described as *pien*, 'eloquent'. The highest proof of this eloquence is having at your fingertips a wealth of historical examples. Robber Chih, after overwhelming Confucius with fourteen such illustrations (which he numbers in groups), continues: 'Of the instances you might use to persuade me . . . '.[4] In the next dialogue in 'Robber Chih' we find four neat pairs of illustrations summed up by 'These are the examples which former generations passed down and recent generations preach'.[5] 'Yielding the throne' turns out when related to the rest of the Yangist miscellany to be an actual handbook of illustrations for use in debate, some of them used in 'Robber Chih'. These are assembled from a variety of older sources. A by-product of the Yangists' interest in literary skills is that their original stories are longer and technically more sophisticated than anything elsewhere in *Chuang-tzŭ*. Indeed 'The old fisherman' is a landmark in the development of narrative technique in China.

The fundamental principle of Yangism is that the life of the body is more important than the things which serve to nurture it. Possessions are replaceable, the body is not; therefore one should never sacrifice as much as a hair of the body in exchange for any object external to it, even the throne of the empire. Not that the Yangist chooses poverty on principle; he may on occasion, after weighing the circumstances, judge it safe to accept a throne, and he especially despises the man so proud of his own incorruptibility that he will commit suicide rather than debase himself by accepting a worldly honour.[6] But he is careful not to be deluded into seeking power and possessions at risk to life by the two great temptations, greed for wealth and the moral demand to contribute to the good government of the people. The 'Robber Chih' dialogues wage campaigns in both directions, first against moralism, then against worldly ambition. The central issue which divides the Yangists from the moralists, whether Confucian or Mohist, shows up most clearly in a story of probably Mohist origin which survives by good luck in *Lieh-tzŭ* (a Taoist book of *c*. AD 300), about a confrontation of Ch'in Ku-li, the chief disciple of Mo-tzŭ, with Yang Chu and his disciple Meng Sun-yang:

'Ch'in Ku-li asked Yang Chu

'If you could help the whole world by sacrificing one hair of your body, would you do it?'

'It would surely be of no help to the world to give one hair.'

'But supposing it did help, would you do it?' Yang Chu did not answer him. When Ch'in Ku-li came out he told Meng Sun-yang.

'You do not understand what is in our Master's heart,' said Meng Sun-yang. 'Let me explain. If you could win 10,000 pieces of gold by injuring your skin and flesh, would you do it?'

'I would.'

'If you could gain a state by cutting off one limb at the joint, would you do it?'

Ch'in Ku-li was silent for a while. Meng Sun-yang continued:

'It is clear that one hair is a trifle compared with skin and flesh, and skin and flesh compared with one joint. However, enough hairs are worth as much as skin and flesh as one joint. You cannot deny that one hair has its place among the myriad parts of the body; how can one treat it lightly?'[7]

What the Mohist calls 'helping the world' the Yangist calls 'gaining a state', and since it is by winning political power that one becomes able to benefit the people, neither party quibbles over the identification. What for Yang Chu is a high-minded indifference to possessions is for Ch'in Ku-li a selfish refusal to help others. The narrator, who seems to be a Mohist, says that according to Yang Chu 'a man of ancient times, if he could benefit the empire by the loss of one hair, would not give it, and if the whole empire were presented to himself alone, would not take it'. The Confucian Mencius says similarly:[8] 'What Yang Chu was *for* was self; if by plucking one hair he might benefit the whole world he would not do it.' This last is a one-sided description of his thesis, but it picks out the point which for moralists was crucial, and which in the story just quoted embarrasses Yang Chu himself. However, the Yangist values self against external things rather than other selves. We are more than once told[9] that it is the man who puts his own life and health before the possession of a throne who deserves to occupy a throne – a point made also by the Primitivist[10] and in *Lao-tzŭ* chapter 13. This may seem a curious claim, but the reasoning is presumably that the Yangist ruler would put the lives of his subjects, like his own, before his throne and any other mere thing, the only function of which is to nurture life. This is exemplified in the story of the Great King Tan-fu.[11]

   Chuang-tzŭ appears once in the Yangist miscellany, as the hero of 'The discourse on swords'. This is sufficient to explain how the Yangist miscellany came to be incorporated into *Chuang-tzŭ*, where it is only slightly incongruous; Taoism after all inherited the Yangist thesis that health and longevity matter more than property and office, even if it inclines rather to the view that you avoid damage to the spontaneous process of life by *not* thinking about it. 'The discourse on swords' is so unlike any story of Chuang-tzŭ elsewhere in the book that many scholars doubt that it can be about the same man, although when he follows the custom of referring to himself by his personal name (which in translation has to be replaced by 'I') he too turns out to be called 'Chou'. But if it is correct to infer from the story of the huge magpie that Chuang-tzŭ was at one time a Yangist[12] it becomes comprehensible that there might be a divergent tradition about him in Yangist literature.

1

Yielding the throne

This chapter is a collection of illustrative anecdotes for use in Yangist disputation, some of them actually applied in the 'Robber Chih' dialogues. Most can be found in the *Lü-shih ch'un-ch'iu* and other extant sources; some items are Confucian, one is from the Tillers,[13] and the first two are evidently different versions of a single story. The editor added no comments of his own, but many of his extracts from the *Lü-shih ch'un-ch'iu* already had Yangist comments which he left intact.

The anecdotes fall into two series, each in chronological sequence.

FIRST SERIES

These stories illustrate the point that life and health are more important than possessions and that you can be happy in poverty.

Yao resigned the empire to Hsü Yu. Hsü Yu refused it. Next he resigned it to Tzǔ-chou Chih-fu.

'It might not be a bad idea to make me Son of Heaven,' said Tzǔ-chou Chih-fu. 'However, at the moment I am worried about a serious ailment. I'm going to put it right, and haven't time just now to put the empire right.'

The empire is the most important thing of all, but he would not harm his life for the sake of it, and how much less for anything else! Only the man who cares nothing for the empire deserves to be entrusted with the empire.

· · ·

Shun resigned the empire to Tzǔ-chou Chih-po.

'At the moment I am worried about a serious ailment,' said Tzǔ-chou Chih-po. 'I'm going to put it right, and haven't time just now to put the empire right.'

So though the empire is the greatest of the tools a man can use, he would not barter away life for it. This is where the man who possesses the Way is quite different from the vulgar.

· · ·

Shun resigned the empire to Shan-chüan.

'All Space and Time are the court in which I stand,' said Shan-chüan. 'In the winter days I wear furs, in the summer days vine-cloth and hemp. In spring I plough and sow, and my body is strong enough for the labour; in autumn I harvest and store, and the yield is sufficient to rest and feed me. I start work with the sunrise, retire with the sunset. As I go my rambling way between heaven and earth, my heart has all it needs to satisfy it. What does the empire matter to me? Alas, that you should so misunderstand me!'

So he would not accept. Then he left and went deep into the mountains, and no one knows where he settled.

* * *

Shun resigned the empire to his friend the farmer of Stone Door.

'What a fidgety person our Emperor is!' said the farmer of Stone Door. 'He's a fellow who can't help working too hard.'

He decided that the Power in Shun was inadequate. Then he and his wife loaded up their belongings, he on his back, she on her head, and leading his children by the hand he went over the sea, and to the end of his life never came back.

* * *

When the Great King Tan-fu was settled in Pin, the Ti tribes attacked him. He offered them tribute in hides and silks but they would not accept, in horses and hounds but they would not accept, in pearls and jades but they would not accept; what the Ti wanted was the land. Said Tan-fu

'To send to their deaths the younger brothers and the sons of those with whom I live, I could not bear to do that. Get on as best you can here, all of you. What difference does it make whether you are subjects to me or to the Ti? I have heard too that one does not let a means of nurture do harm to what it nurtures.'

So he departed from them staff in hand. The people followed in a procession behind him. Then he founded a state at the foot of Mount Ch'i.

The Great King Tan-fu may be pronounced capable of honouring life. One capable of honouring life, however rich and noble, will not let the nurturing of his own person do it injury; however poor and mean, he will not for the sake of gain tie his body by involvements. The men of the present age who occupy high office and an honoured estate all fail at this over and over again. Are they not deluded, when at the sight of gain they so lightly bring ruin on their own persons?

* * *

The men of Yüeh three times in succession murdered their lord. The King's son Sou, expecting it to happen to him, fled away to Cinnabar Cave, and the state of Yüeh was without a lord. When they looked for Prince Sou he was nowhere to be found, until they tracked him down in Cinnabar Cave. Prince Sou would not come out, but the men of Yüeh smoked him out with mugwort and rode him back in the royal chariot.

As Prince Sou was pulling himself by the strap up into the chariot, he looked up to Heaven and cried:

'A king! A king! Why couldn't they leave me alone?'

It was not that Prince Sou hated being a king, he hated the troubles of being a king. One may say of such a man as Prince Sou that he would not for the sake of a state do injury to life; and the result was that he was the very man whom the people of Yüeh wanted as their lord.

*   *   *

Han and Wei were in conflict and raiding each other's borders. When Tzŭ-hua-tzŭ visited Marquis Chao-hsi, the Marquis looked worried.

'Let's suppose', said Tzŭ-hua-tzŭ, 'that the empire were to draw up a document in my lord's presence, and this is how it was worded: "If you grasp this with your left hand you shall lose your right, if you grasp it with your right hand you shall lose your left; but whoever does grasp it shall possess the empire." Would you be able to do it?'

'I would not.'

'Very good. You may see by this that having both your arms is more important than having the empire. Likewise your whole person is more important than your two arms. And Han after all is far less important than the empire, and the land you are contending for now far less important than Han. Are you really going to distress your person and do injury to life worrying and fretting that you can't get it?'

'Excellent! Many have advised me, but no one ever said this to me before.'

We may say that Tzŭ-hua-tzŭ knew the important from the unimportant.

*   *   *

The lord of Lu heard that Yen Ho was a man who had won the Way, and sent a messenger to approach him with presents. Yen Ho kept to himself in a mean quarter, wore a sackcloth coat and fed his cows with his own hands. When the lord of Lu's messenger arrived Yen Ho himself came to the door.

'Is this the house of Yen Ho?'

'It is.'

The messenger handed over the presents.

'I'm afraid you may have heard the name wrong', Yen Ho replied, 'and it will get you into trouble. You had better confirm it.'

The messenger went back to confirm his instructions. When he came looking for him again he did not find him in.

It will be seen that it is by no means the case that someone like Yen Ho hates wealth and rank. As the saying goes: 'The most genuine in the Way is for supporting one's own person, its left-overs are for running a state, its discards are for ruling the empire.' Seen from this viewpoint, the achievements of emperors and kings are the left-over deeds of the sage, they are not the means by which he keeps his person whole and nurtures life. How sad that so many of the worldly gentlemen of today endanger their persons or throw away their lives sacrificing themselves for mere things! Whenever the sage is prompted to act, he will be sure to scrutinise both why and how he is acting. Now suppose we have a man who uses the pearl of the Marquis of Sui as a crossbow pellet to shoot at a sparrow 10,000 feet high in the air. The worldly would laugh at him of course. Why? – Because what he is utilising is more important than what he aims at. And is not life much more important than the pearl of the Marquis of Sui?

•   •   •

Master Lieh-tzŭ was living in distress, with the pinch of hunger in his face. There was a visitor who spoke of him to Tzŭ-yang of Cheng.

'Lieh-tzŭ is known as a knight who has the Way. While living in your state he has fallen into distress. Might not people think that you are uninterested in men of talent?'

Tzŭ-yang at once ordered an official to send him grain. Lieh-tzŭ when he saw the messenger bowed twice and refused it. The messenger left, Lieh-tzŭ went in. His wife gazed after the departing man and said beating her breast

'I had heard that the wife and children of anyone who has the Way live in ease and joy. Now our faces are pinched with hunger, yet when his lordship notices and sends you grain you refuse to take it. What a fate is mine!'

With a smile Lieh-tzŭ said to her

'It was not that his lordship knew me himself, it was on another man's word that he sent me grain. Should he ever find me deserving of punishment, it would again be on another man's word. This is why I did not accept.'

Finally it turned out that the people rose in rebellion and killed Tzŭ-yang.

•   •   •

When King Chao of Ch'u lost his state, his mutton butcher Yüeh was one of those who fled with him. When King Chao regained the state, he intended to reward all who had been loyal to him, even mutton butcher Yüeh.

'His Majesty lost the state, I lost my job,' said Yüeh. 'His Majesty regained the state, I regained my job. My title and salary are already restored, why mention a reward?'

'Make him accept,' said the King.

'That His Majesty lost the state was no fault of mine, so I would not have presumed to offer myself for punishment. That His Majesty regained the state is not to my credit, so I do not presume to claim a reward.'

'Bring him here,' said the King.

'By the law of the state of Ch'u, only men who are being richly rewarded for great deeds are admitted to the presence. Now I was neither clever enough to save the state nor brave enough to die fighting the invaders. When the army of Wu entered Ying I was scared of trouble and fled from the invaders, it wasn't that I deliberately threw in my lot with His Majesty. Now His Majesty desires to grant me an audience which would be a flouting of the law and a breach with precedent; that is not going to make the world think well of me.'

Said the King to his marshal Tzŭ-chi

'Mutton butcher Yüeh has a mean and humble position, but the point he is making is a very lofty one. On my behalf promote him to a placement with three banners.'

'A placement with three banners', said Yüeh, 'is more exalted I know than a mutton butcher's stall, and a salary of 10,000 *chung* is more lavish than a mutton butcher's earnings. But how could I be so greedy for title and salary as to let my sovereign become notorious for indiscriminate liberality? I cannot claim to deserve it, I want to go back to my mutton butcher's stall.'

He never did accept.

•   •   •

Yüan Hsien was dwelling in Lu, in a house 50 cubits by 50 cubits, thatched with growing grass, with a bramble door which let in the wind and had a mulberry stalk for hinge, two rooms which had jars with the bottoms out for windows, and rags stuffing the holes. On the damp floor under the leaking roof he sat straight-backed singing to the zither.

Tzŭ-kung with a team of tall horses, and robed in white over royal blue, in a high-fronted carriage too grand to squeeze into the lane, went to call on Yüan Hsien. Yüan Hsien in a cap split down the middle and heel-less sandals leaning on a goosefoot staff answered the door.

'O, how you have deteriorated!' said Tzŭ-kung.

'As I have heard it, lack of means is called "poverty", proving incapable of living by the Way one was taught is called "deteriorating". The trouble with me now is poverty, not deterioration.'

Tzŭ-kung shuffled his feet and looked embarrassed. Said Yüan Hsien with a smile

'To be on the lookout for worldly prospects, make friends in some gang which can help me along, do my learning with others in mind and my teaching thinking only of myself, and while corrupting Goodwill and Duty put on a splendid show with my carriages and horses, are things I could not bear to do.'

NOTE   Yüan Hsien and Tzŭ-kung were both disciples of Confucius (as was Tseng-tzŭ in the next story).

* * *

When Tseng-tzŭ lived in Wey his quilted gown was down to the lining, his face was swollen and blotched, his hands and feet calloused. He did not light a fire once in three days, did not have a coat cut once in ten years. When he straightened his cap the chin-band snapped, when he pulled on his lapels his elbows showed through the sleeves, when he got into his shoes they burst at the heels.

With shuffling steps he would sing the *Hymns of Shang*. The sound filled heaven and earth, as though from bells and stone chimes. The Son of Heaven could not get him as a minister, the lords of the states could not get him as a friend. So when nurturing your intent forget the body, in nurturing the body forget profit, in perfecting the Way forget the calculations of the heart.

* * *

Said Confucius to Yen Hui
'Hui, come here! Your family is poor, your station humble. Why not take office?'

'I prefer not to take office. I have 50 *mou* of fields out in the country, enough to provide porridge and gruel, and 10 *mou* on the edge of town, enough to keep me in silk and hemp. Strumming on the zither is all the amusement I need, and in the Way I studied under you, sir, I find all my happiness. I prefer not to take office.'

Confucius solemnly composed his face.

'Excellent, that resolve of yours! I have heard it said: "The man who knows when he has enough does not let himself be tied for the sake of profit; the man who understands where satisfaction lies is not afraid of losses; the man who is disciplined in his private conduct is not ashamed to lack position." I have been chanting the words for a long time, and now at last in you I see an example of it. You have done me a service.'

* * *

The Chung-shan Prince Mou said to Chan-tzŭ
'My body is here by the river and the sea, but my heart lingers on under the city gate-towers of Wei. What's to be done?'

'Give weight to life. See life as heavy and profit will be light to you.'

'Well though I know it, still I am unable to conquer myself.'

'If you cannot conquer yourself, let go. Are there not aversions which are from the daemonic in us? To be unable to conquer oneself, yet force oneself not to let go, this is what they call ''being wounded twice over''. Men who wound themselves twice over are the sort that never live long.'

Mou of Wei was a prince of 10,000 chariots, and to hide away in the caves of the cliffs was harder for him than for a commoner. Even though he had not attained the Way, we may say that he had the idea of it.

. . .

When Confucius was caught with no way out between Ch'en and Ts'ai, for seven days he did not eat a cooked meal, he had no grain in his soup of herbs, he was haggard in the face, but he strummed and sang inside the house. While Yen Hui picked vegetables, Tzŭ-lu and Tzŭ-kung were saying to each other

'Twice our Master was chased out of Lu, he had to scrape away his foot-prints in Wey, he had a tree chopped down over him in Sung, he had no way to turn in Shang and Chou, and here between Ch'en and Ts'ai they have him surrounded. His life is at the mercy of anyone, he is outside the protection of the law. To be singing and strumming his zither, never a pause in the sound – is a gentleman so without shame?'

Yen Hui had no answer for them. He went in and told Confucius. Pushing away his zither, Confucius sighed deeply.

'Tzŭ-lu and Tzŭ-kung are petty people. Call them in, I shall speak to them.'

The two men entered. Said Tzŭ-lu

'To be in these straits I would call getting nowhere.'

'What words are these? For a gentleman, to have access throughout the Way is what is meant by getting somewhere, to make no progress in the Way is what is meant by getting nowhere. At present in embracing the Way of Goodwill and Duty I come upon the troubles of a disordered age, what has that to do with getting nowhere? So in looking inwards I have unhindered access to the Way, and in confronting difficulties I do not lose the Power in me. After great cold comes, after frosts and snows fall, that is when I know that the pines and cypresses are thriving. These narrows of Ch'en and Ts'ai, are they not a blessing to me?'

Confucius with a flourish resumed his strumming on the zither and sang. Tzŭ-lu with a swagger took up his shield and danced. Said Tzŭ-kung:

'I never knew that heaven is so high, that earth is so firm under my feet.'

The men of old who had grasped the Way were happy whether they got anywhere or not. Their happiness had nothing to do with failure or success. Wherever the Way is grasped, failure and success belong with the cycles of cold and heat, wind and rain. Therefore Hsü Yu was content on the north bank of the Ying, and Kung-po lived satisfied on the summit of Mount Kung.

• • •

SECOND SERIES

These are stories, again arranged in chronological sequence, of high-minded men who commit suicide rather than disgrace themselves by accepting a throne or office. Such conduct was widely admired, and the Syncretist 'Finicky ideas' mentions a special category of hermits who withdraw from government on moral grounds and 'wither away or drown themselves'.[14] But the Yangist detests them, and is arranging examples to be used as the last of them, the story of Po Yi and Shu Ch'i, is used by Robber Chih.[15] Where his main source the *Lü-shih ch'un-ch'iu* has an approving comment he cuts it out. The series breaks off unexpectedly early, at the very beginning of the Chou, perhaps because of textual mutilation; Robber Chih's other instances are later.

Shun resigned the empire to his friend Wu-tse the Northerner.

'What a strange person our Emperor is!' said Wu-tse the Northerner. 'From the fields where he belonged he came to hang around the court of Yao. Nor is that the worst of it; he wishes to pollute me too with his disgraceful conduct. I should be embarrassed to see him.'

Then he threw himself into the deeps of Ch'ing-leng.

• • •

When T'ang had resolved to smite his lord Chieh, he appealed to Pien Sui to plan the campaign.

'It is no business of mine,' said Pien Sui.

'Who do you think would do?'

'I would not know.'

Next T'ang appealed to Wu Kuang to plan the campaign.

'It is no business of mine.'

'Who do you think would do?'

'I would not know.'

'What about Yi Yin?'

'He is energetic and unscrupulous, that is all I know about him.'

Then T'ang planned the campaign against Chieh with Yi Yin. He defeated him, and resigned the throne to Pien Sui. Pien Sui refused it.

'When the Emperor smote Chieh', he said, 'he was going to plan the campaign with me: certainly he believed me rebellious. Having conquered Chieh he resigns the throne to me: certainly he believes me ambitious. I live on and on in an age of disorder, and twice a man without the Way has come to pollute me with his disgraceful conduct. I cannot bear to hear the same thing over and over again.'

Then he threw himself into the River Ch'ou and died.

Next T'ang resigned the throne to Wu Kuang, saying

'I have heard it said: "That the wise plan it, the warriors execute it, and the benevolent make the settlement, is the Way of old." Why not take the throne yourself?'

Wu Kuang refused.

'To make away with your sovereign is contrary to Duty, to slaughter your people is contrary to Goodwill; and when others have undertaken the hard part, for me to enjoy the profit would not be honesty. I have heard it said: "For deeds contrary to one's duty one does not accept the Emperor's favours, in a reign without the Way one does not tread the Emperor's soil", far less let him elevate one to honours! I cannot bear that my eyes should go on seeing.'

Then he loaded a stone on his back and drowned himself in the waters of Lu.

·   ·   ·

Formerly during the rise of the Chou there were two knights who lived in Ku-chu, called Po Yi and Shu Ch'i. The two men said to each other

'They say that in the West there is a man who seems like someone who would have the Way. Let's go and take a look at him.'

When they arrived south of Mount Ch'i, King Wu heard of them, and sent his younger brother Tan to go and see them. He made a covenant with them, promising "You shall have income of the second class, office of the first rank", smeared it with a victim's blood and buried it.

The two men exchanged glances and smiled.

'Hmm, strange! This is not what we would call the Way. Formerly when Shen-nung possessed the empire, in the seasonal sacrifices he was perfectly reverent but he did not pray for blessings; his dealings with others were loyal, trustworthy, perfectly orderly, but he did not seek anything from them. He delighted in joining with the correct to correct, with the orderly to order. He did not take advantage of other men's deterioration to become successful himself, or of others' degradation to elevate himself, or of the chances of the times to profit himself.

'Now the Chou seeing the disorder of the Yin come running to correct it. They promote conspiracies and distribute bribes, rely on arms and presume on their authority. A covenant with slaughtered victims is their idea of good faith, they brag of their deeds to please the masses, murder and invade to get their hands on profit. This is to exchange tyranny for a misrule pushed farther still.

'We have heard that the knight of old, when blessed with orderly times did not shirk his responsibilities, when he chanced on an age of misrule did not save himself by expediencies. Now the empire is in darkness, the Power in the Chou has decayed. Rather than besmirch ourselves by continuing to side with the Chou, better shun them and keep our conduct unsullied.'

The two men went north as far as the mountain of Shou-yang, and then starved to death there.

The attitude to wealth and rank of men like Po Yi and Shu Ch'i is not to recognise any justification at all for accepting them. With their lofty punctiliousness and harsh code of conduct they take a lonely pleasure in their resolve and refuse to be of service to their age. Such was the punctiliousness of the two knights.

2

Robber Chih

This chapter consists of three dialogues, starting with the famous satire in which the robber gets the better of Confucius. In spite of his ferocity the bandit is used as a spokesman of Yangism, so that his words are a little out of character; he despises appeals to profit and hankers after the peaceful Golden Age before the Yellow Emperor introduced war. The remaining two dialogues are among the few in *Chuang-tzŭ* which are genuine debates, and the spokesmen of moralism (Tzŭ-chang, disciple of Confucius), and of worldliness, are allowed their say before being defeated by the Yangist.

The chapter mentions that the Chou dynasty founded by King Wu has ended (this happened in 256 BC) and that its descendants are extinct.[16] When the robber is described as a tall man 7 feet 5 inches high,[17] the Chinese measure we are converting is that of the Ch'in dynasty and its successor the Han; if we took it for the Chou measure he would be a mere 5 feet 4 inches. This point raises the same difficulty as the dating of the Primitivist, that a writer later than the Ch'in reunification seems to assume that China is still divided into warring states, and the solution is surely the same, that he is writing in the interregnum between Ch'in and Han (209–202 BC). 'Robber Chih' and the Primitivist essays, although unlike in philosophy and style, show a striking variety of common themes and ideas, which suggest a common background in the same brief and very distinctive period. Examples are the Golden Age which lasted until Shen-nung and was destroyed by the Yellow Emperor; the idea that gentleman and knave both make a 'human sacrifice' of themselves, one for reputation and the other for profit; the equal harmfulness of moralist and criminal; the usurpation of the state as a crime which puts morality at the service of the victor; the observation that 'A petty thief goes to gaol, a great thief becomes lord of a state, and at the gates of the lord of a state you'll find your dutiful Knight', which the Primitivist makes in almost the same words;[18] the tone of polemical violence; Robber Chih himself, who appears in the Primitivist essays also, but nowhere else in the book. We can have every confidence that we are hearing the voices of those very Yangists emerging from hiding whom the Primitivist describes as 'just now starting to put on airs and think they are getting somewhere'.[19] If we are right in dating them both in this brief period of furious controversy, it cannot be a coincidence that the story of Confucius trying to sell himself to the robber appeared just when, or within a few years after, K'ung Fu, descendant of Confucius and head of his family, took office under the peasant rebel Ch'en Sheng (209–208 BC). No details survive about this event, but one can imagine the mockery of enemies of Confucianism at the time – or rather, with this contemporary document in front of us, there is no need to imagine it.

Confucius was friendly with Liu-hsia Chi, whose younger brother went by the name of Robber Chih. Robber Chih with 9,000 warriors at his back rampaged throughout the empire, raided and plundered the lords of the states, tunnelled into houses or unhinged doors, drove off people's cows and horses, carried off their wives and daughters. In his greed for spoils he gave nothing to his kin, ignored his father and mother and brothers, refused to sacrifice to his ancestors. In any city that he came by, in a great state they would man the walls, in a small state retreat to the citadel. He was a pest to all the myriads of the people.

Said Confucius to Liu-hsia Chi

'It is necessary that whoever is a father be able to command his son, and whoever is elder brother be able to teach the younger. If fathers cannot command sons or elder brothers teach younger, then kinship between fathers and sons and brothers will no longer be respected. Now you, sir, are the most talented knight of our times, while your younger brother is that Robber Chih who is a danger to the empire, yet you are unable to teach him. I would be so bold as to express my embarrassment on your behalf. Allow me to go on your behalf to advise him.'

'You say, sir, that fathers must be able to command their sons and elder brothers to teach the younger. If a son will not listen to his father's commands or a younger brother will not accept the elder's teaching, then even with the eloquence which you are exhibiting now, sir, what is one to do about it? Besides, Chih is a man with a heart like a bubbling spring and thoughts like the whirlwind, strength enough to defy reprimands, eloquence enough to dress up wrong as right. If you agree with his ideas that's fine, but if you rub him the wrong way he gets into a rage, and is prone to humiliate people with his tongue. It would be a great mistake for you to go, sir.'

Confucius would not listen. With Yen Hui driving the carriage, Tzŭ-kung on the right, he went to visit Robber Chih.

Just then Robber Chih was resting his band on the sunny side of Mount T'ai, and taking an afternoon snack of human livers. Confucius alighted from the carriage and came forward to present himself to the adjutant.

'The man of Lu Confucius, who has heard of the General's lofty reputation as a man of honour.'

Respectfully he bowed twice to the adjutant, who entered with the message. Robber Chih when he heard it was furious, his eyes were like bright stars, his hair bristled up so high it tilted his cap.

'It's that crafty hypocrite Confucius from Lu, isn't it? Tell him from me: "You devise maxims, concoct aphorisms, tendentiously cite King Wen and King Wu, and with that branching tree of a cap on your head and the hide off a dead cow's ribs round your waist, by your verbose phrasings and lying explanations you get your dinner without having to plough and your clothes without having to weave, with quivering lips and pounding tongue you engender whatever it pleases you to call right and wrong, in order to lead the sovereigns of the empire astray and make the scholars of the empire lose sight of the fundamentals – a man who by capriciously inventing filial and fraternal obligations are making your bid to become wealthy and noble with a fief of your own. Your crime is as heavy as a crime can be. Run home as fast as you can, or I'll add your liver to this afternoon's delicacies.'

Confucius sent in another message:

'I have been honoured with an introduction from Chi, and hope to see from a distance your feet under the curtain.'

The adjutant again passed on his message.

'Let him come forward,' said Robber Chih.

Confucius entered briskly, declined a mat, stepped quickly backward and bowed twice to Robber Chih. Robber Chih, furious, with legs spread wide, hand on hilt, eyes glaring, said in a voice like a nursing tigress:

'Come here, Confucius my lad. If what you have to say suits my fancy you shall live, if it offends, you die.'

'I have heard', said Confucius, 'that in the world there are three degrees of Power. To grow up from birth peerlessly tall and handsome, so that everyone young or old, noble or mean, takes pleasure in the sight of you, is to have the highest powers. To have knowledge enough to fasten heaven and earth in their places, capable of discriminating judgements on every kind of thing, is to have middling powers. To be brave, fierce, resolute, daring, a gatherer of hosts and leader of warriors, is to have the lowest powers. Any man who has even one of these degrees of Power deserves to face south and be addressed as Your Majesty. Now in you, General, all these three are joined. You stand 7 feet 5 inches tall, your countenance glows, your lips are like glistening cinnabar, your teeth are like an even row of seashells, your voice is in tune with the *huang-chung* pitch-pipe, yet the name you are known by is 'Robber' Chih. In my embarrassment on your behalf, General, I would make so bold as to disapprove.

'If you have a mind to listen to me, General, I request to be sent on a mission to Wu and Yüeh in the south, Ch'i and Lu in the north, Sung and Wey in the east and Chin and Ch'u in the south, to persuade them to build you a great city several hundred miles round, establish it as a capital of some hundreds of thousand households, and honour you as one of the lords of the states. You will make a new beginning with the world, lay down your arms and give rest to your troops, gather up and care for your brothers, join them in sacrificing to your ancestors. This will be the conduct of the sage and of the knight of talent, and what the world desires of you.'

'Come a bit nearer, Confucius my lad,' said Robber Chih furiously. 'That he can be restrained by appeals to profit and be moralised to in speeches is never to be said except of the stupid, the doltish, the commonplace. Now that I am tall and handsome, and other men take pleasure in the sight of me, is from the powers inherited from my parents, and even without your praise do you suppose that I wouldn't be aware of it myself? I have heard too that people who are fond of praising you to your face are equally fond of slandering you behind your back. Now when you tell me about a great city and a host of subjects, you hope to restrain me by appeals to profit and tame me with the rest of the commonplace people. How long would it last? No city however great is greater than the empire; Yao and Shun possessed the empire but their descendants didn't have enough ground to stick with an awl, T'ang and King Wu reigned as Son of Heaven but their lines have died out. Wasn't it because the profit that came to them was too great?

'Moreover I have heard that of old the birds and animals were many but the men were few. In those days the people all lived in nests to escape them. In the daytime they gathered acorns and chestnuts, and at nightfall perched in the treetops; therefore they were named the ''Nester clan'' people. Of old the people did not know how to clothe themselves, in summer they piled up masses of firewood, and in winter burned it; therefore they were named the ''Life-knower'' people. In the age of Shen-nung

> They slept sound,
> Woke fresh,
> The people knew their mothers,
> But did not know their fathers,
> And lived as neighbours with the deer.

By ploughing they were fed, by weaving clothed, and there was no mischief in their hearts. This was the culmination of utmost Power.

'However, the Yellow Emperor was unable to maintain Power at its utmost, he battled with Ch'ih Yu in the field of Cho-lu, and made the blood stream for a hundred miles. Yao and Shun rose up, and instituted ministers. T'ang banished his sovereign, King Wu killed Chow. From this time on men took advantage of strength to oppress the weak, of numbers to persecute the few. Ever since T'ang and Wu they have all been the troublemaking sort.

'Now you cultivate the Way of King Wen and King Wu, and with all the eloquence in the world at your disposal you teach it to a later generation. In your spreading robe and narrow belt you bend words and falsify deeds, to delude and lead astray the princes of the empire, hoping to get riches and honours from them. There's no robber worse than you. Why doesn't the world call you Robber Confucius instead of calling me Robber Chih?

'You coaxed Tzŭ-lu with sweet phrases and made him do as you said, made him put off his jaunty hat and unfasten his long sword to be taught by you. The whole world said, ''Confucius is able to check violence and forbid wrong.'' But the end of it was that Tzŭ-lu tried to kill the lord of Wey but didn't bring it off, and his pickled body hung from the East Gate of Wey. Such are the failures of your teaching. Is it a knight of talent, a sage, you call yourself? Well, you were twice chased from Lu, had to scrape away your footprints in Wey, were at your wits' end in Ch'i, were besieged between Ch'en and Ts'ai, nowhere in the world is there any room for you. You taught Tzŭ-lu to get pickled, that was what it cost him, for

> If you can't look after yourself first,
> You can't look out for others either.

How can that Way of yours deserve to be honoured?

'Of those whom the age esteems, the greatest was the Yellow Emperor, but even the Yellow Emperor could not keep Power intact, he battled in the field of Cho-lu and sent the blood streaming for a hundred miles. Yao was not a good father, Shun was not a good son, Yü became paralysed down one side, T'ang banished his sovereign, King Wu smote Chow. These are the six whom the world esteems, but consider them closely, all of them were men who for profit confused what was genuine in them, persistently flouted what was essential and natural in them. Their conduct was utterly embarrassing.

'As for those whom the world calls excellent knights, the greatest were Po Yi and Shu Ch'i. Po Yi and Shu Ch'i resigned the princedom of Ku-chu and starved to death on Mount Shou-yang, where their flesh and bones lay unburied. Pao Chiao, acting to impress, condemning the age, died with his arms round a tree. Shen-t'u Ti, when his criticisms were ignored, jumped into the Yellow River with a stone on his back, and was eaten by the fish and turtles. Chieh Tzŭ-t'ui was so extreme in his loyalty that he hacked flesh from his own thigh to feed Duke Wen; when later Duke Wen turned his back on him, Tzŭ-t'ui left in anger, and with his arms round a tree let himself burn to death. Wei Sheng made a tryst with a girl under a bridge; the girl did not come, when the rising waters reached him he would not leave, and died clinging to a post of the bridge. These six are worth no more than a dead dog in the street, a stray pig, a beggar with his bowl. They were all men who, to get themselves a name, made light of death, and did not remember to nurture life from the roots to their destined old age.

'Of those whom the age calls loyal ministers the greatest were Prince Pi-kan and Wu Tzŭ-hsü. Tzŭ-hsü drowned in the Yangtse, Pi-kan had his heart cut out. These two the age calls loyal ministers, but they ended up as laughing-stocks for the whole empire. Observing them from the first I mentioned down to Tzŭ-hsü and Pi-kan, not one deserves to be honoured. Of the instances you might use to persuade me, if you tell me tales about spirits, I don't pretend to know about that; but if you tell me tales about men, there are none more to the point than these, I've heard them all.

'Now let me tell you what man essentially is. The eyes desire to look on beauty, the ears to listen to music, the mouth to discern flavours, intent and energy to find fulfilment. Long life for man is at most a hundred years, at the mean eighty, at the least sixty; excluding sickness and hardship, bereavement and mourning, worries and troubles, the days left to us to open our mouths in a smile will in the course of a month be four or five at most. Heaven and earth are boundless, man's death has its time; when he takes up that life provided for a time to lodge in the midst of the boundless, his passing is as sudden as a thoroughbred steed galloping past a chink in the wall.

Whoever cannot gratify his intents and fancies, and find nurture for the years destined for him, is not the man who has fathomed the Way.

'Everything you say I reject. Away with you, quick, run back home, not a word more about it. Your Way is a crazy obsession, a thing of deception, trickery, vanity, falsehood. It will not serve to keep the genuine in us intact, what is there to discuss?'

Confucius bowed twice and hurried out. Outside the gate, when he climbed into the carriage, he let the reins slip three times before he could hold them; his dazed eyes saw nothing, his face was like dead ashes, he leaned on the crossbar with drooping head, could not let out a breath. When he arrived back outside the East Gate of Lu, Liu-hsia Chi happened to be there.

'I've missed seeing you for several days now,' said Liu-hsia Chi. 'By the look of your horse and carriage you have been travelling. Surely you can't have gone to see Chih?'

Confucius looked up at the sky and sighed.

'I did'

'He surely didn't shout you down as I said he would?'

'He did. I burned moxa on my skin when I wasn't ill, as the saying goes. I was in a hurry to pat the tiger's head, braid the tiger's whiskers, and very nearly didn't escape the tiger's mouth.'

. . .

Tzŭ-chang put a question to Greedyguts Grabitall.

Q. 'Why not take doing the done thing as your end in life? Unless you do the done thing you cannot be trusted; unless you can be trusted you will not be given office; unless you are given office there will be no profit for you. So recognise it by its reputation or estimate it by its profitability, either way it is being dutiful which is really the right way to live. And if you ignore both reputation and profit, and refer the question to your own heart, can the knight who takes doing the done thing as his end abandon it as his end even for a single day?'

A. 'The shameless get rich, the most trusted get noticed. The greatest reputation and profit belong I should think to the official who is shameless but can be trusted. So recognise it by its reputation or estimate it by its profitability, either way it is getting trusted which is really the right way to live. And if you ignore both reputation and profit, and refer the question to your own heart, does the knight who takes doing the done thing as his end hold on to what is in him from Heaven?'

Q. In former times Chieh and Chow had the most honoured title, Son of Heaven, and the richest of possessions, the empire; but now if you tell a slave or a groom ''You behave like Chieh and Chow'' he looks shamefaced and feels misjudged, for even knaves despise them. Confucius and

Mo Ti stayed stuck as commoners; but now if you say to the Prime Minister ''You behave like Confucius and Mo Ti'' he will look bashful and disclaim the compliment, for knights are sincerely honoured. So you can be enthroned as Son of Heaven without being sure of honour, or stay stuck as a commoner without necessarily being scorned. Your share of honour or scorn depends on how fair or foul your conduct is.'

A.   'A petty thief goes to gaol, a great thief becomes lord of a state, and at the gates of a lord of a state you'll find your dutiful knight. Formerly Hsiao-po, the Duke Huan, killed his elder brother and tumbled his sister-in-law, but Kuan Chung became his minister. Tzǔ-kao, who was T'ien Ch'eng, killed his lord and stole his state, but Confucius took a present from him. When we scorn them in theory but in practice serve them, isn't it too much of a contradiction having the facts of what we say and what we do so at war inside our breasts? As the book says, ''Which is foul, which is fair? Bring it off and you're the head, lose and you're the tail.'' '

Q.   'Unless you take doing the done thing as your end, you will cease to grade close above distant kin, observe the duties of base to noble, give precedence to elder over younger, and what will happen to the distinctions of the Five Relationships and Six Degrees?'

A.   'When Yao killed his eldest son and Shun exiled his younger brother, were the close being graded above distant kin? When T'ang banished his lord Chieh and King Wu killed his lord Chow, were the base being dutiful to the noble? When Wang Chi was promoted to Heir Apparent and the Duke of Chou killed his elder brother, were the elder being given precedence over the younger? When Confucians are phrasing their hypocritical appeals to anyone who will listen, and Mohists are practising their equal love of all, do you find them distinguishing the Five Relationships and the Six Degrees?

'I would add that in the last resort your end in life is reputation, and in the last resort mine is profit. When reputation or profit is taken too seriously, we neither accord with the pattern of things nor have a clear view of the Way. I propose that you and I refer the case to Never-committed.'

Said Never-committed

'The knave sacrifices himself for possessions, the gentleman for reputation. In the reasons why they tamper with the essential in them and barter away their nature they differ; but when it comes to casting aside what is our end in life and becoming a sacrifice for something which is not, they are as one. Hence I say

> Never be a knave,
> Return and seek what is from Heaven in you.
> Never be a gentleman,
> Take your course from Heaven's pattern.

> Whether you go crooked, whether you go straight,
> Minister to the Pole of Heaven in you.
> Turn your gaze through all the four directions,
> In accord with the times diminish and grow.
>
> Whether you do right, whether you do wrong,
> Through the cycles grip the winding handle in you.
> Fulfil alone the purpose which is yours,
> In accord with the Way walk your meandering path.

Do not reduce your conduct to a principle, do not make your dutifulness too perfect, or you will miss your end in life. Do not be in too much of a hurry for your wealth, do not pursue your successes too far, or you will throw away what is from Heaven in you. Pi Kan had his heart cut out, Tzǔ-hsü had his eyeballs gouged; they suffered for being too loyal. Upright Kung bore witness against his father, Wei-sheng drowned; they got into trouble by being too trustworthy. Pao-tzǔ stood until he withered, Shen-tzǔ entombed himself; they were harmed by being too honest. Confucius did not see his mother or K'uang-tzǔ his father; they lost by being too dutiful. These are the examples which former generations passed down and recent generations preach. Whoever has this conception of the knight is absolute in word and unvarying in deed, and therefore submits to the same calamities, runs up against the same misfortunes.'

. . .

Insatiable put a question to Temperate.

Q. 'In all mankind there was never anyone who did not push for reputation and pursue profit. If someone is rich others set their hopes on him, setting their hopes on him they put themselves under him, putting themselves under him they honour him. Having others under him and honouring him is the Way by which he lives long, satisfies the body, delights the fancy. Now if you alone have no mind for that, is it that you are too ignorant? Or is it that you do know, and are too weak to act on the knowledge? Is that why you are so meticulous about pushing just to the exact degree?'

A. 'The sort of man you mention as an instance will be thinking of himself as acknowledged by everyone born in his own times and living in his own neighbourhood as the one among them who is out of the ordinary and ahead of the rest of them. The result is that for forming his own opinions he has nothing in himself to master what comes into him from others or direct what goes out from him to others. How he regards times past and present, and the spheres of the right and of the wrong, transforms with customary opinion. The worldly dismiss the weightiest, discard the most venerable, in conceiving their ends in life. But will not the Way by which someone like that grades long life, satisfaction of the body, delighting the fancy, be after all wide of the mark? In the miseries of stress or the comforts of ease, he will not have a clear view of what they are doing to his body; in the palpitations of fear or excitements of joy, he will not have a clear view of what they are doing to his heart. He knows how to make his ends his ends, but does not know why they are his ends. This is why, even enthroned as Son of Heaven, with all the riches of the empire, he does not escape from troubles.'

Q. 'If a man has wealth it is profitable to him in everything, he has all that can be had of glory and position, more than the Utmost Man succeeds in reaching, more than the sage is able to attain. The courage and strength of the men whom he controls become his own majesty and might, the knowledge and resourcefulness of the men he manipulates become his own brilliance and discernment, the powers of the men on whom he depends become his own cleverness and skill. Without ever being presented with a state he has as much authority as a ruler or a father. In any case, when it comes to music, beauty and tastes, to sway and position, man's heart does not have to learn before delighting in them, man's body does not await a model before being satisfied by them. It is inherent in our desires and dislikes, inclinations and aversions, that they do not require a teacher; these are from the nature of man. Though all the world declares me wrong, which of you is capable of renouncing them?'

A. 'When the wise man deals with affairs, he has the motives of ordinary people, he does not stray from the average. This is why, as soon as he has enough of something, he refrains from competing for it; he has no more use for it, so does not seek it. It may be that he does not have enough, so does seek it, and competes for it wherever he finds it without thinking himself greedy; or it may be that he has too much, so refuses it, tosses away the empire itself without thinking what an honest man he is. What is really honesty or greed he judges not by pressures from outside him but by the measure of which he has a clear view when he reflects. Enthroned as Son of Heaven, he would not use the honour to be arrogant to others; owning all the riches of the empire, he would not use his wealth to trifle with others. If he estimates the trouble something will cost, anticipates reverses, concludes that it might be injurious to his nature, and therefore refuses it, that will not be out of a need for praise and repute. When Yao and Shun resigned possession of the throne, it was not out of goodwill to the world, they wouldn't for the sake of vainglory injure life. When Shan Chüan and Hsü Yu would not accept the offer of the throne, it was no empty gesture of humility, they would not by taking on its tasks injure their own selves. All those men preferred the *profitable* choice and refused the harmful one, and if the world cites them as examples of men of excellence, by all means let us give them the credit, but it was not to win praise and reputation that they did it.'

Q. 'Of course it was to sustain reputation. If tormenting the body, renouncing luxuries, reducing diet, is for sustaining life, you can be sure the man is somebody lingering on in sickness or penury who refuses to die.'

A. 'An even measure is a blessing, excess is an injury; that is so of all things, but most of all of possessions. Now in the case of the rich man, his ears dote on the sounds of bells and drums, flutes and pipes, his mouth drools over the tastes of fine meats and wines, stirring his fancy until he overlooks and neglects his serious business. You can call that "lassitude". He is choked and flooded by the swelling of his energies, it is like climbing a slope with a heavy load on his back. You can count that as "strain". Out of greed for riches he chooses to risk his health, out of greed for mastery he chooses to wear himself out; when he rests at home he spoils himself, and as his body gets fatter his temper gets worse. That comes under "ill health". His end in life is desire for wealth, the urge for profit, so when his coffers are as tight as the stones in a wall he doesn't know how to do anything else, however full they are he won't leave off. That amounts to "ignominy". With more wealth in store than he can use, he clings to it and won't part with a penny, his heart is full of stresses and cares, he cannot stop seeking more and more. Put that down as "anxiety". At home he is suspicious of being plundered by cadgers and pilferers, abroad is in dread of being murdered by bandits; at home he is surrounded by towers and moats, abroad does not dare to walk alone. That comes under the heading of "fear".

'These six are the world's worst harms, yet he ignores them all and is too ignorant to examine them. When disaster comes to him, if he should use up all the resources of his nature and every penny of his property simply trying to recover one carefree day it will be too late. So if you recognise the right way to live by its reputation, there's no sign of that; if you seek it for its profitability, there's no trace of that. Is it not a delusion to submit your body and your thoughts to such bondage competing for this?'

3

The discourse on swords

Of all the chapters in *Chuang-tzŭ* this is the one most remote from Taoism. But if we think of it in relation to the Yangist miscellany rather than the book as a whole, it ceases to be puzzling. Yangists, who see the preservation of life as the supreme value, would naturally disapprove of sword-fighting as a sport. This chapter is a denunciation of such duelling, pervaded throughout by disgust at the pointless shedding of blood, and exhibiting that subtle persuasive rhetoric adapted to the listener in which the Yangists take such pride.

There is one troublesome detail. Why does Chuang-tzŭ wear 'scholar's garb', which ought to mark him as not Yangist or Taoist but Confucian? Perhaps the term is used generally, to contrast with martial dress without distinguishing schools, but elsewhere it refers specifically to the uniform of the Confucians.[20]

In former times, King Wen of Chao delighted in the sword. The swordsmen who flanked his gate as retainers were 3,000 men or more; day and night they duelled in his presence, and the dead or wounded in a single year were 100 men or more. His lust for it was untiring. It had been like this for three years, the state was in decline, the princes of other states were plotting to take advantage.

The Crown Prince K'uei was troubled, and summoned the men on his left and right.

'Who can dissuade the King from his fancy? To the man who rids us of the swordsmen I give 1,000 in gold.'

'Chuang-tzŭ might be able,' they said.

Then the Crown Prince sent a man to Chuang-tzŭ with a present of 1,000 in gold. Chuang-tzŭ would not accept it, but went with the messenger to see the Crown Prince.

'What is it that Your Highness requires of me, that you should give me 1,000 in gold?'

'I heard that you are an illumined sage, sir, and presented it in all due respect for you to give away to your retinue. You did not accept it, so what more would I presume to say?'

'I hear that the purpose for which Your Highness wishes to employ me is to make the King give up his greatest delight. Suppose that on the one hand I offend His Majesty by my advice, and on the other fail to satisfy Your

Highness, I shall die at the hands of the executioner, and what use would I have for the gold? Suppose that on the one hand I do convince His Majesty, and on the other do satisfy Your Highness, is there anything in the whole state of Chao which would not be mine for the asking?'

'As you please. You know our King will see no one but swordsmen.'

'No difficulty there, I can handle a sword.'

'Very well then. The swordsmen whom our King does see all have tousled hair bristling at the temples, tilted caps, stiff chin-straps, coats cut short at the back, glaring eyes and rough speech, that's what pleases His Majesty. Now if you insist on seeing him in scholar's garb, the thing is sure to go wrong from the start.'

'Excuse me while I kit myself up as a swordsman,' said Chuang-tzŭ.

After three days kitting himself up he went to see the Crown Prince, and then the Crown Prince went with him to see the King. The King awaited him with his naked blade drawn.

As he entered the gate of the hall, Chuang-tzŭ did not quicken his step, seeing the King he did not bow.

'What is it you wish to tell me, now you've got my son to introduce you?'

'I hear that Your Majesty delights in the sword, and it is about the sword that I have come to see you.'

'What sort of fight can you put up with that sword of yours?'

'My sword, if there were a man every ten feet, would keep straight on going for a thousand miles.'

The King was delighted with that.

'Then you're a match for anyone in the world.'

'The master swordsman', said Chuang-tzŭ,

'Lays himself wide open,
Tempts you to take advantage,
Is behind in making his move,
Is ahead in striking home.

Give me an opportunity to prove myself.'

'Enough, sir. Go to your quarters and await my command. I'll get ready for the sport and call for you.'

Then the King matched his swordsmen against each other for seven days. When the dead or wounded were sixty or more, he picked five or six men, and had them present themselves sword in hand in the hall. Then he summoned Chuang-tzŭ.

'Today we shall see how you measure up against my swordsmen.'

'I have been looking forward to it for a long time.'

'In your choice of arms which do you favour, sir, the long sword or the short?'

'As far as I am concerned either will do. But I have three swords, which are at the service of Your Majesty. Allow me to describe them before I try them out.'

'I am eager to hear about your three swords.'

'I have the sword of the Son of Heaven, the sword of the prince of a state, the sword of the common man.'

'The sword of the Son of Heaven, what is that like?'

'The sword of the Son of Heaven has Yen Valley and Stone Wall Mountain as its point, Ch'i and Tai as its edge, Chin and Wey as its spine, Chou and Sung as its handguard, Han and Wei as its hilt. It is wrapped by the barbarians of the four borders, sheathed in the four seasons, wound round by the Sea of Po, hung at the belt of Mount Heng. It is designed in accord with the Five Phases, assessed by its punishment and bounty, drawn by means of the Yin and Yang, wielded in spring and summer, and strikes its blow in autumn and winter. This sword,

> Thrust and there's nothing ahead,
> Brandish and there's nothing above,
> Press down on the hilt and there's nothing below,
> Whirl it round and there's nothing beyond.

Up above it breaks through the floating clouds, down below it bursts through the bottom of the earth. Use this sword once and it will discipline the lords of the states, the whole empire will submit. This is the sword of the Son of Heaven.'

King Wen was amazed and lost in thought.

'The sword of the prince of a state, what is that like?'

'The sword of the prince of a state has clever and brave knights for its point, clean and honest knights for its edge, worthy and capable knights for its spine, loyal and wise knights for its hand-guard, dashing and heroic knights for its hilt. This sword,

> Thrust and there's nothing ahead,
> Brandish and there's nothing above,
> Press down on the hilt and there's nothing below,
> Whirl it round and there's nothing beyond.

Up above it has the round heavens as its model, takes its course from sun, moon and stars; down below it has the square earth as its model, follows the course of the four seasons. In between it harmonises the wants of the people, to bring security to the four quarters. Use this sword once, and it will be like the quake after a clap of thunder, within the four borders none will refuse to submit and obey your commands. This is the sword of the prince of a state.'

'The sword of the common man, what is that like?'

'The sword of the common man is to have tousled hair bristling at the temples, a tilted cap, stiff chin-strap, coat cut short at the back, have glaring eyes, be rough of speech, and duel in your presence. Up above it will chop a neck or slit a throat, down below it will burst lungs or liver. This is the sword of the common man, it is no different from cockfighting. In a single morning a man's fated span is snapped. It is no use whatever in matters of state. Now the throne of the Son of Heaven is yours to have, yet Your Majesty prefers the sword of the common man; I venture to deplore it on behalf of Your Majesty.'

Then the King drew him up to the top of the hall. When the steward was serving dinner, the King walked three times round and round.

'Sit down at your ease and calm your spirits, Your Majesty,' said Chuang-tzǔ. 'About matters of the sword I have no more to say.'

Afterwards the King did not leave the palace for three months. Back in their quarters, the swordsmen all died on their sword points.

4

The old fisherman

'Protecting one's genuineness' is mentioned in *Huai-nan-tzŭ* as one of the tenets of Yang Chu.[21] In this story the fisherman symbolises the genuine, which is identified as the true feeling, whether of joy, grief, anger, love, which is so easily submerged by Confucian ritualism. The genuine is also a Taoist concept; but, granted that Taoism never wholly repudiated the passions in the manner of Buddhism, the positive value ascribed to the passions here seems alien to the rest of the book.

The writer, whoever he may have been, is a remarkable literary innovator, who took the historic step from narrative as summary to narrative as scene almost at one bound. Throughout the rest of *Chuang-tzŭ* fiction is not yet distinguished in form from true anecdote, in which one expects names, titles, the place, the time, and a tale advancing as a procession of basic facts. Yet here we have a story with a nameless, mysterious hero designed to tantalise curiosity, about whom our first information is how he *looks* as he leaves his boat and walks up the bank. Since he has never heard of Confucius, we then have the sage described as though we were being informed about him for the first time. This writer, unlike Chuang-tzŭ or any other contributor to the book, can present a changing scene to both ear and eye:

'"...I leave you! I leave you!" Then he poled the boat out. While he lingered picking his way among the reeds, Yen Hui turned the carriage round, Tzŭ-lu held out the strap for Confucius to pull himself up. Confucius did not turn his head. He waited until the ripples settled on the water and he did not hear the sound of the oar, before he ventured to mount.'

Confucius on an excursion in the woods of Tzŭ-wei had sat down to rest on the top of Apricot Mesa. The disciples studied their books, Confucius strummed on the zither and sang. Before the piece was half over, an old fisherman stepped down from his boat and came forward, whiskers and eyebrows glistening white, hair loose on his shoulders, hands tucked into his sleeves. He walked up from the level ground and stopped when he reached the summit, left hand resting on his knee, right hand propping his chin, listening.

When the piece finished he beckoned to Tzŭ-kung and Tzŭ-lu. Both responded. The stranger pointed at Confucius.

'What sort would he be?'

'A gentleman of Lu,' Tzŭ-lu replied.

The stranger asked about his clan.

'The clan K'ung.'

'What does Mr K'ung do?'

Tzŭ-lu would not reply, but Tzŭ-kung answered

'Mr K'ung is by nature devotedly loyal and truthful, in his personal life is benevolent and dutiful; he is embellishing Rites and Music, and codifying rules of conduct, in the first place out of loyalty to our present sovereign, and in the second to reform the common people, with the purpose of benefiting the world. That is what Mr K'ung does.'

The man had another question.

'Is he a prince with land of his own?'

'No.'

'Is he adviser to a lord or a king?'

'No.'

Then the stranger smiled and turned away, saying as he walked off

'Benevolent he may be, but I'm afraid he won't escape with his life. By such exertions of heart and body he is endangering the genuine in him. Alas, how far he has diverged from the Way!'

Tzŭ-kung returned and reported to Confucius. Confucius thrust aside his zither and rose to his feet, said 'Could he be a sage?'. Then he rode down to look for him, as far as the shore of the lake. The man was just leaning on the oar to pull out the boat. Glancing over his shoulder he saw Confucius, and turning to face him stood up. Confucius stepped quickly back, bowed twice and came forward.

'What do you want of me?' said the stranger.

'Just now before you went away you hinted at something, and I am not clever enough to know what you meant. Allow me to stand waiting in all humility, in the hope of hearing your sublime eloquence, so that your help to me will not have been in vain.'

'Hmm, extraordinary how you love to learn!'

Confucius bowed twice, stood up straight.

'From my childhood I have cultivated learning, by now for sixty-nine years, and found none from whom to learn the ultimate doctrine. What can I do but keep the space open in my heart?'

> 'The same in kind go along with each other,
> The same in sound respond to each other.

That indeed is a pattern which is in us from Heaven. I propose not to talk about what belongs to my own sort, but to put you right on what concerns yourself. What concerns you is the affairs of men. The Son of Heaven, the lords of the states, the administrators, the common people, the self-rectifying of these four is excellence in government; and misrule is never worse than when these four depart from their stations.

> Let officials mind their own departments,
> Let the people stick to their own affairs.

Then they will not bother anyone else.

'For example, that the fields are unweeded or there's a hole in the roof, that he is ill-fed, ill-clothed, can't pay his taxes, that his wife and concubine don't get along, the youngsters are cheeky to their elders, these are the worries of the common man. That someone isn't good enough for his job, the department is badly run, there's dishonesty somewhere, the clerks are lazy, he isn't getting credit for what he does, might lose his title and salary, these are the worries of an administrator. That his court lacks loyal ministers, there are plots and dissensions in his state and his family, inefficiency among the artisans, that tributes and services are below standard, he's ranked below his station in spring and autumn visits to the capital, falling out of favour with the Son of Heaven, these are the worries of the lord of a state. That the Yin and Yang are discordant, and cold and heat untimely, damaging the crops; that the lords of the states are unruly and go to war on their own authority, bringing ruin to ordinary folk; that Rites and Music are irregular, the public coffers depleted, public morals deteriorating, the peasants rebellious; these are the worries of the chancellors of the Son of Heaven.

'Now you have neither the position of ruler or chancellor above nor the office of high minister or bureaucrat below, yet on your own authority you are embellishing Rites and Music and codifying rules of conduct, in order to reform the common people. Aren't you meddling in what isn't your business?

'I would add that there are eight blemishes in a man and four mischiefs in affairs, of which it is most important to be aware. Being busy in what isn't your business one calls "officiousness". Begging attention for what nobody cares about one calls "wheedling". Doting on someone's ideas and citing his words one calls "fawning". Repeating them without picking the right from the wrong one calls "toadying". Taking pleasure in talking about the faults of others one calls "backbiting". Breaking up friendships and estranging kinsmen one calls "troublemaking". Flattering and deceiving in order to get the better of the wicked one calls "intriguing". Not choosing between good men and bad, finding room for both, being comfortable with either, and appealing to their tastes as occasion offers, one calls being "slippery". By these eight blemishes

> Outside you disarrange others,
> Within do injury to yourself.
> A gentleman will not have you as a friend,
> A clear-sighted prince will not have you as minister.

'As for what I mean by the four mischiefs, being fond of taking charge of great affairs, and altering or replacing accepted practice in order to win credit and renown, one calls "presumption". Thinking you know best, doing things your own way, encroaching on others to make things your own

business, one calls "wanting what doesn't belong to you'. Refusing to
amend what you see to be a mistake, and with every criticism that you hear
becoming more obstinate, one calls "stubbornness". If others agree with
you, approving of them, but if they don't, pronouncing them bad however
good they are, one calls "bigotry". There you have the four mischiefs. Not
until you get rid of the eight blemishes and avoid the four mischiefs will you
become teachable.'

Confucius sighed solemnly, bowed twice and stood up straight.

'Twice I was chased out of Lu,' he said, 'I had to scrape away my footprints in Wey, a tree was chopped down over my head in Sung, I was
besieged between Ch'en and Ts'ai. How is it that, without knowing where I
was at fault, I suffered calumny these four times?'

A melancholy look came over the stranger's face.

'How very hard it is to wake you! There was a man who shrank from his
own shadow, loathed his own footprints, and ran to get away from them. The
more quickly he lifted his foot the more prints he left, however fast he ran the
shadow would not part from his body. He thought he was still too slow, ran
faster and faster and never stopped till he fell dead with exhaustion. He didn't
have the sense to sit in the shade and obliterate his shadow, sit still and put an
end to making footprints, such an utter fool he was! You search out distinctions between Goodwill and Duty, scrutinise the borderlines of the similar
and the different, watch for the moment to act or refrain, measure what you
give against what you receive, rearrange your essential likes and dislikes,
readjust your occasions for pleasure and anger; it looks as though you will
never make your escape.

> Earnestly cultivate your own person,
> Carefully guard the genuine in you,
> Turn back and leave other things to other people,

and then you will no longer be tied by involvements. What now you are
seeking in others without cultivating in your own person, can it be more
than the externals?

Confucius said solemnly

'Let me ask what you mean by "genuine".'

'The genuine is the most quintessential, the most sincere. What fails to be
quintessential and sincere cannot move others. Thus, forced tears however
sorrowful fail to sadden, forced rages however formidable do not strike awe,
forced affection however much you smile will not be returned. Genuine
sorrow saddens without uttering a sound, genuine rage strikes awe before it
bursts out, genuine affection is returned before you smile. The man who is
inwardly genuine moves the external daemonically. This is why we value the
genuine.

'When it is applied to relations between men, in service within the family the son is filial and the father compassionate, in service within the state the minister is loyal and the lord just, in a wine-feast you enjoy, in mourning you grieve. What matters in being loyal or just is that you do fulfil the charge, in a wine-feast that you do enjoy, in mourning that you do grieve, in serving parents that you do please them. To the glory of fulfilling the charge you can pick your own route; in serving parents, if you do please them they won't raise difficulties about how you did it; in the wine-feast, if you do enjoy you won't be finicky about the cups; in mourning, if you do grieve no one quibbles about the rite.

'The rites are what the custom of the times has established. The genuine is the means by which we draw upon Heaven, it is spontaneous and irreplaceable. Therefore the sage, taking Heaven as his model, values the genuine and is untrammelled by custom. The fool does the opposite; incapable of taking Heaven as his model he frets about man, ignorant of how to value the genuine he timidly lets himself be altered by custom, and so is an unsatisfied man. What a pity you were steeped so soon in man's artificialities, and are so late in hearing the greatest Way!'

Again Confucius bowed twice and stood up straight.

'Today I have been fortunate, it is like a blessing from Heaven. If, sir, it would not disgrace you to have me in the ranks of your underlings and teach me in person, I will be so bold as to ask where you live. I request that I may take this opportunity to become your apprentice and learn at last about the greatest Way.'

'I have heard it said: "The right man to go with, stay with as far as the profoundest Way: the wrong man to go with, since you do not know the Way proper to him be careful to stay away from, simply for your own protection." Do the best you can. I leave you! I leave you!'

Then he poled the boat out. While he lingered picking his way among the reeds, Yen Hui turned the carriage round, Tzŭ-lu held out the strap for Confucius to pull himself up. Confucius did not turn his head. He waited until the ripples settled on the water and he did not hear the sound of the oar, before he ventured to mount.

Running beside the carriage Tzŭ-lu asked

'I have been in your service a long time, Master, but never yet did I see you in such awe of any man you met. The lord of 1,000 or of 10,000 chariots never fails when he sees you to grant you the seat and the rites proper to his peers, and even then you have a proud air. Today an old fisherman stands insolently leaning on his oar, and you, Master, bending at the waist to the angle of a chiming-stone bow twice every time you reply. Surely you went too far? All your disciples wondered at you, Master. Why should an old fisherman deserve this?'

Confucius leaned on the crossbar and sighed.

'Tzŭ-lu, how hard it is to make another man of you! You have been steeped so long in Rites and Duty, but even now that rude and coarse heart of yours will not be gone. Come forward, I shall tell you. To be irreverent when you meet an elder is to fail in the Rites. Not to honour excellence when you see it is Ill-will.

> Whoever falls short of utmost Goodwill
> Is unable to defer to another man.

If deference is not refined to its quintessence

> He fails to attain the genuine in him,
> And so inflicts a lasting wound on himself.

Alas, to fall into Ill-will is the greatest misfortune which can happen to a man, and you alone are responsible for bringing it on yourself.

'Moreover it is from the Way that the myriad things take their courses. Everything which loses it dies, which finds it lives; enterprises which defy it fail, which follow it succeed. Hence to anyone in whom the Way is present the sage pays homage. It can be said of that old fisherman just now that he did possess the Way; would I dare not to treat him with reverence?'

NOTES TO PART FIVE

1 *Lü-shih ch'un-ch'iu*, chapter 1/2, 'Taking life as basic'; 1/3, 'Giving weight to self'; 2/2, 'Valuing life'; 2/3, 'The essential desires'; 21/4, 'Being aware of what one is for'. This text is available in a German translation, Richard Wilhelm, *Frühling und Herbst des Lu Pu We* (Jena, 1928).
2 cf. p. 200 above.
3 cf. p. 240f above.
4 cf. p. 238 above.
5 cf. p. 241 above.
6 cf. pp. 231–3, 238 above.
7 *Book of Lieh-tzŭ*, translated A. C. Graham (London, 1960), pp. 148f.
8 *Mencius*, translated D. C. Lau (Penguin Classics, 1970), 7A/26; cf. also 3B/9.
9 cf. pp. 224, 226 above.
10 cf. p. 212 above.
11 cf. p. 225 above.
12 cf. p. 117 above.
13 cf. p. 199 above.
14 cf. p. 264 below.
15 cf. p. 238 above.
16 cf. p. 237 above.
17 cf. p. 236 above.
18 cf. pp. 208, 240 above.
19 cf. p. 202 above.
20 cf. p. 122 above.
21 cf. p. 221 above.

Part Six

The Syncretist writings

The reunified Chinese empire of the Ch'in dynasty (221–209 BC) and the Han (206 BC–AD 220) required a unified ideology for a new political establishment. Between the fall of the Ch'in, which favoured Legalism, and the final adoption of Confucianism by the Emperor Wu (140–87 BC), there was an interval in which various kinds of eclecticism or syncretism flourished. It must have seemed that a system blending the most persuasive elements in the doctrines of the various schools would have the best chance of success. This is the period of the latest parts of the *Chuang-tzŭ*, many of which are syncretistic in character:

(1) The last of a series of miscellanea tacked on to the Primitivist essay 'Keep it in place and within bounds' (chapter 11) and the introductory essays of the next three chapters, 'Heaven and earth', 'The Way of Heaven' and 'The circuits of Heaven' (chapters 12–14), together with three rhapsodies on the Way ascribed to an unnamed 'Master' in chapters 12 and 13.

(2) The short chapter 'Finicky notions' (chapter 15). This contrasts the syncretistic philosophy with five less comprehensive world-views, distinguishes it by the slogan 'The Way of Heaven and Earth',[1] and expounds it with close verbal parallels to 'The Way of Heaven'.

(3) The very important 'Below in the empire' (chapter 33), the earliest general history of the philosophical schools. (The chapter title is literally 'Under Heaven', recalling the titles of chapters 12–14). Here too a rival school, the Sophists, is condemned 'from the viewpoint of the Way of Heaven and Earth'.[2]

The prevalence of eclectic tendencies in the second century BC makes it likely that the *Chuang-tzŭ* collection would come to completion in the hands of Syncretist editors. We may credit them with the strange three-word titles of the *Inner chapters*, which resemble those of the Han apocryphal books (*wei-shu*). These titles include several two-word phrases found in the Syncretist essays but not in the *Inner chapters* themselves: 'even things out', 'ultimate ancestor', and the very characteristic 'emperor and king'.[3]

There is no guarantee of single authorship, so we shall speak of the 'Syncretists' as of the 'Yangists'. But we need not hesitate over the capital letter, for the documents expound a coherent and distinctive set of ideas, by no means identical with those, for example, of the equally eclectic *Huai-nan tzŭ* compiled not much later by the clients of the Prince of Huai-nan (died 122 BC). Basic concepts which we have encountered throughout the book have been reshuffled to make a new system. 'Heaven' is now the superior member in the pair 'Heaven and earth', and the 'Way' assumes a secondary position as the 'Way of Heaven and Earth'. Since the capacity to act according to the Way is what a Taoist understands by 'Power', the capacity of the cosmos to proceed on its regular course is the 'Power which is in heaven and earth'. In the ultimate depths out of which their mysterious operations issue heaven and earth are 'daemonic', and they are inhabited by a hierarchy of beings called 'daemonic-and-illumined' (*shen-ming*), presumably the gods of the official cultus. The sage himself becomes companion to these presences when he has refined to perfect purity the vitalising energies in him, his 'quintessence' (*ching*), also described as the 'quintessential-and-daemonic' (*ching-shen*). He then possesses the 'Power which is in emperor or king', and, without ever allowing a residue of knowledge to accumulate from past experience and clog his spontaneous reactions, he dispassionately mirrors events and responds to them unthinkingly. This is the Taoist principle of 'Doing Nothing'; his actions are not deliberately chosen in the light of goals, they belong to the natural processes of the cosmos.

Thus far the system is Taoist. However, below the sage emperor there are ministers, officials and people who do have to think and to apply rules. In the Syncretists' scheme there is room for only one Taoist in public life, and they are unique among the writers in *Chuang-tzŭ* in being essentially political thinkers for whom private life is secondary. Their ideal rulers are the Yellow Emperor, Yao and Shun, the designers of a moral code and an administrative hierarchy, the very men from whom both the Primitivist and the Yangists date the decline of government. The Syncretists recognise as indispensable both the Confucian code of behaviour ('Goodwill' and 'Duty') and the administrative methods of the Legalist school ('law', 'reward and punishment', and the checking of an official's 'performance' against his 'title'). However, they react strongly against the Ch'in reliance on punishment (in this alone resembling the Primitivist), and exemplify the swing from law to morality which culminated in the conversion of the Han dynasty to Confucianism. In 'The Way of Heaven' a list of nine steps in the application of the Way gives the first place to Heaven, the next to the Taoist concepts, the Way and the Power, the third to Confucian Goodwill and Duty, the rest to administrative measures; and afterwards we are explicitly reminded that the Legalist checking of performance against title did not come until the fifth step, and that reward and punishment had the last place of all.[4]

'Finicky notions' contrasts the comprehensive 'Way of Heaven and Earth' with five one-sided views of life, the fourth of which is that of idlers who prefer to sit fishing by the river instead of taking part in government – Chuang-tzŭ himself and every other writer in the book. The task of allotting all the philosophical schools their places in the Syncretists' scheme is undertaken in 'Below in the empire'. A modern reader sees the thought of these schools as the most creative in Chinese history, but the ideologists of a reunited empire have a very different viewpoint. They assume that the ancient sage emperors, who knew all that there is to know, possessed a unified system of lore rooted in the Way and ramifying out into the detail of rites, morals and administration. In the present decadence some of this lore survives where it belongs, in officially recognised circles, as administrative techniques preserved by the historiographers or as the teaching of Confucian scholars qualified in the classics, but the rest has been fragmented and scattered over the 'Hundred Schools' of the philosophers 'below in the empire'. Each school recommends the 'tradition of its own formula', which however is only one facet of the primordial 'tradition of the Way'. 'Below in the empire' discusses the uses and limitations of five schools, the fourth headed by Old Tan (Lao-tzŭ) and the fifth by Chuang-tzŭ, and concludes by rejecting the Sophists altogether, as having no share in the 'tradition of the Way'. It is interesting to find that at this period, perhaps well into the second century BC, there was still no conception of a Taoist school embracing both Lao-tzŭ and Chuang-tzŭ, and that each is seen as merely displaying one facet of the comprehensive Way of Heaven and Earth. Chuang-tzŭ appears as the poet of the sage's union with heaven and earth and his ecstatic journeys with the 'daemonic-and-illumined', to be read with caution, on the lookout for the extravagances of his language. Having placed him in this safe setting, the official-minded authors of the eclectic documents were able to come to terms with the genius of Chuang-tzŭ. 'The Way of Heaven' has a quotation from the *Inner chapters* explicitly credited to Chuang-tzŭ,[5] who was probably also the author of the fine poem which introduces 'The circuits of Heaven'.[6]

1

The Way of Heaven

The Way of Heaven as it circuits is not clogged by precedents, and so the myriad things come to full growth. The Way of the Emperor as it circuits is not clogged by precedents, and so the whole world pays allegiance to him. The Way of the Sage as it circuits is not clogged by precedents, and so all within the four seas submit to him.

The man who, being clear about Heaven and versed in sagehood, has an understanding which ranges in the six directions and is open through the four seasons, by the Power which is in emperor or king – in his own spontaneous actions, as though he were unseeing he never ceases to be still. When the sage is still, it is not that he is still because he says 'It is good to be still'; he is still because none among the myriad things is sufficient to disturb his heart. If water is still, its clarity lights up the hairs of beard and eyebrows, its evenness is plumb with the carpenter's level: the greatest of craftsmen take their standard from it. If mere water clarifies when it is still, how much more the stillness of the quintessential-and-daemonic, the heart of the sage! It is the reflector of heaven and earth, the mirror of the myriad things.

Emptiness and stillness, calm and indifference, quiescence, Doing Nothing, are the even level of heaven and earth, the utmost reach of the Way and the Power; therefore emperor, king or sage finds rest in them. At rest he empties, emptying he is filled, and what fills him sorts itself out. Emptying he is still, in stillness he is moved, and when he moves he succeeds. In stillness he does nothing; and if he does nothing, those charged with affairs are put to the test. If he does nothing he is serene; and in whoever is serene, cares and misfortunes cannot settle, his years will be long.

Emptiness and stillness, calm and indifference, quiescence, Doing Nothing, are at the root of the myriad things. To be clear about these when you sit facing south is to be the kind of lord that Yao was; to be clear about these when you stand facing north is to be the kind of minister that Shun was. To have these as your resources in high estate is the Power which is in emperor, king, Son of Heaven; to have these as your resources in low estate is the Way of the obscure sage, the untitled king. Use these to settle in retirement or wander at leisure, and the hermits of river, sea, mountain and forest submit to you. Use these to come forward and act in order to bring comfort to the age, and your achievement is great and name illustrious, and the empire is united. In stillness a sage, in motion a king, you do nothing yet are exalted, you are simple and unpolished yet no one in the empire is able to rival your glory.

Seeing in the clearest light the Power which is in heaven and earth – it is this that is meant by being, from the ultimate root and ultimate ancestor, in harmony with Heaven; it is the means to adjust and attune the empire and be in harmony with men. Being in harmony with men is called 'the joy from man', being in harmony with Heaven is called 'the joy from Heaven'. In the words of Chuang-tzŭ, 'My teacher, O my teacher! He chops fine the myriad things but it is not cruelty, his bounty extends to a myriad ages but it is not goodwill, he is elder to the most ancient but it is not living long, he overhangs heaven and bears up earth and cuts up and sculpts all shapes but it is not skill.'[7] It is such that is meant by the joy from Heaven.

Hence it is said that 'whoever knows the joy from Heaven

> In his life proceeds with Heaven,
> In his death transforms with other things,
> In stillness shares the Power in the Yin,
> In motion shares the surge of the Yang.'

So for one who knows the joy from Heaven

> There is no wrath from Heaven,
> No blame from man,
> No being tied by other things,
> No retribution from ghosts.

And so it is said: 'In his motions, heaven, and in his stillness, earth: by the fixity of his unified heart he reigns over the empire. His anima does not sicken, his animus does not tire; to the fixity of his unified heart the myriad things submit' – meaning that by being empty and still he extends his understanding throughout heaven and earth and becomes conversant with the myriad things. It is this that is meant by the joy from Heaven. The joy from Heaven is the sage's heart being thereby pastor to the empire.

The Power which is in emperor or king has heaven and earth for its ancestors, the Way and the Power as its masters, Doing Nothing as its norm. Doing *nothing*, one has more than enough to be employer of the empire; doing *something*, one is inadequate for more than to be employed by the empire. That is why the men of old valued Doing Nothing. If as well as the man above the men below did nothing, the men below would share the Power in the man above; and if the men below share the Power in the man above, they do not minister. If as well as the men below the man above did something, the man above would share the Way of the men below; and if the man above shares the Way of the men below, he is not sovereign. The man above must do nothing and be employer of the empire, the men below must do something and be employed by the empire; this is the irreplaceable Way.

Therefore those who of old reigned over the empire, though wise enough to encompass heaven and earth would not do their own thinking, though discriminating enough to comprehend the myriad things would not do their own explaining, though able enough for all the work within the four seas would not do their own enacting. Heaven does not give birth, but the myriad things are transformed; earth does not rear, but the myriad things are nurtured; emperors and kings do nothing, but the world's work is done. Hence the saying: 'Nothing is more daemonic than heaven, nothing has richer resources than earth, nothing is greater than emperor or king.' And the saying: 'Emperor or king is by the Power in him peer of heaven and earth.' This is the Way by which to have heaven and earth as your chariot, set the myriad things galloping, and employ the human flock.

The root is in the man above, the outermost twigs are in the men below; the crux is in the sovereign, the details are in the ministers. The operations of the Three Armies and the Five Weapons are twigs which have grown from the Power in him. The proclamations of reward and punishment, benefit and harm, the Five Penalties, are twigs from his teaching. The details of rites and laws, measures and numbers, title and performance, are twigs from his government. The sound of bells and drums, the display of plumes and yak-tails, are twigs from his joy. The clothes differentiated for degrees of wailing and mourning are twigs from his sorrow. These five sorts of twig are outcomes which await the circuitings of the quintessential-and-daemonic, and the motions from the workings of the skilled heart. The study of the outer-most twigs did exist among the men of old, but was not what they put first.

The ruler comes first, the minister follows; the father comes first, the son follows; the elder brother comes first, the younger follows; the senior comes first, the junior follows; the man comes first, the woman follows; the husband comes first, the wife follows. Being exalted or lowly, first or last, belongs to the progressions of heaven and earth; therefore the sage takes his model from them. Being exalted if of heaven, lowly if of earth, are the stations of the daemonic-and-illumined; spring and summer first, autumn and winter last, is the sequence of the four seasons; the myriad things originating by transformation, and assuming form according to the direction of their growth, is the passing through degrees of flourishing and fading, the process of alteration and transformation. Heaven and earth are supremely daemonic yet have sequences of the exalted and the lowly, the first and the last, and how much more the Way of Man! If you expound a Way without their sequences, it is not their Way; and if you expound a Way which is not their Way, from what will you derive a Way? Therefore the men of old who made clear the great Way

(1) first made Heaven clear,
(2) and the Way and the Power were next:
(3) and when the Way and the Power were clear, Goodwill and Duty were next:
(4) and when Goodwill and Duty were clear, portions and responsibilities were next:
(5) and when portions and responsibilities were clear, title and performance were next:
(6) and when title and performance were clear, putting the suitable man in charge was next:
(7) and when putting the suitable man in charge was clear, inquiry and inspection were next:
(8) and when inquiry and inspection were clear, judging right or wrong was next:
(9) and when judging right or wrong was clear, reward and punishment were next.

When reward and punishment were clear, wise and foolish were properly placed, noble and base occupied their stations, worthy and inadequate were seen for what they were; invariably they were allotted tasks according to their abilities, invariably their tasks derived from their titles. This is how one served the man above or was pastor to the men below, put other things in order or cultivated one's own person. Cleverness and strategy were unused, they invariably referred back to what was from Heaven in them. It is this that is meant by supreme tranquillity, the utmost in government.

Therefore, when the book says 'There is the performance, there is the title', though performance and title did exist among the men of old, they are not what they put first. When the men of old expounded the great Way, at the fifth of the stages title and performance deserved a mention, by the ninth it was time to talk about reward and punishment. To be in too much of a hurry to expound performance and title is to be ignorant of the root of them, to be in too much of a hurry to expound reward and punishment is to be ignorant of their origin. The men whose words turn the Way upside down, whose explanations run counter to the Way, it is for others to govern, how would they be able to govern others? To be in too much of a hurry to expound performance and title, reward and punishment, this is to have the tools for knowing how to govern, it is not the Way of knowing how to govern. Such men are employable by the empire but inadequate to be employers of the empire; it is these that are meant by 'the subtle advisers, each with his own little corner'. The details of rites and laws, numbers and measures, title and performance, did exist among the men of old, but as means for those below to serve the one above, not for the one above to be pastor to those below.

Formerly Shun asked Yao:

'To what use does Your Majesty put the heart?'

'I do not disdain those who have none to complain to, do not neglect the most wretched of the people. I suffer when a man dies, give hope to the children, grieve for the wife. This is the use to which I put the heart.'

'Fine, as far as it goes, but not yet great.'

'What should I do then?'

> 'Heaven is bountiful, earth firm,
> Sun and moon shine, the four seasons run their course.
> To accord with rule, be like night succeeding day.
> By the clouds running their course the gift of the rain falls.'

'All my bustling, meddling! You have joined yourself to Heaven, I to man.'

It is the scope of heaven and earth which of old was recognised as greatness, which the Yellow Emperor, Yao and Shun in common glorified. So what did they do at all, those who of old reigned over the empire? They were nothing else but heaven and earth.

2

Finicky notions

In the Syncretist scheme, to follow the Way of Heaven and Earth is to perform one's social functions as ruler or subject without personal ambitions. But five kinds of people diverge from this Way either by refusing office or by using it to further their careers:

(1) Embittered moralists who will die rather than serve a government of which they disapprove (a category especially detested by the Yangists).[8]
(2) Self-absorbed moralists more interested in improving their own characters than in serving the state.
(3) Ambitious politicians.
(4) Idlers who prefer the comforts of private life. (Chuang-tzŭ himself fits the description of them as fishing by riverside or seaside.)[9]
(5) The cultivators of health and longevity by 'guide-and-pull' exercises ('guiding' the breath and 'pulling' on the limbs).[10]

After declaring that all five can fulfil their aims by following the comprehensive Way of Heaven and Earth, the writer proceeds to an exposition, much of it in the same words as in 'The Way of Heaven'.

To have finicky notions and superior conduct, to be estranged from the age and different from the vulgar, to discourse loftily and criticise vindictively, interested only in being high-minded – such are the tastes of the hermits of mountain and valley, the condemners of the age, who wither away or drown themselves.

To expound Goodwill and Duty, loyalty and keeping one's word, to be respectful, temperate, modest, deferential, interested only in improving themselves – such are the tastes of the fellows who go putting the world to rights, the teachers and instructors, the itinerant and the stay-at-home scholars.

To talk of great deeds and establish great reputations, to make ruler and minister observe the forms and have everyone above and below exactly in his place, interested only in governing – such are the tastes of the men at court, the exalters of princes and strengtheners of states, the doers of deeds, the annexers of lands.

To head for the woods and moors, settle in an untroubled wilderness, angle for fish and live untroubled, interested only in Doing Nothing – such are the tastes of the recluses of the riverside and seaside, the shunners of the age, the untroubled idlers.

To huff and puff, exhale and inhale, blow out the old and draw in the new, do the 'bear-hang' and the 'bird-stretch', interested only in long life – such are the tastes of the practitioners of 'guide-and-pull' exercises, the nurturers of the body, Grandfather P'eng's ripe-old-agers.

As for being lofty without having finicky notions, improving oneself without bothering about Goodwill and Duty, governing without caring about deeds and reputations, living untroubled not by riverside or seaside, living to a ripe old age without 'guide-and-pull', and forgetting them all and possessing them all, being serene and unconfined and having all these glories as the consequences, this is the Way of Heaven and Earth, the Power which is in the sage.

Hence it is said that calm and indifference, quiescence, emptiness and nothingness, Doing Nothing, these are the even level of heaven and earth, the substance of the Way and the Power; therefore the sage finds rest in them. At rest he is even and unstrained; being even and unstrained he is calm and indifferent. If he is even and unstrained, calm and indifferent,

> Cares and misfortunes cannot enter,
> The deviant energies cannot make inroads.

Therefore his Power is intact and his daemon unimpaired. Hence it is said that the sage

> In his life proceeds with Heaven,
> In his death transforms with other things.
> In stillness shares the Power in the Yin,
> In motion shares the surge of the Yang.

> He will not to gain advantage make the first move,
> Will not to avoid trouble take the first step:
> Only when stirred will he respond,
> Only when pressed will he move,
> Only when it is inevitable will he rise up.
> Rejecting knowledge and precedent
> He takes his course from Heaven's pattern.

Consequently, for him

> There is no wrath from Heaven,
> No being tied by other things,
> No blame from man,
> No retribution from ghosts.

His living is like drifting,
His dying is like going to rest.
He refuses to think things out,
Refuses to plan ahead,
Is bright without dazzling,
Is trusted without promising,
Sleeps without dreaming,
Wakes without cares.

His daemon is pure and delicate, his animus does not tire; in emptiness and nothingness, calm and indifference, he joins with Heaven's Power.

It may be said then that sadness and joy are deviations from the Power, being pleased or angry are transgressions of the Way, likes and dislikes are failings of the heart. Therefore when the heart neither worries nor delights, Power is at its utmost; when it is unified and unaltering, stillness is at its utmost; when nothing bumps against it, emptiness is at its utmost; when it does not engage with other things, indifference is at its utmost; when it does not thwart other things, delicacy is at its utmost. As the saying goes

The body if not rested from strain wears out,
The quintessence if used incessantly dries up.

Water by its nature
If unmixed is clear,
If nothing disturbs is level.
But when, being clogged or dammed, it does not flow
It never can be clear.

This is an image of the Power from Heaven. Hence it is said that to be unmixed in purity and delicacy, unaltering in stillness and oneness, indifferent and doing nothing, and when moved proceeding with Heaven, this is the Way to nurture the daemonic.

The owner of a sword from Kan or Yüeh keeps it in its case, not daring to use it lightly, for it is supremely precious. The quintessential-and-daemonic courses in the four directions, flows on with everything, is everywhere unconfined; it borders heaven above, coils round earth below, transforms and fosters the myriad things and cannot be conceived as an image, is to be named the 'sharer with God'.

By the Way of the pure and simple
Only with the daemon do you abide.
Abide with it, do not let it go.
May you and your daemon become one.

The quintessence when it is one courses without obstruction, tallying with the grading which is Heaven's. In the words of the proverb,

> The vulgar man gives weight to profit,
> The honest man to reputation.
> The intelligent man esteems high intent,
> But the sage values the quintessence.

That it is 'simple', then, means that it is unmixed with anything; that it is 'pure' means that he has kept his daemon unimpaired. One who is able to identify himself with the pure and simple we call the 'True Man'.

3

Syncretist fragments

They are mean but must be employed, 'things'; they are lowly but must be your basis, the 'people'.

It is irksome but must be done, 'work'; they are crude but must be promulgated, 'laws'.

It ranges far but you must be at home in it, 'Duty'; it draws you close but must be spread wide, 'Goodwill'; they are discrete but must be accumulated, the 'Rites'.

It is within but must be looked up to, the 'Power'; it is one yet you must change courses, the 'Way'; it is daemonic in its workings yet they must be acted out, 'Heaven'.

Therefore the sage, having a full view of *Heaven* will not give it a helping hand, being full-formed by the *Power* is not tied by involvements, coming out along the *Way* does not plan what to do.

He hits the course which is *Goodwill* but does not depend on it, approximates to *Duty* but is not clogged by precedents, answers to the *Rites* but does not taboo.

He is aware of the *work* and does not shirk it, he applies the *laws* evenly and does not misrule.

Being dependent on the *people* he does not despise them, having *things* as his basis he does not reject them. As for things, none is important enough to be worth what is done about it, which however must be done.

Whoever is unclear about Heaven is impure in his Power, whoever is unversed in the Way is at fault whatever course he takes. Alas for the man who is unclear about the Way! What do we mean by the 'Way'? There is the Way of Heaven, there is the Way of Man. To be exalted by Doing Nothing is the Way of Heaven, to be tied by doing something is the Way of Man. The sovereign's is the Way of Heaven, the minister's is the Way of Man. That the Ways of Heaven and of Man are far apart is not to be overlooked. (*Chuang-tzŭ*, chapter 11)

· · ·

Though heaven and earth are so vast, their transformations are regular; though the myriad things are so many, their ordering is unified; though mankind is so numerous, it shares the ruler for its master. The ruler finds his source in the Power and is full-formed by Heaven. We say then that in profoundest antiquity ruling the empire was Doing Nothing; it was simply a matter of the Power which is from Heaven.

Use the Way to examine words, and names throughout the empire will be correct; use the Way to examine portions, and the duties of ruler and minister will be clear; use the Way to examine abilities, and the offices of the empire will be ordered; use the Way to examine no matter what, and the responses of the myriad things will be at your disposal.

What runs through heaven then is the 'Way', what accords with earth is the 'Power', what is exercised on the myriad things is 'Duty', men being ordered from above is 'work', ability having its speciality is 'skill'. Skills are annexed to the work, the work to Duty, Duty to Power, Power to the Way, the Way to Heaven.

Hence it is said of those who of old were pastors of the empire that they desired nothing, yet the empire had enough; they did nothing, but the myriad things were transformed; they were still from the depths, but the Hundred Clans were settled. As the record says: 'Everywhere be conversant with the One, and the myriad tasks will all be done; succeed without resort to the heart, and the spirits will submit to you.' (Introduction to *Chuang-tzŭ*, chapter 12, 'Heaven and earth')

· · ·

'Heaven turns circles, yes!
Earth sits firm, yes!
Sun and moon vie for a place, yes!
Whose is the bow that shoots them?
Whose is the net that holds them?
Who is it sits with nothing to do and gives them the push that sends them?

'Shall we suppose, yes, that something triggers them off, then seals them away, and they have no choice?
Or suppose, yes, that wheeling in their circuits they cannot stop themselves?
Do the clouds make the rain?
Or the rain the clouds?
Whose bounty bestows them?
Who is it sits with nothing to do as in ecstasy he urges them?

'The winds rise in the north,
Blow west, blow east,
And now again whirl high above.
Who breathes them out, who breathes them in?
Who is it sits with nothing to do and sweeps between and over them?

Allow me to ask the reason for all this.'

The shaman Hsien beckons, 'Come! I shall tell you. Heaven has the Six Calamities and Five Blessings; if emperor or king complies with it there is order, if he defies it disaster. By the policies of the Nine Lo, order is brought to perfection and the Power is fully at his disposal. His mirror reflects the whole earth below, he is carried on the heads of the whole empire; such a one is to be called supremely august.' (Introduction to *Chuang-tzŭ*, chapter 14, 'Circuits of Heaven')

NOTE   This mysterious dialogue is unique in *Chuang-tzŭ* in failing to introduce the inquirer. The cause is not textual mutilation, for the chapter 'Circuits of Heaven' must always have started with the first words of the inquiry, from which (by the convention followed in all the *Outer chapters*) it takes its title. We have already noticed evidence that the questions once stood in the *Inner chapters*, where we restore them (p. 49 above). One can only suppose that the Syncretist has quoted the poem (as another rhapsodic passage is quoted from the *Inner chapters* in 'The Way of Heaven'), and then put an answer into the mouth of the shaman in the *Inner chapters* who knew the day of every man's death (pp. 96, 260 above).

The answer can be taken to mean 'Don't ask questions, simply respond to the fortune and misfortune sent by Heaven.' The Nine Lo are probably the nine sections of the 'Great Plan' in the *Book of documents*, which according to legend were symbolised by the nine numbers in the 'Lo document', a diagram on the back of a tortoise which came out of the Lo river in the time of the sage Yü. If so, the Six Calamities are premature death, sickness, care, poverty, ugliness, weakness, and the Five Blessings are longevity, wealth, health, Power, natural death.

4

Three rhapsodies on the Way

1 THE WAY AND THE GENTLEMAN

The Master said:

'The Way is the shelterer and sustainer of the myriad things. Vast, vast is its greatness! The gentleman has no choice but to scrape out everything in his heart for it.

'It is the doer of it by Doing Nothing that we call "Heaven", the teller of it by Doing Nothing that we call "Power". It is loving other men and benefiting other things that we call "Goodwill", bringing all dissimilars within the scope of the similar that we call "Greatness", acting without compartmentalising that we call "Flexibility", having the myriad dissimilars in oneself that we call "Wealth".

'Therefore it is having a grip on the *Power* that we mean by "being in control", the maturation of the *Power* that we mean by "getting a footing", accord with the *Way* that we mean by "having everything at one's disposal", refusal to let other things blunt one's *intent* that we mean by being "unharmed".

'If the gentleman has a clear vision of these ten, then overwhelming is the greatness of his heart as he puts it to work, torrential is its flow on behalf of the myriad things.

'Such a man as that

> Stores his gold in the mountain,
> Sinks his pearls in the deep,
> Neither treasures goods and chattels
> Nor courts the rich and noble,
> Is neither glad to live long
> Nor sorry to die young,
> Neither glorifies success,
> Nor vilifies failure.

He will not reserve what would benefit the world
    as a private portion for himself.
He will not think of the kingship of the empire
    as an illustrious position for himself.
For him the myriad things are a single storehouse,
Life and death the same state.'

            (*Chuang-tzŭ*, chapter 12)

2 THE WAY AND KINGLY POWER

The Master said:

'The Way, in what profundity it dwells! How translucent is its purity! If metal and stone failed to get it, they would have no means to ring, and that is why

> Though there's sound in metal and stone,
> Unless they are struck they will not ring.

'The myriad things, who can fix them in their places? The man of Kingly Power flows on in simplicity and does not deign to be too thoroughly conversant with affairs, sets them up firm at their root and source and knows how to be thoroughly conversant with the daemonic; hence the Power in him ranges wide. Whatever comes forth from his heart, some other thing brought on itself.

> So the body without the Way would not be living,
> The living without the Way is not illumined.

Whoever by preserving the body lasts out his span of life, and by making Power stand firm is illumined about the Way, is he not one of Kingly Power?

'So mighty! In a moment it comes forth, in an instant he is moved, and the myriad things follow him! Such a one we call the man of Kingly Power. He goes on gazing into the darkness, listening to the noiseless; within the darkness he alone sees the dawning, within the noiseless he alone hears the harmony. Hence he is able to be the thing in the deepest of the deep, the quintessence in the most daemonic of the daemonic. Therefore in his dealings with the myriad things, from utmost nothingness he supplies their needs, as he gallops with the times he is at the crux within reach of all their one-night stops. The big and the small, the long and the short, he has provision for each of them.' (*Chuang-tzŭ*, chapter 12)

3 THE WAY AND THE UTMOST MAN

The Master said:

'As for the Way, throughout the greatest it never comes to an end, within the smallest is never left out; by it one has all the myriad things at one's disposal. So wide, wide, that it has room for everything, so profound that it is immeasurable! Punishment and bounty, Goodwill and Duty, are the outermost twigs from the daemonic; who but the Utmost Man can fix them in their places?

'For the Utmost Man, to be possessor of the whole world is a great thing indeed, but not enough to become a tie to him. Everyone in the empire is eager to grasp the handles, but he refuses to compete; he remains aware of the Flawless and does not shift position with the profitable, he is at the apex of the genuine in things, and is able to abide at the root of them.

'Therefore he puts heaven and earth outside him, leaves the myriad things behind, and the daemonic in him is never pent in anywhere.

> He has access throughout the Way,
> Remains joined to the Power,
> Retires Goodwill and Duty from their offices,
> Has no more use for Rites and Music.

The heart of the Utmost Man has a place where it is fixed.' (*Chuang-tzŭ*, chapter 13)

5

Below in the empire

Down below in the empire there are many who cultivate the tradition of some formula, and all of them suppose that there is nothing to add to what they have. In which of them is it finally to be found, that which of old was called the tradition of the Way? I say it is to be found in them all. I say:

> From where does the daemonic descend?
> From where does illumination come forth?
> Sagehood is born from something,
> Kingship forms out of something:
> All have their source in the One.

Whoever does not part from the ancestral we call 'Heaven's man'. Whoever does not part from the quintessential we call the 'daemonic man'. Whoever does not part from the genuine we call the 'utmost man'. Whoever recognises Heaven as his ancestor, the Power as his root, the Way as his gateway, who has escaped beyond the alterations and transformations, we call the 'sage'. Whoever uses Goodwill to do kindnesses, Duty to pattern, Rites to conduct, Music to harmonise, and is serenely compassionate and benevolent, we call the 'gentleman'. As for using laws to apportion, names to mark, checks to test, verification to decide, that is what it is for its number to become 1, 2, 3, 4. . . . The hundred offices use these to grade each other, and take service as their routine, and feeding and clothing as their object, set their thoughts on breeding, growing, rearing, storing, on the old, the feeble, the orphan, the widow, and all have their own patterns of action to nurture the people.

Did not the men of old provide for everything? They were peers of the daemonic-and-illumined and equals of heaven and earth, they fostered the myriad things and harmonised the empire, their bounty extended over the Hundred Clans. They had a clear vision of the Number at the root and connected it to the measurements of the outermost twigs, their understanding ranged in the six directions and was open through the four seasons; throughout small and great, quintessential and crude, there was nothing they missed out in their circuitings. Of what they clarified in the realm of number and measure, much is still possessed by the historiographers who preserve the antique laws and the records handed down through the generations. As for what resides in the *Songs* and *Documents, Rites* and *Music*, there are many among the gentry of Tsou and Lu, the teachers with memorandum tablets in their sashes, who are able to clarify it. (The *Songs* serve as guide to the intent, the *Documents* to the work, the *Rites* to conduct, the *Music* to harmony, the *Changes* to the Yin and Yang, the *Spring and autumn annals* to names and portions.) As for what became available in the central states when its number divided out in the empire below, the scholars of the Hundred Schools at times cite and expound some of it.

The empire is in utter confusion, sagehood and excellence are not clarified, we do not have the one Way and Power; below in the empire there are many who find a single point to scrutinise and delight in as their own. There is an analogy in the ears, eyes, nose and mouth; all have something they illuminate but they cannot exchange their functions, just as the various specialities of the Hundred Schools all have their strong points and at times turn out useful. However, they are not inclusive, not comprehensive; these are men each of whom has his own little corner. They split the glory of heaven and earth down the middle, chop up the patterns of the myriad things, and scrutinise some point in what for the ancients was a whole. There are few who are able to have the whole glory of heaven and earth at their disposal, and speak of the full scope of the daemonic-and-illumined. Therefore the Way to be inwardly a sage and outwardly a king becomes darkened and is not clarified, becomes clogged and does not issue forth, and below in the empire each man studies whatever he prefers in it, and turns it into a formula of his own. Alas, if the Hundred Schools go off in their own directions and do not return, it is certain that they will never join up! If scholars of later generations unhappily fail to see what is purest in heaven and earth, and the grand corpus of the ancients, the tradition of the Way will be ripped to pieces below in the empire.

NOTE This Syncretist essay begins by declaring that the ancients possessed a grand corpus of rules and institutions which was the 'tradition of the Way'. It was multiple, but rooted in the oneness of the Way out of which it divided. The moral code of the Confucian 'gentleman', and the institutions of the Legalist administrators (both approved within their limits in 'The Way of Heaven', cf. p. 258 above), are surviving portions of this corpus, preserved by the Confucian teachers of Lu and Tsou and by the court historiographers. The rest has become fragmented and scattered beneath the level of authorised teachers and scribes, 'below in the empire', where each of the Hundred Schools teaches the 'tradition of a formula', valid within its limits but one-sided and extreme. The purpose of the essay is to sort out the good from the bad in five major schools, in order to recover the integrity of the ancient tradition.

Not being extravagent in a decadent age – nor wasteful with the myriad things – nor pointlessly elaborating numbers and measures – self-disciplined with the rigour of the carpenter with his ink and cord – but providing for every need of the age which is urgent –

some of the ancient tradition of the Way is to be found in these, and Mo Ti and Ch'in Ku-li got wind of them and delighted in them. But in what they did they went much too far, and in what they did away with were much too consistent. They originated 'rejection of music' and put it under the heading 'thrift in expenditure', they would not sing a song for the living or wear mourning for the dead. Mo-tzŭ loved no matter whom and benefited indiscriminately, and he condemned fighting, it belonged to his Way not to get angry. Also he was fond of learning and widely informed, but he did not agree with the former kings, he demolished the rites and music of the ancients.

The Yellow Emperor had the Hsien-ch'ih music, Yao the Ta-chang, Shun the Ta-shao, Yü the Ta-hsia, T'ang the Ta-huo, King Wen the Pi-yung, and King Wu and the Duke of Chou originated the Wu. By the ancient rites of mourning there was an etiquette for noble and for base, there were degrees for superior and inferior. The Emperor had seven coffins one inside another, the lord of a fief five, a grandee three, a knight two. Now Mo-tzŭ alone refused to sing a song for the living or wear mourning for the dead, and made it a regulation to have a coffin of three-inch paulownia wood and no outer coffin. Teaching this to others I am afraid that he was not loving to others, and practising it in his own case most certainly he was not loving to himself. I would not slander Mo-tzŭ's Way; however, if you sang he condemned you for singing, if you wept he condemned you for weeping, if you made music he condemned you for making music, was he really the same sort as the rest of us? With the living he took such pains, with the dead he was so niggardly, his Way was too impoverished, he made men worry, made them pine, his code was hard to live up to, I am afraid it cannot be the Way of a sage. It went counter to the hearts of the empire, the empire would not bear it. Even if Mo-tzŭ himself could take up such a burden, what of the rest of the empire? Alienated from the empire, he was a long way from kingship.

Mo-tzŭ cited and expounded, saying:

'Formerly, when Yü dammed up the great flood, made breaches for the Yellow River and the Yangtse, and circulated water throughout the Nine Provinces and the regions of the barbarians around them, the notable rivers amounted to 300, the tributaries to 3,000, the rivulets were countless. Yü put his own hands to basket and shovel and nine times made the tour of the rivers of the empire, till there was no flesh on his calves and no down on his shins, and washed by heavy rains and combed by fierce winds he instituted 10,000 fiefs. Yü was a great sage, and this is how he wore out his body for the empire.'

The result was that many of the Mohists of later generations dressed in furs or coarse wool, wore clogs or hemp sandals, never rested day or night, and thought of self-torment as the noblest thing of all. 'If you are incapable of such effort,' they said, 'it is not the Way of Yü, you do not deserve to be called a Mohist.'

The disciples of Hsiang-li Ch'in, the followers of Wu Hou, and the Mohists of the South, K'u Huo, Chi Ch'ih, Teng-ling-tzŭ and their like, all recited the Mohist canons but diverged and disagreed, they called each other heretical Mohists, abused each other in disputation about 'the hard and the white' and 'the same and the different', answered each other with propositions at odds and evens which do not match. They regarded their Grand Masters as sages, all of whom wished to become their acknowledged head, aspiring to lay down the line for the future generations of the school; even today the issue is undecided.

As far as the idea of Mo Ti and Ch'in Ku-li is concerned, they were right; but in putting it into effect they were wrong. The result was simply that Mohists of later generations had to urge each other on to torment themselves until there was no flesh on their thighs or down on their shins. It was a superior sort of disorder, an inferior sort of order. However, Mo-tzŭ was truly the best man in the empire, you will not find another like him. However shrivelled and worn, he would not give up. He was a man of talent, shall we say?

NOTE Mo Ti (Mo-tzŭ) of the late fifth century BC was the first to emerge as a rival of Confucius, Ch'in Ku-li (cf. p. 222 above) was his chief disciple. The book *Mo-tzŭ*, the corpus of his school, is extant in 71 chapters; for partial translations, see Y. P. Mei, *The ethical and political works of Mo-tse* (London, 1929) (for chapters 1–39 and 46–50); Burton Watson, *Mo Tzu: basic writings* (New York, 1963) (14 chapters from chapters 8–39); A. C. Graham, *Later Mohist logic, ethics and science* (London, 1978) (for chapters 40–5). The school lasted until the suppression of the philosophers by the Ch'in and revived briefly after the fall of Ch'in in 209 BC (cf. p. 197 above). If we are right in dating the Syncretist after the Han reunification in 202 BC, it would seem from the present passage that they also resumed their sectarian struggles. However, in the literature of the second century BC Mohists are mentioned only in conjunction with Confucians ('Confucians-and-Mohists' as a general label for moralists), suggesting that as an organised movement Mohism was already moribund or dead.

Establishing a pattern which is repeated throughout the next four episodes, the Syncretist first formulates in his own words Mohist tenets which belong to the true tradition of the Way, then proceeds to criticise the errors of the school in terms of its own slogans. 'Rejection of music' and 'Thrift in expenditure' are two of the ten Mohist doctrines, expounded in *Mo-tzŭ*, chapters 20–2, 32–4. In what senses things may be called 'same' or 'different', and whether or not two properties are mutually pervasive like the hardness and whiteness of a stone, are themes discussed in *Mo-tzŭ*, chapters 40–5.

The Syncretist, unlike Chuang-tzŭ, thinks of thrift, practicality and moral rigour as admirable qualities in a subject, even if they are irrelevant to the sage ruler. He praises the Mohists for them but deplores their extremes of self-denial, dwelling in particular on their rejection of music and fine funerals, which are attacked as useless luxuries in *Mo-tzŭ*, chapters 23–5, 32–4. The central Mohist doctrine, 'Love of everyone', and its corollary, 'Rejection of aggression' (expounded in *Mo-tzŭ* chapters 14−16, 17−19) are mentioned only in passing.

•   •   •

Not being tied by the custom − nor ostentatious with possessions − nor oppressive towards the people − nor offensive towards the crowd − wishing for peace and security in the empire in order to revive the people − others and oneself all having as much as and no more than they need to eat − and by these attitudes laying bare what belongs to the heart −

some of the ancient tradition of the Way is to be found in these, and Sung Hsing and Yin Wen got wind of them and delighted in them. They invented the 'Mount Hua' cap as their token. For dealing with the myriad things they took 'farewell to narrowness' as the starting-point, they spoke of the heart as widening to find room, and named this 'the conduct which is the heart's', in order that we should be harmonious and happy together, in order that all within the four seas should be in tune. As for 'the desires which are essential', it was to the locating of these that they attached most importance. By 'To be insulted is not disgraceful' they helped the people not to quarrel, by 'Forbid aggression and disband troops' they helped the age to avoid war. They travelled all over the empire to preach these tenets, advising the high and teaching the low, and even if the empire would not be converted, they were the sort that persist in making a fuss and will not give up. As the saying goes, 'High and low are sick of the sight of you but you persist in showing up.'

However, they cared too much for others, too little for themselves. 'When the desires which are essential are definitely located, five pints of rice are enough,' they said. Even the teachers, I am afraid, didn't get a good meal, but the disciples hungry as they were would not forget the empire. Unresting day and night they told everyone, 'Life is sure to revive for us!' Fellows with such proud hopes to save the world! They said, 'The gentleman does not make bothersome inquiries, he does not put his own person in pawn for other things', thinking that if something is of no advantage to the empire, there is no point in bringing it to light. They treated 'Forbid aggression and disband troops' as the outside of their doctrine, 'The essential desires are few and shallow' as the inside, and in the big and the small and the coarse and the fine of it, the practice of it never got further than this.

NOTE   Sung Hsing and Yin Wen were among the philosophers in the Chi-hsia academy of King Hsüan (319−301 BC) of Ch'i. Both left writings catalogued in the Han Imperial library but no longer extant. It would seem from this and other early testimony that they continued the moralistic tradition of the Mohists (the do-gooder attitude for which the Syncretist has a mixture of sympathy and distaste), but shifted attention from external conduct to the inward motions of the heart from which it starts. This internalisation of ethical thinking pervaded the philosophies of the fourth century BC, and is evident in Confucianism, between Confucius himself and his successor Mencius who taught the goodness of human nature. The slogans of Sung Hsing and Yin Wen appear often enough in the early literature to be intelligible. 'Farewell to narrowness' was an appeal to widen one's outlook and transcend prejudices. 'To be insulted is not disgraceful' was an affirmation that no external accident, only one's own actions, should matter for one's self-respect. 'The essential desires are few' declared that the desires which bring men into conflict are for the most part inessential, and called for a rediscovery of the few needs of eye, ear and mouth which are indispensable to life.

Sung Hsing is the Sung Jung of 'Going rambling without a destination (p. 44 above). Chuang-tzŭ both respected his indifference to other men's approval or disapproval, and deplored his moralism.

• • •

Being impartial, not partisan – treating one thing as interchangeable with another, without favouritism – being as ready to burst out in one direction as another – inclining to one or another without posing them as alternatives – not interested in thinking ahead – not hatching schemes out of knowledge – not selecting from things but going along with them all –

some of the ancient tradition of the Way is to be found in these, and P'eng Meng, T'ien P'ien and Shen Tao got wind of them and delighted in them. It was to evening out the myriad things that they gave head place, saying:

'Heaven can cover over but cannot hold up, earth can hold up but cannot cover over, the greatest Way can embrace but cannot judge between alternatives.'

They knew that all the myriad things in some circumstances are allowable, in others unallowable. So they said: 'If you prefer some to others you cease to be comprehensive, if you lay down a doctrine you fall short. As for the Way, nothing is missing from it.'

Therefore Shen Tao discarded wisdom and dismissed self, to set his course by the inevitable; it was letting other things carry him along that he took as the pattern of his Way. He said 'When you do know you don't know'; he was a man who intended not just to disparage knowledge but to deal it a mortal blow. Shameless, admitting responsibility for nothing, he laughed at the empire for promoting men of worth; loosed from restraints, without a code of conduct, he denied the great sages of the empire.

> Hammer and pound to round off the corners,
> Roll smoothly along with other things.
> Cast off ''That's it', cast off 'That's not',
> Fit in with the moment and you'll always get by.

He did not recognise the authority of knowledge and deliberation, did not know what comes first or last; he simply put everything below him.

> Proceed only when pushed,
> Start off only when dragged,
> As the whirlwind spins,
> As the feather turns,
> As the grindstone revolves.
> Being perfect you will have no flaw,
> Moving or still you will not err,
> Never will you be blamed for anything.

Why would that be? A thing without knowledge does not have the troubles which come from establishing selfhood or the ties which come from utilising knowledge; whether moving or still it does not depart from pattern. That is why as long as it lasts nobody praises it. So he said:

'Simply attain to being like a thing without knowledge. Have no use for excellence or sagehood; a clump of soil does not miss the Way.'

The distinguished people agreed in laughing at him, saying:

'Shen Tao's Way isn't for live men to act on, he's attained the pattern which sets the course for dead men.'

He merely got himself regarded as odd.

It was the same with T'ien P'ien. He studied under P'eng Meng and gained unteachable things from him. The teacher of P'eng Meng said:

'The men of the Way in antiquity simply got so far that nobody judged "That's it", nobody judged "That's not". But the wind of it is hushed, from where would it be sayable?'

By constantly thwarting people, and making themselves unwelcome, they had no escape from that 'rounding off the corners'. That which they called the Way was not the Way, and even in the right things they said they did not escape from being wrong. P'eng Meng, T'ien P'ien and Shen Tao did not know the Way. However, speaking broadly, they were all men who had heard something about it.

NOTE Like Sung Hsing and Yin Wen, T'ien P'ien and Shen Tao were members of the Chi-hsia academy of King Hsüan of Ch'i (319–301 BC). Both left writings catalogued in the Han Imperial library, lost except for considerable fragments of Shen Tao edited and translated by Paul Thompson, *The Shen Tzu fragments* (London, 1979).

The account of them here is at first sight puzzling. Their thoughts seem to be those familiar throughout *Chuang-tzŭ*; why are they rejected much more forcibly than the rest of the Syncretist's five schools, even the Mohists? However, it is clear from Shen Tao's writings, and from all other early information about the school, that they were not Taoists but political theorists of the type classed as 'Legalist', exceptional only in that, while most Legalists were administrators who seem to treat their writings as arcana to be kept in governing circles (which is why the Syncretist sees them as outside the Hundred Schools), T'ien P'ien and Shen Tao were members of the Chi-hsia academy who exposed themselves to public debate. They were the first to circulate the thought that the institutions of the state compose a mechanically functioning system, which the ruler manipulates by reward and punishment in the confidence that they will respond as impersonally as the arm of the balance which goes up or down according to the weights placed on either side. In this depersonalised order the moral or intellectual quality of individuals does not matter, it is enough that they are placed in positions which they are suited to fill. Legalists can talk about this system in Taoist-sounding language, but there is the fundamental difference that Taoists claim to find for man his natural place in the cosmos, Shen Tao his allotted role in an artificial system into which administrators are fitted as though they were dead matter, 'rounding off the corners'. The Syncretist is writing in the time of reaction against Ch'in Legalism; he has a use for Legalist institutions, allowed a humble but acknowledged place in 'The Way of Heaven', but there is nothing for which he has a profounder distaste than a Legalist metaphysic dressed up as Taoism.

•   •   •

Deeming the root to be quintessential – in contrast with the crudity of the things which grow from it – deeming it inadequate to be guided by accumulation of precedents – serenely swelling alone with the daemonic-and-illumined –

some of the ancient tradition of the Way is to be found in these, and Kuan-yin and Old Tan got wind of them and delighted in them. They founded them in that which for ever is nowhere anything, and recognised as the sovereign of them the Supreme One, they deemed gentleness and weakness, modesty and inferiority to be their manifestations, and emptiness, tenuity, not damaging the myriad things, to be their substance.

Kuan-yin said:

> 'Within yourself, no fixed positions:
> Things as they take shape disclose themselves.
> Moving, be like water,
> Still, be like a mirror,
> Respond like an echo.
> Blank! as though absent:
> Quiescent! as though transparent.
> Be assimilated to them and you harmonise,
> Take hold of any of them and you lose.
> Be never ahead of others, for ever in the train of others.'

Old Tan said:

> 'Knowing the male, abide by the female.
> Become the world's ravine.
> Knowing the white, abide by the sullied.
> Become the world's valley.'

Others all prefer to be ahead, he alone preferred to be behind, saying:

> 'Accept humiliation from the world.'

Others all prefer to be full, he alone preferred to be empty; he stored up nothing and therefore had more than enough. (In his self-sufficiency he had more than enough.) Unhurried in conducting his own life he refused to squander himself, and by Doing Nothing mocked at cunning. Others all sought good fortune, he alone by bending remained whole, saying:

'By doing what suits the moment you escape calamity.' He deemed the profoundest to be the root, all threads to derive from the knot, saying:

'If hard, you crumble; if sharp, you get blunted,' and always widened to find room for other things, did not encroach on the territory of other men.

Although they failed to attain to the highest, Kuan-yin and Old Tan in their breadth and greatness were indeed True Men of old!

NOTE   Old Tan (Lao-tzŭ) is the legendary instructor of Confucius, the supposed author of *Lao-tzŭ*, claimed by Taoists as their founder as soon as they came to distinguish themselves as a school. The Syncretist account of him is put together out of quotations and echoes from *Lao-tzŭ*[11] But the Syncretist sees Lao-tzŭ and Chuang-tzŭ as belonging to separate schools, both of which (like all the rest from the Mohists downwards) appear onesided from the viewpoint of his own 'Way of heaven and earth'. He does not yet have the idea of a 'Taoist school', which first appears in the classification of the 'Six Schools' (Yin-Yang, Confucian, Mohist, Sophist, Legalist, Taoist) by Ssŭ-ma T'an (died 110 BC). It is remarkable that throughout the episode Old Tan is mentioned *after* the obscure Kuan-yin, whose book in the Han Imperial library catalogue is no longer extant (perhaps because the Syncretist likes Kuan-yin's concept of the mind as a clear mirror more than Old Tan's doctrine of yielding, cf. p. 259 above). There must have been a short period when this *Kuan-yin-tzŭ* could be seen as more important than *Lao-tzŭ*. The name 'Kuan-yin' means 'keeper of the pass', and in some way connects with the legend in Ssŭ-ma Ch'ien's biography of Lao-tzŭ that the latter travelled to the West and disappeared after leaving his book *Lao-tzŭ* with 'the director of the pass Yin Hsi'.

For the words 'Although they failed to attain to the highest . . . ' we follow a variant reading, so unexpected in a Taoist book that we cannot doubt that it is original. It fits the Syncretist's scheme, in which all five schools are one-sided, but no later Taoist could have written it. The standard text reads 'They may be said to have attained the highest . . . ', a pious correction.

.   .   .

> Vast and vague, without shape,
> Altering and transforming, never constant!
> Is it death? Or is it life?
> Am I side by side with heaven and earth?
> Or setting out with the daemonic-and-illumined?
> In a haze! Where am I going?
> In a daze! Where shall I arrive?
> The myriad things all spread out before me.
> And none deserves to be my destination.

Some of the ancient tradition of the Way is to be found in this, and Chuang Chou got wind of it and delighted in it. With his outrageous opinions, reckless words, extravagant formulations, he was sometimes too free but was not partisan, he did not show things from one particular point of view. He thought that the empire was sinking in the mud, and could not be talked with in too solemn language. He thought that 'spillover' saying lets the stream find its own channels, that 'weighty' saying is the most genuine, that saying 'from a lodging-place' widens the range. Alone with the quintessential-and-daemonic in heaven and earth he went to and fro, but was not arrogant towards the myriad things. He did not make demands with a 'That's it, that's not', and so he got along with conventional people.

Although his writings are extraordinary there is no harm in their oddities. Although his formulations are irregular, their enigmas deserve consideration. What is solid in them we cannot do without. Above, he roamed with the maker of things; below, he made friends with those for whom life and death are externals and there is neither end nor beginning. As for the Root, he opened it up in all its comprehensiveness, ran riot in the vastness of its depths; as for the Ancestor, it may be said that by being in tune he withdrew all the way back to it. However, when one assents to transformation and is released from things, the body has not exhausted its pattern, having come it will not be shaken off. Abstruse! Obscure! A man who did not succeed in getting it all.

NOTE   Chuang-tzǔ is seen as the poet of an ecstasy which transcends life and death, the side of him most prominent in 'The teacher who is the ultimate ancestor' (the chapter quoted in the Syncretist 'Way of Heaven', p. 260 above). It is notable that, compared even with the others later classed as Taoists, he is treated as a writer rather than as a thinker. He is admired, but with the reservation that he may tempt you to lose sight of the real world and its practical problems. The Syncretist warns us not to take his wild words too literally, and calls attention to the three uses of words distinguished in one of the *Mixed chapters* fragments (p. 106f above).

• • •

Hui Shih had many formulae, his writings filled five carts, but his Way was eccentric, his words were off centre. He tabulated the ideas of things, saying:

'The ultimately great has nothing outside it, call it "the greatest One". The ultimately small has nothing inside it, call it "the smallest one".

'The dimensionless cannot be accumulated, yet its girth is 1,000 miles.

'The sky is as low as the earth, the mountains are level with the marshes.

'Simultaneously with being at noon the sun declines, simultaneously with being alive a thing dies.

'Being similar on a large scale yet different from the similar on a small scale, it is this that is meant by "similarity and difference on a small scale". The myriad things to the last one being similar, to the last one being different, it is this that is meant by "similarity and difference on the large scale".

'The south has no limit yet does have a limit.

'I go to Yüeh today yet arrived yesterday.'

'Linked rings can be disconnected.

'I know the centre of the world; north of Yen up in the north, south of Yüeh down in the south, you are there.

'Let your love spread to all the myriad things; heaven and earth count as one unit.'

Hui Shih thought of these as opening up a comprehensive view of the world and a new dawn for disputation; and the sophists below in the empire shared his joy in them.

An egg has feathers.

A chicken has three legs.

In the city of Ying there is the whole empire.

A dog may be deemed to be a sheep.

A horse has eggs.

A frog has a tail.

Fire is not hot.

Mountains issue from holes.

A wheel does not touch the ground.

The eye does not see.

What we point out we fail to arrive at, what we arrive at we do not detach.

A tortoise grows longer than a snake.

The L-square is not square, compasses cannot make a circle.

The hole in the chisel does not circumscribe the handle.

The shadow of a flying bird has never moved.

Fast though the barbed arrow flies, there is a time when it is neither moving nor at rest.

A whelp is not a dog.

A yellow horse and a sable ox make three.

A white dog is black.

An orphan colt has never had a mother.

A stick one foot long, if you take away a half every day, will not be exhausted for a myriad ages.

The Sophists used these in debate with Hui Shih, and never for the rest of their lives got to the end of them.

Huan T'uan and Kung-sun Lung of the sophists' party put elaborate thoughts into men's hearts, changed round their ideas; that they were able to make men submit from the mouth but not from the heart was the limitation of the sophists. Hui Shih day after day used his wits in disputation with others, but it was only in the company of the sophists down below in the empire that he distinguished himself as extraordinary; that is all it amounted to.

But Hui Shih's chatter seemed to him supremely clever. 'What nobler theme is there than heaven and earth?' he said. 'I keep to the male role, I depend on no tradition.' There was a strange man of the South called Huang Liao, who asked why heaven does not collapse or earth subside, and the causes of wind, rain and thunder. Hui Shih answered without hesitation, replied without thinking, had explanations for all the myriad things, never stopped explaining, said more and more, and still thought he hadn't said enough, had some marvel to add. He took whatever contradicted common opinion as fact, and wished to make a name for himself by winning arguments; that is why he came to be so unpopular.

Weak in the Power within, strong on the things outside, his was a crooked path. If we consider Hui Shih's abilities from the viewpoint of the Way of Heaven and Earth, yes, his were no more than the labours of a mosquito or a gnat. Even within the realm of things, what use were they?

The ones who excelled in a single direction were still commendable, one says of them: 'If he had honoured the Way more he would be almost there.' Hui Shih was incapable of satisfying himself with this, he never tired of scattering all over the myriad things, and ended with no more than a reputation for being good at disputation. What a pity that Hui Shih's talents were wasted and never came to anything, that he would not turn back from chasing the myriad things! He had as much chance of making his voice outlast its echo, his body outrun its shadow. Sad, wasn't it?

NOTE The section on the Sophists abandons the form of the previous five episodes, but on closer inspection can be seen to follow on to them. Unlike the other schools, the Sophists do not even have a one-sided 'tradition of a formula' revealing one aspect of the 'tradition of the Way'. Their founder Hui Shih had 'many formulae' and declared with pride, 'I depend on no tradition.' But he had nothing to offer but barren analysis and speculation about heaven and earth, which compared with the Syncretist's 'Way of Heaven and Earth' are negligible.

The writings of the Sophists are lost, except for a couple of genuine essays (the 'White horse' and 'Meanings and things') preserved in a book forged between AD 300 and 600 in the name of Kung-sun Lung, translated complete by Y. P. Mei in *Harvard Journal of Asiatic Studies*, 16 (1953), 404–37, the very controversial 'Meanings and things' also in my *Later Mohist logic* 457–68. It is lucky that the Syncretist, in spite of his contempt for logic-chopping, has been kind enough to preserve a selection of sophisms for us, although without their explanations.

NOTES TO PART SIX

1 cf. p. 265 above.
2 cf. p. 285 above.
3 cf. 'the ultimate root and the ultimate ancestor' (p. 260 above), 'evening out the myriad things' (p. 279 above). The phrase 'emperors and kings' does occur elsewhere in *Chuang-tzŭ* but is especially common in the Syncretist writings.
4 cf. p. 267 above.
5 cf. pp. 91, 260 above.
6 cf. p. 270 above.
7 Quoting p. 91 above.
8 cf. pp. 231–3, 238 above.
9 cf. p. 122 above.
10 cf. p. 177 above.
11 cf. Lao Tzu, *Tao te ching*, translated D. C. Lau (Penguin Classics, 1963), XXVIII, 63; LXVIII, 188.

List of Characters

chi	幾,機	germ, 'thing which makes it go'
ch'i	氣	breath, energy
ch'i wu	齊物	even things out
chien pai	堅白	hard and white
ching	精	quintessence
ching	静	still, quiet
ching-shen	精神	quintessential and daemonic
fang-shih	方士	magician
fei	非	'That's not'
hsing	性	nature
hsing	行	proceed
hsü	虚	tenuous, unreal
jan	然	so
jen	人	man
k'o	可	allowable

lei	累	ties, involvements
li	理	pattern, arrangement
lun	論	sort out
pien	辯	disputation
pien-che	辯者	sophist
pu te yi	不得已	inevitable
shen	神	daemon, daemonic
sheng	生	be born
shen-ming	神明	daemonic and illumined
shih	實	solid, real
shih	是	'That's it'
ta fang	大方	Great Scope
ta jen	大人	Great Man
ta tsung	大宗	ultimate ancestor
tao	道	way
tao-yin	導引	guide and pull

te	德		Power
ti	帝		God
ti wang	帝	王	Emperors and Kings
t'ien	天		Heaven
wan	萬		10,000, myriad
wei	為		deem
wei shih	為	是	'The "that's it" which deems'
wu	無		lack, there is not
wu wei	無	為	Doing Nothing
yi	義		duty
yin	因		go by
yin shih	因	是	'The "that's it" which goes by circumstance'
yu	遊		roam, travel
yu	有		have, there is
yüeh	樂		music

Index